RICHARD
THE
LIONHEART

RICHARD THE LIONHEART

Second Edition

John Gillingham

Weidenfeld and Nicolson
London

For Kate and Emma

George Weidenfeld and Nicolson Ltd
91 Clapham High Street, London sw4 7ta

Printed in Great Britain by
Butler & Tanner Ltd
Frome and London

CONTENTS

ILLUSTRATIONS

ACKNOWLEDGEMENTS

The illustrations are reproduced by kind permission of the following: Archives Nationales, Paris (and Photographie Giraudon), p. 1 above and below, p. 6 below; British Museum, p. 1 centre, p. 3 above, p. 6 above; Musée du Mans, p. 2 above; Archiv für Kunst und Geschichte, p. 2 below; Cim, p. 3 below; Burgerbibliothek, Bern, p. 4 above; Bibliothèque Nationale, Paris, p. 4 below, p. 5 above; Bernd Lohse, Munich, p. 5 below; Archives Photographiques, Paris, p. 7 below. Maps drawn by Peter White.

MAPS

PREFACE TO THE SECOND EDITION

This book presents an entirely new Richard. It cuts through the tissue of myth and misinterpretation with which he has long been surrounded and demonstrates that, far from being a feckless knight-errant kind of a king, he was, in reality, a masterful and businesslike ruler. Richard's own contemporaries recognised his greatness but in the course of the nineteenth and twentieth centuries academic historians learned to take a very different view. They came to see in him a wilfully negligent absentee, a king who chose to flit abroad in vain pursuits of chivalrous dreams rather than stay at home and get on with the much less exciting, but much more vital, work of government, the high domestic duty of a ruler to do justice and keep the peace. Even today this is still how he is generally portrayed: the king who neglected his kingdom. It is, however, a mistaken view. Richard no more shirked his responsibilities than does a modern politician who, in the Europe of the late twentieth century, decides to spend most of his time at Brussels, Strasbourg or Luxemburg, choosing to devote his energies to the business of all the members of a nascent political community rather than to just one of the member states. For Richard too, England was just one part of a wider whole, the Angevin Empire, a far-flung territory which stretched from the Pyrenees to the Scottish border. Thus the fact that he spent very little time in England only means that his own order of priorities was very different from that of a nineteenth or early twentieth century statesman – or academic.

Moreover as head of the Plantagenet royal house, a dynasty which had family interests in the Kingdom of Jerusalem, he owed a special responsibility to the crusading movement, a responsibility which he fully acknowledged and which, entirely rightly, won him the respect and admiration of contemporaries. His brilliant generalship on the Third Crusade enabled him to negotiate a treaty which was to prolong the life of the crusader states, against all the odds, for another century. This, in the judgment of a modern historian of the crusades, was an 'almost incredible success'.

As crusader and as Angevin ruler Richard confronted head-on challenges far greater than those facing most – if not all – kings of England. We only have to think of his two chief political and military opponents: Philip Augustus, the most successful king of France ever, and the great Saladin, the outstanding statesman of medieval Islam. But in Richard both of them met their match.

One of the ways by which Richard met these challenges was by projecting an image of himself, the image of the knight as Christian hero. This he did by deliberate and skilful manipulation of the media of the day, the political commentators and the song-writers – and Richard, of course, was a song-writer himself, with – in the opinion of a recent writer on the medieval lyric – a poetic voice that was very much his own. He managed this so successfully that he made himself a legend in his own lifetime, and a prisoner of legend he has remained ever since, with new legends about his supposed sexual preferences being created even in our own day. But eight hundred years later it is surely time to set him free.

There are two respects in which my own re-appraisal of Richard differs from the views expressed in all earlier modern studies of his life. In the first place earlier studies have tended to reflect the fact that the overwhelming bulk of the surviving evidence relates to Richard in two of his roles only: as a crusader and as an absentee king of England. By comparison there is very little evidence for his activities on the continent. Yet it was on the continent that he spent by far the greater part of his political life. Thus any book which simply 'follows' the evidence inevitably produces a distorted picture. In a deliberate attempt to redress the balance I have emphasised the importance of Aquitaine and of Richard's experience as Duke of Aquitaine.

In the second place my assessment of Richard's qualities as a ruler is an unusually high one. Undeniably a tendency to over-praise one's subject is the besetting sin of biographers and it may be that I have done no more than succumb to the temptation. On the other hand this is an area in which I am consciously 'following' the evidence – for there is no doubt that, in the middle ages, men believed that Richard had been a great ruler, that he had brilliantly succeeded in living up to contemporary ideals of kingship. It may be, of course, that by conforming to the twelfth century model of kingship he failed to live up to the expectations of observers who lived seven hundred years or more later. But it is patently unjust as well as absurd to judge anyone by standards as anachronistic as this.

The case for this revisionist view of Richard the Lionheart was first stated some ten years ago now, and I remain deeply indebted to those who helped me then. To Christopher Falkus who encouraged me to write it; to Nett Capsey, Irene Leon and Pat Welch for finding time, among other more pressing duties, to type my manuscript; to Tommy and Joan Arkell, David Corner, Hans Eberhard Mayer, Jinty Nelson and Rowan Watson for their help and advice.

I am very grateful to the publishers and, in particular, to Juliet Gardiner for deciding to issue a second edition in 1989, the 800th anniversary of Richard I's accession to the throne. I have taken the opportunity to write a new preface, to revise the bibliography and to re-write the chapter notes in order to take account of work published since 1978.

I would like to dedicate this edition to the memory of Richard Benjamin, a young scholar killed by a careless driver just a month before his first piece of historical writing appeared in print. It was he who discovered important new evidence relating to Richard as Duke of Aquitaine (see below p. 293). Were he still alive today Plantagenet studies would be both richer and more entertaining.

JOHN GILLINGHAM
1989

1

THE LIONHEART
OF LEGEND

MORE than any other King of England Richard the Lionheart belongs, not to the sober world of history, but to the magic realm of legend and romance. The picture we have of him is still shaped by the images of a child's view of the Middle Ages: knights in armour, crusaders fighting a desert war beneath a burning sun, minstrels, forest lairs and castle dungeons. Most historians, on reaching adult years, cast aside their childhood fantasies and turn instead to themes which they believe to be of greater significance. They write about castles as though they were banks where treasure was stored and accounted for by office clerks, not as military strong-holds where men performed deeds of courage or cowardice, of loyalty or treachery. In reality castles were both these things. Increasingly they write about society and government, whether in north-western Europe or in the Middle East, not about the human drama of the struggles between Richard and Philip Augustus and Saladin. In other words they prefer to study man as a socio-political animal rather than as a fighting animal, though of course he is both these things. Indeed in the opinion of a highly cultivated twelfth-century Arab, Usamah, Europeans were animals who were good at fighting – but at nothing else. Naturally no one will deny that the underlying structures of economy and society, government and administration, and religious and secular thought are all important subjects and that grown-ups ought to study them. But we should also recognize that, as a result, historians have turned their backs on a king who was at home on the field of war.

Even that venerable, if misleading, academic tradition which places kings at the centre of the story of the development of nations like England and France has not saved Richard from the neglect of historians. In part this is because most academics have come to value more highly the king who is a crowned civil servant rather than a front-line soldier. But in part it is also because Richard ruled a political structure which no longer exists, and which indeed began to break up immediately after his death: the Angevin Empire. Today we think and write in political categories like 'England' and 'France', and if we are historically minded we may be interested in the past of these countries. Where does that leave Richard? Although he was indeed crowned king in Westminster Abbey he has never attracted the attention of students of English history, for almost the whole of his life was spent abroad; in his ten-year reign he spent only six months in England. He stands accused of 'neglecting his kingdom'. On the other side of the Channel French historians are interested either in regional studies or in the rise of the Capetian monarchy. If the former, they may write about social change in twelfth-century Anjou, but they are less inclined to write about the empire built up by the Counts of Anjou, since that sprawling conglomeration of territories was so much more ephemeral than the individual provinces of which it was comprised. If the latter, they concentrate upon the massive achievements of King Philip Augustus. Richard is just one of the figures at the side of the stage who have to be swept away to make room for the heroes of the drama – the Capetian Kings of France. If Richard has been seriously considered at all it is by historians of the crusades, but even here, though for a moment he held the centre of the stage, his part was a very short one. He spent little more than a year in Outremer, the land of the crusaders, and in that time he did not recapture Jerusalem. Richard's career does not fit into any of their favourite fields of study and so, as far as professional historians are concerned, he remains a forgotten king.

For nearly eight hundred years Richard has been left in the hands of the myth-makers. Even today the legendary picture of Richard is the one which predominates. Precisely because they have done no serious work on him it is accepted even by academic historians. This does not, of course, mean that they bubble over with enthusiasm for the crusader king. Instead they tend to combine a child's view of Richard's character with an adult's moral disapproval of it. Thus for the great English historian of the nineteenth century, William Stubbs, Richard was 'a man of blood and his crimes were those of one whom long use of warfare had made too familiar with slaughter'. So far as the leading French authority on the Angevin Empire, Jacques Boussard, is concerned, Richard's reign was 'entirely given up to deeds of prowess' and he characterizes these deeds as 'brilliant but sterile'. The same sense of distaste is evident in the description of him by a recent biographer, the American historian, James Brundage, as 'a peerlessly efficient killing machine ... in combat he was brilliant and courageous; in the council-chamber he was a total loss'. They do no more than echo the enlightened words of Edward Gibbon: 'If heroism be confined to brutal and ferocious valour, Richard Plantagenet will stand high among the heroes of the age.'

Of course there can be no doubt that in some ways the real Richard was very like the figure of romance. He did return from crusade in disguise and was captured and thrown into a German prison. He was a king who led from the front, who inspired admiration because he was so often to be found in the thick of the fray. There is some historical justification for the dramatic image conjured up by an Elizabethan playwright:

> O, still, methinks, I see King Richard stand
> In his gilt armour stain'd with Pagan's blood,
> Upon a galley's prow, like war's fierce God.

But was he just that and nothing more? If we remove the Lionheart's helmet will we find revealed only the battered face of a prize-fighter? 'Certainly one of the worst rulers that England has ever had.' In passing this sentence upon him, Brundage was echoing the famous verdict of Stubbs: 'a bad son, a bad husband, a selfish ruler, and a vicious man'. Is this the truth behind the legend?

If we are to answer this question we must clearly start by deciding what is legend and what is not. Once we look a little more closely at some of the stories about Richard it soon becomes obvious that the coat of legendary paint which conceals him is a very thick coat indeed and that there is an enormous amount of colouring to strip away before we can feel confident that we are even beginning to uncover the historical figure. He was the first king since the Norman Conquest to become a folk hero, a status he had achieved as early as the mid-thirteenth century. Tough and intelligent rulers they may have been, but none of his predecessors, not William the Conqueror, nor Henry I, nor Henry II, possessed the magnetic quality which attracted legend and story. But Richard certainly possessed it. No sooner was he dead than the process of legend-making got under way with an attempt to explain the puzzling circumstances of his death. Most remarkable of all is the fact that the legend-making still goes on today. It is only in the last forty years that the story has gone around that Richard was a homosexual. Although this is now generally accepted as the 'plain, unvarnished truth' about Richard, repeated in works as staid as the *Encyclopaedia Britannica*, it is in fact no more than a highly coloured assertion which cannot be substantiated – in other words a new legend which tells us more about our own times than it does about the character of the man whom it ostensibly concerns.

Of course some of the legends about Richard have never been taken seriously. Take, for example, the following story from a thirteenth-century romance. Returning from the Holy Land Richard was captured and imprisoned by King Modred of Almain (Germany). Modred's daughter, Margery, fell in love with him and bribed the jailer to allow him to spend his nights in her chamber, but on the seventh night they were discovered. Modred wanted to have Richard killed there and then, but his counsellors were alarmed by the idea of executing a king, and preferred to arrange an 'accident'. The lion in the royal menagerie was to be starved for a few days and then allowed to 'escape' into the captive's cell. Margery learned of the plan and begged Richard to attempt an escape, but he would not hear of it. Instead he asked her for forty silk handkerchiefs, which he then bound round his right arm. When the lion burst into his cell and leapt hungrily upon him Richard simply thrust his hand down the lion's throat and tore his heart out. Then, pausing only to give thanks to God, he strode up to the great hall, still bearing the warm heart in his hand. Before the astonished gaze of Modred and his court, Richard thumped the heart down on the banqueting table, sprinkled salt over it and proceeded to eat it with relish.

Clearly this story was invented in order to explain the name Lionheart, and although it is told again in later ballads, as early as the sixteenth century a debunking historian was remarking that 'Of the learned it is thought that this is but a fable, but rather that he was so called for his invincible courage and strength.' Nor have historians taken very seriously the report, based upon no less than three visions vouchsafed to a thirteenth-century bishop of Rochester, that after thirty-three years in purgatory, Richard ascended into heaven in March 1232.

But not all the legends are so transparent. Some are still taken as fact and repeated as such in book after book, whether scholarly monograph, popular biography or school textbook. Chapter Two will deal with one story of this kind, the story of Richard's death. To begin at the death is, of course, a dramatic cliché but it is also, I believe, the best way to understand Richard's life, because it takes us straight into Aquitaine and into the turbulent politics of the duchy of Aquitaine. It was here, after all, that Richard spent at least two-thirds of his active political life. We must learn to see him on his home ground and not just as a crusader or an absentee King of England.

2

AT THE CASTLE OF CHALUS-CHABROL

THE legend of Richard's death is the legend of buried treasure and of a king's greed. A peasant from the Limousin unearthed a treasure-hoard and took it to his lord, but news of the marvellous find reached King Richard and he claimed it as treasure-trove. Forgetting everything else he hurried south from Anjou, determined that it should be his. He came to the small town of Chalus, not far from Limoges, and there he besieged the castle of Chalus-Chabrol where the treasure had been deposited. The garrison realized that they had no hope of being able to hold out against the most famous destroyer of castles in Europe, so they offered to surrender on condition that their lives, arms and armour were spared. But Richard rejected this offer; he swore that he would capture and hang them all. In this brutal and over-confident mood he took one risk too many and was struck in the shoulder by a crossbow bolt. Eleven days later, on 6 April 1199, he died. The King of England, the greatest crusader of his age, had been killed in a trivial quarrel in Aquitaine when nothing of any significance was at stake; arrogance and greed had brought about his downfall in an obscure sideshow over buried treasure. He had devoted his life to 'sterile deeds of knightly prowess' and now he lost it while 'in pursuit of a gaudy bauble' – James Brundage's phrase. It was an entirely appropriate end to the reign of a king who lacked political sense, was a brave soldier certainly, but no statesman, a legendary warrior but an irresponsible king who understood little of the true art of government.

This is the version of Richard's death which is repeated in all the biographies – including my own – and in all the history textbooks. The question is, is it true? Was it really treasure-trove which drew Richard to Chalus? Several contemporary chroniclers tell us that this is what happened, but how well informed were they? Did they know what they were talking about or were they merely repeating rumours? Were they reasonably accurate and objective in what they wrote – or were they moralists or propagandists content with a story which served to show that an arrogant king had met with the fate which he deserved? We must try to answer all of these questions if we are to understand what happened outside the walls of the castle of Chalus-Chabrol. There is, after all, at least one very odd thing about the treasure-trove story. What became of the treasure? The castle was captured but no chronicler says anything about a treasure being found in it. Was it simply forgotten in the shadow of the still more dramatic news of Richard's death? Or was no treasure found because there was no treasure?

We have to begin with some detective work. As in all the best detective stories, the key problem is one of motive – though in this case it is not the killer's motive, but the victim's. Why did Richard go to Chalus-Chabrol? Detective work seven hundred and eighty years after the event is not easy. That, however, is no reason to shirk it. Our chief sources of information will be the chroniclers who wrote at the time or soon afterwards. Not surprisingly their accounts of the death differ very considerably one from another. What are we to do in the face of such discrepancies? What most historians have in fact done is to take the versions written by the major English and French chroniclers and piece together a patchwork, using one detail from one, adding another from a second, and throwing in yet another from a third. But the major chroniclers, writing at Paris or in England, are not necessarily the best informed about events in the Limousin. Rather than creating a mosaic from many sources, would it not be better to 'cross-question' them, decide which source was the most reliable, and then stick to his version, refusing to succumb to the temptation to embroider the story with picturesque details taken from those who were less well informed? This, at any rate, will be the method adopted here.

First let us investigate the major French and English chroniclers, those who seem to stand closest to the rival royal courts and whom therefore we might reasonably expect to be well informed about the deaths of kings. We shall begin with the writer who gives the most detailed description of the treasure. This is Rigord, a monk from the royal abbey of St Denis, just outside Paris, who wrote a book called the *Gesta Philippi Augusti*, The Deeds of Philip Augustus. Since Philip Augustus was Richard's most ruthless enemy and Rigord saw himself as the French king's 'official' biographer, it is clear that Richard could expect little sympathy from the monk of St Denis. According to Rigord the treasure consisted of a set of figures made of gold, representing an emperor and his family seated around a golden table. This marvellous find – which modern historians have suggested may have been a relic of the wealth of Roman Gaul – was unearthed by an unnamed knight. When Richard demanded the treasure the knight took refuge with his lord, the Viscount of Limoges, the most powerful baron in this part of Aquitaine. So, despite the fact that it was Lent, when war was prohibited by the Church, Richard laid siege to Chalus-Chabrol, a castle belonging to the Viscount. There he was shot by an unknown crossbowman. This account is clear and straightforward enough but it is worth noting that Rigord introduced his description of the treasure with the phrase *ut ferebatur*, which means 'as men said' or 'according to the story which I have heard'.

Rigord wrote his version of Richard's death before 1206 and possibly quite soon after the event. Some years later it was revised by William the Breton, the second of our informants. Since William was one of King Philip's chaplains he reflected the outlook of the French court even more closely than the monk of St Denis. Between Rigord's original account and William the Breton's revision of it, there are some important differences. Where Rigord had written that 'a treasure had been found there by a certain knight', William put 'a treasure had, so it is said, been found there'. Moreover he omitted altogether Rigord's description of the treasure. In other words he seems to have regarded Rigord's version with a certain amount of caution.

But William also wrote another work, a long Latin poem called the *Philippidos*, and in this poem he threw caution to the winds. It is, in fact, not meant to be a history of King Philip's reign so

much as a series of dramatic episodes, building up to a triumphant
climax in the description of his greatest victory, the Battle of Bouvines in 1214. In other words its purpose is to justify and glorify
its hero, and Philip's enemies are treated accordingly. Thus
Richard's death is celebrated in a long literary set-piece which
begins with fifty lines devoted entirely to moralizing about his false
pride and the wrong he is committing in making war against his
overlord, the King of France. Then William tells us about something marvellous which happened near Limoges. A peasant plough-
ing his fields stumbled across a hoard of coins and took them to
his lord, Achard of Chalus. The rumour of this reached Richard
and, putting everything else aside, he determined to possess the
treasure. In the face of Richard's overwhelming military might,
Achard begged for a truce during the holy days of Lent and offered
to submit the quarrel between them to the court of the King of
France. Infuriated by this suggestion, Richard pressed on with the
siege and very soon the walls of Chalus began to crumble. The tiny
garrison fought on with the courage born of desperation, peppering
the besiegers with any improvised missiles which came to hand. At
this point William interrupts his narrative of the siege in order to
introduce his readers to the Fates, the three Old Sisters who control
man's destiny, either spinning out the thread of his life or deciding
to cut it short. Into the mouth of one of the three, Atropos, he puts
a thirty-line speech explaining why it was that Richard no longer
deserved to live: he is greedy, has no respect for God or for holy
days, he has broken treaties made with his lord and, by making war
against his own father, has offended against the law of nature. Having convinced her sisters that it was time to stop their spinning,
Atropos herself then took a hand in the siege. She showed Achard
where he could find a bolt and told him to give it to a crossbowman
called Dudo. 'This is how I want Richard to die, for it was he who
first introduced the crossbow into France. Now let him suffer the
fate he has dealt out to others.'

It is obvious that all this is not history but long-winded moral
drama. Moreover it can in no way be said to confirm Rigord's
account of events at Chalus-Chabrol. Rigord and William (in the
Philippidos) agree that a treasure was found but as soon as they de-

scend to details they begin to contradict each other. Above all, whereas for Rigord Richard's chief antagonist was the Viscount of Limoges, William never mentions him. These conflicting stories do not suggest that people at the Capetian court had any very clear idea of the circumstances of Richard's death. And since both Rigord and William the Breton were writing on behalf of his great enemy we can afford to believe anything they say to Richard's detriment only if it is confirmed by other sources with different prejudices.

But it is not just French writers who tell the treasure-trove story. So also do English historians, and among them is Roger of Howden, who is generally considered to be the most reliable and well informed of all the historians of the late twelfth century. In Howden's version the Viscount of Limoges reappears, though he does have the wrong name. Howden calls him Widomar, whereas in fact his name was Ademar or Aimar. (His eldest son and heir was called Guy or Wido, so Widomar may be the composite result of a confused memory of the two names.) According to Howden Viscount Widomar sent Richard a considerable part of the large treasure of gold and silver which was found on his land, but the King demanded it all, and came to Chalus-Chabrol with an army in order to take it by force. The garrison offered to surrender on condition their lives and weapons were spared, but Richard would have none of it. He swore to hang them all. That same day he was shot by a crossbowman called Bertrand de Gurdon and retired, mortally wounded, to his tent. When the castle fell all the defenders were hanged, excepting only Bertrand de Gurdon. Richard had him brought before him. 'What wrong have I done you that you should kill me?' 'With your own hand you killed my father and two brothers, and you intended to kill me. Take your revenge in any way you like. Now that I have seen you on your deathbed I shall gladly endure any torment you may devise.' Upon this Richard forgave him and ordered him to be released. But the dying King's orders were disobeyed. Bertrand was held a prisoner and after Richard's death he was flayed alive.

What are we to make of this story? True, in details it is very different from Rigord and William the Breton. None the less it seems to confirm the essential fact of a treasure at Chalus. Moreover most historians believe that in Roger of Howden they have found the reliable authority they are looking for – a sober, factual chronicler who had access to many official documents. But a historian may be trustworthy in some respects and not in others, well informed on some matters and not on others. As a royal clerk frequently employed on the King's business in the 1170s and 1180s, Roger was certainly well informed on political and administrative matters in the reign of Henry II. He accompanied Richard on the Third Crusade, though he seems to have returned to England before its end. But then he retired to his vicarage at Howden in Yorkshire and stayed there until he died (probably in 1202). As a result, from 1192 onwards his chronicle concentrates on events in England and particularly on events in the north. He knows something about Normandy in the 1190s, but almost nothing about the more distant parts of the Angevin Empire. What he did learn about events in the south was clearly based upon rumour and romance. We hear the story of a Moorish princess, daughter of the 'Emperor of Africa', who falls in love with Richard's brother-in-law, the Christian King of Navarre. From Anjou we hear of fifteen assassins sent by Philip Augustus on a mission to murder Richard. From Poitou we hear of the floods of tears shed by a statue of Christ on the cross which was kept in the cathedral of Poitiers. The dramatic confrontation between Richard and Bertrand de Gurdon belongs in the same category as Howden's other tales from the deep south. It is romantic historical fiction and should be treated as such.

But if we cannot after all safely look to Roger of Howden to confirm the treasure-trove story told by Rigord and William the Breton, there is another contemporary English account which does apparently do this. This is a chronicle written in the Cistercian monastery at Coggeshall in Essex. It looks very much as though its author learned about the siege of Chalus-Chabrol from someone who was there: Milo, the King's almoner, and abbot of the Cistercian house of Le Pin near Poitiers. Indeed it was Milo who heard Richard's last confession, ministered Extreme Unction and then closed the dead man's mouth and eyes. With an eyewitness report to go on the Coggeshall writer compiled what is by far the most detailed account of the siege. And not only is it packed with information, it is also written in a sober and untheatrical fashion; no heroic dialogues invented, no moral attitudes struck. So here we have evidence which must be taken very seriously indeed – and this writer *does* mention the treasure. But first let us see precisely what he says. 'At Lent in the year 1199 the two kings, after holding a peace conference, at length arranged a truce for an agreed period of time. Then, during Lent, King Richard took advantage of this opportunity to lead an army of his own against the Viscount of Limoges, who had rebelled against his lord and made a treaty of friendship with Philip while the two kings were at war. Moreover there are some people who say that a treasure of incalculable value was found on the Viscount's lands; that the King ordered it to be handed over to him; and that when the Viscount refused the King's anger was further aroused. Then he devastated the Viscount's land with fire and sword, as though he did not know that arms should be laid aside during Lent, until at last he came to Chalus-Chabrol ...' There then follows an account of the siege.

Two things are clear. First, the writer knew that the Viscount of Limoges had rebelled against Richard. Second, the writer had also heard rumours of a treasure-trove, but was careful to distinguish this information – 'there are some people who say' – from the fact of rebellion. It is also worth noting that only in one other place in his long description of the siege of Chalus-Chabrol does the Coggeshall chronicler use this phrase 'as people say' and that is where he writes that for almost seven years Richard had abstained from communion 'because of the mortal hatred which he bore in his heart for the King of France'. But there is a great deal of evidence to show that this is simply not true; Richard was assiduous in his attendance at Mass. From all this it appears that the story of treasure-trove may well be no more than a widespread rumour and that there is an alternative explanation for Richard's presence at Chalus-Chabrol.

The next question must be: is this story of a revolt in Aquitaine supported by any other evidence, or must we rely upon the authority of Coggeshall and Abbot Milo alone? In fact no less than five other writers mention a rebellion as the cause of Richard's presence in Aquitaine. By far the most important of these writers is one who is very little known to English historians, Bernard Itier. In 1199 Bernard was in his mid-thirties, a monk in the great Benedictine abbey of St Martial in Limoges, where he later became librarian. Relations between the Viscounts of Limoges and St Martial's, though often tense, were also extremely close; the Viscounts' castle stood cheek by jowl with the abbey and the abbey was the traditional burial place of the Viscounts. Moreover Chalus was only a few miles away from Limoges. Thus there can be no doubt that Bernard Itier was in a much better position to understand the local background to the events at Chalus than any other chronicler. Moreover, he was a careful and conscientious writer who took trouble to check and correct his own work. Once again it would be useful to look at his exact words:

Bernard Itier wrote this on the Friday before the feast of St John the Baptist in the year that King Richard, known as Cœur de Lion, died and was buried with his father in the abbey of Fontevraud, to the joy of many and the sorrow of others. In the year of our Lord 1199 Richard, the most warlike King of the English, was struck in the shoulder by an arrow while besieging a keep at a place in the Limousin called Chalus-Chabrol. In the castle there were two knights with about thirty-eight others, both men and women. One of the knights was called Peter Bru, the other Peter Basil, of whom it is said that he fired the arrow which struck the King so that he died within twelve days, that is to say, on the Tuesday before Palm Sunday, on 6 April, in the first hour of the night. In the meantime while on his sickbed he had ordered his forces to besiege a stronghold called Nontron belonging to Viscount Ademar and another town called Montagut. This they did, but when they heard of the King's death they withdrew in confusion. The King had planned to destroy all the Viscount's castles and towns.

Two points are worth emphasizing. First Bernard Itier says nothing about a buried treasure. Second, it is clear that we are not dealing with the siege of just one, rather minor, castle. Richard attacked three of the Viscount's castles and, in Limoges, men believed that he had intended to attack them all. This fits with what the Coggeshall writer said about the King 'devastating the Viscount's land with fire and sword'.

It fits also with what the author of a long biographical poem, *The*

Story of William Marshal, tells us about Richard's motives in going to the Limousin. Although this poem was not composed until the 1220s and is the work of a minstrel, not of a historian, it is none the less an exceptionally valuable source. William Marshal was one of King Richard's most trusted lieutenants, the man to whom the dying King entrusted the custody of the castle and treasury at Rouen – a vital military and political command. *The Story of William Marshal* was based upon the memories, and possibly the memoirs, of one of William's squires and it includes a vivid and remarkably accurate account of the way in which the news of Richard's death reached Rouen. William Marshal had been with the King only a fortnight before the siege of Chalus-Chabrol and, as one of his closest advisers, he must have known what had taken Richard south. So this poem, emanating from the circle around William Marshal, must be taken seriously. It tells us that Richard went to the Limousin, where the Viscount was holding castles against him – in other words was in revolt – but it says nothing about a treasure. If there really had been one it is hard to imagine a competent minstrel letting the chance of a good story pass him by.

The third of our other writers is a chronicler-monk, Gervase of Canterbury. He states that Richard met his death while besieging Nontron, a castle which belonged, he says, to the Count of Angoulême. In fact Nontron was held by the Viscount of Limoges but since it was situated on the border between the Limousin and the Angoumois and the Viscount held it as a tenant of the Bishop of Angoulême it is a mistake which it was easy to make. Despite this error Gervase's account should be taken seriously since it was based upon the report of a Canterbury monk who was on his way to meet Richard and was either in Normandy or possibly further south still when he heard the news of the King's death and decided to turn back. The introduction into the story of the Count of Angoulême, neighbour and half-brother of the Viscount of Limoges, may be important. It is an addition which does not depend on the evidence of Gervase of Canterbury alone. A fourth writer, Adam of Eynsham, was in Anjou in the spring of 1199. He was there in the company of his friend and master Bishop Hugh of Lincoln, a saintly man who was canonized because of the way he lived, not, like Becket, because of the way he died. In later years Adam wrote a Life of Saint Hugh and he reports that they were on their way to see the King, but stopped at Angers when they heard of disturbances further south caused by the war which Richard was waging against the Count of Angoulême. So not only do we once again find the Count of Angoulême involved, but it is worth pointing out that if the siege of Chalus-Chabrol had been just a minor affair it is not likely that Hugh of Lincoln – who never lacked courage – would have halted for safety's sake at Angers.

The fifth writer to mention a revolt in Aquitaine is Roger of Wendover, chronicler and monk of St Alban's. If his evidence stood alone it would have to be treated with great scepticism since he did not begin to compose his chronicle until the 1230s and he has a greater reputation for the strength of his prejudices than for the accuracy of his historical writing. But it is clear that his account of the year 1199 was based upon a source which is now lost and to that extent it might have a certain value. According to Roger of Wendover, in that year Richard marched an army against some rebel barons in Aquitaine; he burned down their castles and towns, cut down their vineyards and orchards and slaughtered some of them without pity. Once again there is no reference to a treasure. Moreover the accumulated weight of evidence makes it plain that at Chalus Richard was not on a trivial errand but in the thick of a major campaign.

The brief accounts given in *The Story of William Marshal* and by Gervase of Canterbury, Adam of Eynsham and Roger of Wendover are, by themselves, nowhere near substantial enough to outweigh the story as told by Rigord, William the Breton and Howden. Only when read in the light of the evidence supplied by Bernard Itier can their true significance be seen. And it is Bernard Itier's version which forces us to re-read Coggeshall, and to make the crucial distinction between the information derived from Milo of Le Pin and the information based upon rumour. Thus there can be no doubt that Bernard Itier's testimony is of the utmost importance, both for what he says and what he does not say. But by an extraordinary chance, as the result of an apparently trivial slip of the pen, it happened to escape the attention of nearly all modern historians. Much of Bernard's historical writing took the form of brief marginal notes or memoranda jotted down here and there among the manuscripts in the library of St Martial's. Very often these notes began with a phrase such as 'Written by Bernard Itier' or something similar. He added one note of this kind to the library's copy of the chronicle of Geoffrey de Vigeois, an account of events in the Limousin up to the year 1184. That copy of Geoffrey de Vigeois' chronicle no longer exists, but in the early seventeenth century it – or possibly a copy of it – was transcribed by a rather incompetent copyist. He mis-read the opening words of this note and instead of 'B. Itier wrote' – in the Latin it was 'Scripsit B. Iterii' – he put down 'Beati wrote'. This was complete nonsense and as a result, when the seventeenth-century French antiquarian, Père Labbe, printed the chronicle he decided to omit this meaningless sentence. As he printed it the note began with the words 'In the year of our Lord 1199' and it is only in this anonymous form that it has been known to the vast majority of scholars. In consequence no one took it very seriously. But if historians had realized that it had actually been written by Bernard Itier the story of treasure-trove would long ago have been treated with the scepticism which it deserves. Such are the strange consequences which can flow from the misreading of one phrase.

There can be no doubt that those chroniclers who report a rebellion by Viscount Aimar of Limoges and the Count of Angoulême early in 1199 were correct. Their reports are confirmed by a group of four documents which announce a treaty of alliance between the rebels and the King of France, Philip Augustus. Two of these documents, one drawn up in the name of the Count and the other in the name of the Viscount, are dated April 1199 and they justify the alliance by referring to the injuries which they had suffered at the hands of Richard 'formerly King of England'. The third document, drawn up in the name of Aimar of Limoges and his son Guy, is undated. It is worth noting, however, that it refers to the injuries done to them by Richard, King of the English – not Richard, formerly King. The fourth document, drawn up in the name of King Philip, was issued at Paris in April 1198. Unfortunately it is not quite as simple as it seems. At the French court the year ran from

Easter to Easter – and Easter is a moveable feast. This means that by their reckoning 1198 ran from what we would call 29 March 1198 to 17 April 1199. A royal charter dated April 1198 could belong either to April 1198 or to early April 1199. The editors of Philip's charters chose to place it in April 1199 but the balance of probabilities is in favour of April 1198. According to the well-informed Coggeshall chronicler the treaty between Philip and Viscount Aimar had been made 'while the two kings were at war'. In January 1199 Richard and Philip had agreed on a truce for five years, and the truce seems to have been observed. The most reasonable interpretation of these documents would be that two were issued in April 1198, announcing the alliance between King and Viscount, and that two more were added in April 1199, by which time Count Ademar of Angoulême had decided to join his half-brother in revolt.

If, then, Richard travelled south in March 1199 in order to deal with a rebellion, where did the story of buried treasure come from? Was there both a rebellion and a treasure? It may be so, but in that case the treasure was of subsidiary importance. What really mattered was the rebellion; what drew Richard south was not greed but politics. On the other hand, the story of treasure may be nothing more than a legend. Like the death of Kennedy at Dallas the death of Richard took men by surprise. The King was only forty-one years old and he had come unscathed through all the dangers of a crusade and imprisonment. Although it was, of course, always possible that a king who engaged actively in war would die by the sword, it happened, in fact, very rarely. There were more risks involved in going hunting than in going to war. Moreover, so far as men in England knew, there was no war in the spring of 1199. The truce agreed in January 1199 had brought a temporary lull in the great struggle between Richard and Philip. But if a kind of peace had been made why then was the King dead? What had he been doing at a place no one had ever heard of? Such questions could not remain unanswered. For English chroniclers who knew nothing of the politics of Aquitaine the story of buried treasure provided an easy and irresistibly dramatic explanation for his presence in an obscure and distant place. In the hands of Rigord and William the Breton it provided a peg on which to hang denunciations of a greedy and high-handed king whose real offence was that he was a greater man than Philip Augustus. But although stories of the discovery of hidden treasure have commonly been used in many societies to explain the apparently inexplicable, it is still the case that *other* tales might have performed the same function. So why did hidden treasure lie behind the siege of Chalus-Chabrol? It is unlikely that we shall ever be able to answer this question with any degree of certainty, though at times of danger men did, of course, bury hoards of coin and valuables, hoping to recover them when the danger had passed. Indeed in 1892 a major hoard, including nearly a thousand silver pennies minted during Richard's reign, was uncovered at Nontron and it has been plausibly suggested that it may have been concealed at the time of the attack on Nontron by a detachment of Richard's troops in the spring of 1199. But it is possible to speculate and it is worth pointing out that, according to Rigord, the castle which the King besieged was known to the people of the Limousin as the *Castrum Lucii de Capreolo* (i.e. Chalus-Chabrol). In the opinion of seventeenth-century antiquarians from Limoges this name was derived from Lucius, Roman proconsul of Aquitaine in the time of Caesar Augustus, and a man of fabulous wealth. His skill in mountain warfare earned him the name 'Capreolus' – the Goat. He, it was believed, built the castle which was named after him. If the seventeenth-century stories of the wealth of Lucius Capreolus were in circulation as early as 1200 – as seems possible given Rigord's version of the name Chalus-Chabrol – then this might explain why Richard's siege came to be associated with the pursuit of hidden treasure.

This, of course, is no more than guess-work, but what is clear beyond all reasonable doubt is that Richard died while suppressing a rebellion of Aquitainian barons, not in a sideshow, nor in a petty or trivial quarrel. Just how important, however, was the rebellion of Viscount Aimar of Limoges and Count Ademar of Angoulême? It will be one of the main arguments in the following chapters of this book that Richard saw Aquitaine as an integral part of the Angevin Empire, and that he was right to do so. This is to argue that Richard saw the political realities of his day more clearly than historians writing in the nineteenth and twentieth centuries have done, and above all more clearly than English historians. When English medieval historians have looked abroad they have rarely gone beyond Normandy, the land on the other side of that sea which they are accustomed to call the *English* Channel. It is not hard to see why this should be so. In the first place, the events of 1066 made it impossible for them to ignore Normandy. Secondly, one of the effects of the Norman Conquest was to create an Anglo-Norman aristocracy, a single ruling elite with lands on both sides of the sea. Thirdly, the twelfth-century administrators of Normandy left behind some of the kinds of evidence – charters, writs and account rolls, the records of central government – with which English historians are familiar from their study of English history. Thus they could cross the Channel and still remain insular in outlook – and still find cider to drink. But to go further south beyond Normandy would have been to take a leap into an unknown and ill-documented world. Their response has generally been to write off the rest of the Angevin Empire as a nuisance – unproductive, troublesome, and altogether nothing like as important as England and Normandy. This, I think, is a mistake. Anjou and Aquitaine, the valleys of the Loire and the Garonne, were wealthy and civilized parts of the world, where an ambitious ruler could prosper and become famous. But in order to govern effectively the duchy of Aquitaine it was essential to control the roads through Limoges and Angoulême, for these were the vital lines of communication between Poitiers in the north of the duchy and Bordeaux and Gascony in the south. Moreover, for reasons which derive from the history of the eleventh and early twelfth centuries this central region of Aquitaine – the Limousin, the Angoumois and Périgord – was the most independent and turbulent part of the duchy. To a shrewd and hostile observer like Philip Augustus it was clear that here – and not on the heavily fortified frontier between Rouen and Paris – lay the soft underbelly of the Angevin Empire. Thus the rebellion of Aimar of Limoges and Ademar of Angoulême was not just any rebellion of 'feudal' barons chafing against the authority of their overlord; strategically it was vital. When Richard went to Chalus in March 1199 he was attacking a major political problem, perhaps indeed the greatest single problem facing the Angevins.

Bearing in mind the circumstances of his death we can now retrace our steps and hope to make sense of the story of Richard's life. It is a story which begins and ends in Aquitaine, where he was conceived and where he died.

3

THE HOUSES OF
ANJOU AND AQUITAINE

RICHARD was born on 8 September 1157 at Oxford, presumably in the royal palace of Beaumont. But although he was born in England neither his parents nor his grandparents were English. His father King Henry II was a Frenchman from Anjou, the descendant of a long line of counts who had ruled Anjou for two hundred and fifty years. His mother Eleanor was, in her own right, Duchess of Aquitaine, the duchy which her forefathers had ruled since the tenth century. To find an English ancestor it was necessary to go a long way back in Richard's genealogy – to one of his great-grandmothers, Edith, the wife of King Henry I. This English link, slight as it was, was none the less well known to the men who frequented the princely courts of Europe, for in their world family connection was all-important. It shaped the destinies not just of individuals but of entire provinces and kingdoms. One contemporary student of these matters, the learned historian Ralph of Diss, traced Richard's ancestry through Edith to the Anglo-Saxon Kings of Wessex, the line of Alfred the Great and Cerdic, and then, through them, back to Woden and Noah.

But remarkable though they were, his English forefathers seem to have meant little to Richard himself – and this despite the fact that the old Germanic god of war was among their number. When he jokingly referred to the story that he was descended from the Devil he meant no disrespect to his ancestor Woden. He was referring to an Angevin legend, the story of Mélusine. She was a lady of unearthly beauty who married a Count of Anjou and bore him four children. Everything about her and about her marriage seemed to be perfect, apart from one disquieting fact: she hated going into churches and she absolutely refused to be present at the consecration of the Host. Jealous voices reminded the Count of this again and again; eventually he decided to put her to the test. He summoned her to attend church and then, at the moment of consecration, just as she was about to leave, four armed men stopped her. But as they seized her by the mantle, she shook it from her shoulders, folded two of her children in her arms and floated away through a window, never more to be seen by her husband and the two children she had left behind. The point is that Richard's closest family associations, whether real or legendary, were with western France and not with England or Normandy.

Throughout the tenth and eleventh centuries the Counts of Anjou had belonged to a group of princes who were alternately enemies and allies in the struggle for land and power in northern and western Gaul. Their most striking success had been the gradual acquisition of the Touraine, inch by inch, castle by castle, at the expense of their eastern neighbours, the Counts of Blois. The possession of Tours, the city of St Martin, an important market and a vital communications centre, gave the Angevins a tremendous strategic advantage; and the building of the great castles of Chinon, Loches and Loudun showed that they were determined to hold on to it. By the thirteenth century and perhaps by the twelfth Anjou and the Touraine were a single regional society with a common body of custom. Other territorial gains had been short-lived. To the north they had obtained the county of Maine only to lose it to William the Conqueror, Duke of Normandy. To the south they held the Saintonge for a while but the Counts of Poitou (who were also Dukes of Aquitaine) soon won it back again. As a dynasty the Angevins had done well, but noticeably less well then either of their main rivals, the Normans (who had conquered England) and the Poitevins (who had acquired Gascony). All this was to change in a few explosive years of expansion in the mid-twelfth century, shortly before Richard's birth.

It began with the marriage of Geoffrey Plantagenet, otherwise known as *le Bel* (the Handsome), the heir to Anjou, to Matilda, daughter of King Henry I and probable heiress to England and

Normandy. This was in 1128 but any expectations of a swift entry into the inheritance when Henry I died in 1135 were immediately dashed by the dramatic political coup brought off by Stephen of Blois – a member of the family which had earlier lost Touraine to the Angevins. Count Geoffrey, by concentrating his forces on the conquest of Normandy, was able to recover the continental part of his wife's inheritance by 1144, and in 1150 he passed it on to his eldest son Henry Plantagenet, now twenty years old. But for all his troubles Stephen, an amiable and gallant king, had managed to hold on to England and it took three strange twists of fortune to transform the situation.

The first was the premature death of Count Geoffrey, still under forty, in September 1151. If he had lived long enough to see Henry crowned king at Westminster he would have been able to carry out his plan of leaving Anjou to his second son Geoffrey. As it was, the dying Count could do no more than give instructions that his body should not be buried until Henry had promised to observe the terms of his father's will. When Henry, who had not been present at the death-bed, arrived for the funeral, he at first refused to take the oath but eventually, confronted by his father's decomposing body, he agreed to do so. The second remarkable event was Henry's marriage in May 1152 to another great heiress – not for nothing has the twelfth century been called the 'Century of Heiresses'. This was to Eleanor of Aquitaine and it was celebrated just eight weeks after her first marriage, to King Louis VII of France, had been annulled. As a ruler of the vast duchy of Aquitaine, covering something like one-third of the area of modern France, she brought a tremendous accession of wealth and prestige to her new husband. The third event was the unexpected death of King Stephen's elder son Eustace in August 1153. Disheartened by this blow the old King was persuaded to recognize Henry Plantagenet as his heir. In December 1154 Henry II was crowned King of England. Now he was supposed to hand over Anjou to his younger brother. But that oath had been taken while Eleanor of Aquitaine was still married to Louis VII. Whether or not Henry would have kept his promise if she had remained so is an open question, but it is clear that once he had also acquired Aquitaine he would never relax his grip on the territories which served as the vital bridge connecting his mother's lands in the north and his wife's lands in the south. Thus Henry kept Anjou and found himself ruler of an immense empire stretching all the way from the Scottish border to the Pyrenees. Between 1144 and 1154, as the result of a series of flukes unscrupulously exploited, the position of the Count of Anjou had been transformed. From being one prince among many others he became the most powerful ruler in Europe, richer even than the Emperor, and completely over-shadowing his own nominal overlord, the King of France.

The assemblage of lands which he ruled is traditionally called the Angevin Empire and the name is important. For though some historians doubt whether such a loose conglomeration of territories, each with different traditions and customs, cobbled together by 'an unholy combination of princely greed and genealogical accident' and just as likely to fall apart again, can properly be called an empire, none doubts the accuracy of the term Angevin. Its heartland lay in the valley of the Loire, in Anjou, not in England. In English histori-cal atlases the Angevin Empire, like the nineteenth-century British Empire, is often coloured red, but this is misleading. It was not the first British Empire. Henry II was born at Le Mans, died at Chinon and was buried at Fontevraud – all places which lay within the borders of his patrimony, the lands he inherited from his father.

But the phenomenal surge of Angevin power way beyond its fami-liar frontiers in the mid-twelfth century inevitably left behind a trail of disappointed and resentful men. Chief among them were Henry's brother Geoffrey and the ex-husband of Henry's wife, Louis of France. Geoffrey had been cheated of his rights; Louis was alarmed and angered by Eleanor's choice of a new husband, particularly since she had not asked for his consent despite the fact that he con-tinued to style himself 'Duke of Aquitaine' and regarded her as his ward. By the time of Richard's birth, however, Henry seemed to have overcome both of these difficulties. He was absolved from the obligation to carry out his father's wishes by a dispensation obtained from the English Pope, Adrian IV. In February 1156 he met Louis VII on the border between Normandy and France and there did homage for Normandy, Anjou and Aquitaine. In the summer he crushed Geoffrey's rebellion and compelled him to renounce his

claim. Later in the same year he was able to compensate his brother
in handsome style. The citizens of Nantes rebelled against their
lord, Count Hoël, and appealed for Henry's help. It was given and,
in return, Geoffrey was installed as the new Count of Nantes. This
was a notable acquisition, long sought after by the Angevins. Not
only was Nantes the largest town in Brittany, it was also an important sea-port, indeed for the Angevins a vital one. Situated at the
mouth of the Loire, it was their chief outlet for exports of all kinds
– the fine metalwork for which Tours was famous, for example,
but, above all, the wines of Anjou and Touraine. Right up to the
nineteenth century the winegrowers of Anjou and Touraine would
refer to their best wines as 'vins pour la mer', the wines which were
going to be taken down to the sea via Nantes. With these gains under
the belt of the young ruler and the land route to Aquitaine secured,
all seemed well when Henry and Eleanor celebrated the Christmas
of 1156 at Bordeaux. But although they had been settled for the
moment the two great political problems of the next half-century
had already been foreshadowed: first, the tensions within the
Angevin family; second, the feudal question of the relationship
between lord and vassal, between Capetian and Angevin. Henry II,
moreover, had performed homage while King and although it was
homage for his continental possessions and not for his kingdom,
this was a step to which none of his predecessors as Kings of England
had ever steeled themselves. But whatever the future might hold,
the friendly relationship between Henry and Louis which that act
of homage had helped to establish was an important contributory
factor in the happy and optimistic atmosphere in which Richard
was conceived – the fourth child born to Eleanor and Henry in five
years of marriage.

For Eleanor the contrast between her first and second husbands
must have been immense. Her marriage in 1137 to the heir to the
French throne seemed at first to be an ideal match. In political terms
it was a sensible alliance for a fifteen-year-old heiress deprived of
a father's or an uncle's protection. Her father, Duke William X of
Aquitaine, had died suddenly, and without sons, while on a pilgrimage to Compostella. Her uncle Raymond, Count of Tripoli, was
ruler of one of the crusader-states and too far away either to help

her or to threaten to take her inheritance for himself. Moreover contemporaries believed that, as a husband, Louis VII gave her love as well as protection. But as time went by the marriage turned sour. Louis became an extremely devout and ascetic man. The story went around that once, when he was seriously ill, he was advised by his doctors that it would improve his chances of survival if he were to sleep with a woman. An attractive young lady was taken to him but Louis would have nothing to do with her, saying that he would rather die than commit the sin of adultery, even for medicinal purposes only. Eleanor, on the other hand, was said to be beautiful and lively; she was certainly headstrong and indiscreet. Whether or not there was any truth in them, the fact remains that rumours about her affairs became common gossip. In time they reached legendary, almost Messalina-like proportions. She, wrote one historian, was the real Mélusine. Not surprisingly she is said to have complained that Louis was more like a monk than à king.

That the two were incompatible was clear by the late 1140s but this of itself would not have brought about the annulment. At all times the social function of marriage has been to produce heirs and this their marriage had failed to do. After an early miscarriage she bore Louis just two children in fourteen years, and both of them were girls. The lesson to be learned from the recent history of England and Normandy was that it was virtually impossible for a daughter to keep a hold on her inheritance. If Louis VII were to prevent a repetition of Stephen's reign from happening in France then he needed sons. In 1154, after the clergy of France had put an end to his marriage to Eleanor, he married Constance of Castile. She too, however, bore only girls and then died, in childbirth, in 1160. The need for a male heir to the throne of France was now desperate and it took Louis only five weeks to find a third wife, Adela of Champagne. Eventually, in August 1165, a son was born. The mood of the Parisians, when they heard the news for which they had been waiting so long, was recorded by a young Welshman living in a rented room on the Ile de la Cité. The fame of Peter Abelard had helped to make Paris the centre of the intellectual world of the twelfth century, the Mecca of all students. So Gerald of Wales went to Paris and there, on a warm summer's night, he was abruptly awoken when all the bells of the city began to peal. Through his window he could see the flickering light of flames. His first thought was that Paris was on fire – an ever-present threat when wood was the chief building material. He rushed to the window. But the fires were bonfires and the bells told not of danger but of joy. The narrow streets were crowded and it was not long before Gerald had discovered the cause of the exultant bedlam. 'By the grace of God there is born to us this night a King who shall be a hammer to the King of the English.' The newborn boy was given the name of Philip. In the course of time he and Richard were to become fellow-crusaders and bitter enemies.

But in the late 1150s that night in August 1165 was still far away, and it is not difficult to imagine Louis VII's exasperated mood. In fourteen years Eleanor had not produced an heir to his kingdom, but in the first six years of her second marriage she had had five children and four of them were boys: William, who died in 1156, Henry, Richard and Geoffrey. Altogether Henry II and Eleanor had eight children, the last of whom, John, was born in 1167. Henry, it was clear, was no monk. In 1157, the year of Richard's birth, he was a solidly built young man of twenty-four, twelve years younger than his wife. He was to be a great king, for thirty-five years the master-politician of Western Christendom, able to overwhelm or out-manœuvre all his rivals. Only at the end, when in the grip of his last illness, was he defeated. He was an intelligent and well-educated man who enjoyed argument and conversation, whether in French or Latin. Impatient of court ceremonial and indifferent to the trappings of majesty, he felt most comfortable in the hard-wearing clothes of the huntsman. Like all members of the aristocracy he was addicted to hunting and liked nothing better than to be in the saddle and away before the crack of dawn. On the other hand he could work at all hours of the day and night – much to the dismay of his advisers and household servants who would have preferred a more predictable routine. He hated sitting still, and remained constantly on the move, restless and seemingly tireless, preferring to call for needle and thread to mend his own clothes rather than do nothing.

Quick-tempered and at times reduced to mindless fury – for example by what he regarded as Becket's betrayal of him – he could also be marvellously patient. This is how he was described by one of his courtiers, Walter Map: 'Whatever way he goes out he is seized upon by the crowds and pulled hither and thither, pushed whither he would not and yet, surprising to say, he listens to each man with patience, and though assaulted by all with shouts and pullings and rough pushings, does not threaten anyone because of it, nor show any sign of anger; only, when he is hustled beyond bearing, he silently retreats to some place of quiet.' Generally he seems to have dealt with those who came to him with requests by saying that he would do something for them, and then repeating this promise whenever he had to, postponing action for as long as possible. According to Walter Map this was his mother's teaching: he should keep aspirants waiting in hope, she said, deliberately spinning out their affairs, for an unruly hawk, if meat is held out to it and then snatched away or hid, will become keener and more inclined to be attentive and obedient. But a king could not simply sit back and wait for people to come to him. To ensure that his subjects acquired the habit of carrying out his instructions he had to visit them as often as possible, and although the king's itinerary was normally publicized in advance – so that merchants and tradesmen, as well as petitioners, could frequent his court without difficulty – it was sometimes useful to turn up without warning. Thus the education of a king's son was supposed to include learning to sleep in a hard or badly made bed to prepare him for the rigours of a life of non-stop, and sometimes unexpected, movement. With the whole of the Angevin Empire to govern Henry II had to travel further and faster than most ruling princes. Despite the rumour that he could fly, all this really meant for Henry was that he was in the saddle so much that he suffered from sore legs.

In these circumstances it was inevitable that for Richard and his brothers and sisters their father was a distant figure, always in a hurry. It seems likely that as small children they stayed in the relative security of England while Henry spent most of his time abroad, immersed in what was always to be the central concern of his life, governing his continental dominions. In a letter written in the summer of 1160 Archbishop Theobald of Canterbury asked the King to return to England. Among other arguments he reminded Henry of his children. 'Even the most hard-hearted father could hardly bear to have them out of his sight for long.' But the letter failed to achieve its object. Not until January 1163 did Henry again set foot in England, after an absence of four and a half years. There is not much, at this stage of his life, to suggest that Henry was fond of his children. In May 1165 the Queen took Richard and his elder sister Matilda (born 1156) to Normandy; a fortnight later King Henry crossed the Channel in the other direction, leaving his family behind while he mounted a major campaign, albeit an unsuccessful one, against the Welsh. Everything about his later life shows that Richard was much closer to his mother than to his father. But Eleanor too had to travel a great deal, and in his earliest years it was almost certainly Richard's nurse who provided love and security on a day-to-day basis. Twelfth-century romances make it plain that for a noblewoman to suckle her own child implied a quite exceptional degree of love. Undoubtedly Richard was handed over to a wet-nurse. We know a little about her. She was called Hodierna and Richard seems to have remembered her with affection. More than thirty years later, when he became king, he granted her a generous pension. She became a wealthy and, in her own part of the world, a famous woman – perhaps the only wet-nurse in history to have a place named after her: the Wiltshire parish of Knoyle Hodierne.

Although there is no direct evidence on the subject of Richard's upbringing and education – we do not even know the names of his tutors as we do in his father's case – it is none the less possible, by using romances and treatises, to reconstruct the type of education which he must have undergone. As soon as he could walk he would be taught to ride, for horse-riding was inseparable from high social rank. At first he would have remained chiefly in the care of women, learning how to behave, how to speak in a courtly fashion, when to keep silent, how to play and sing. Then, when he was five or six years old, he entered a masculine world and his formal schooling began. The description of Tristan's education given by the great medieval German poet Gottfried of Strasbourg bears witness to the fact that this change in the pattern of a child's life could be intensely felt and vividly remembered. 'In his seventh year his [foster] father took him and placed him in the care of a man of experience and promptly sent him abroad with him to learn foreign languages and begin at once to study books. This was his first loss of freedom ... Just when he was entering the springtime of life his best life was over . . . he had tasted freedom only to lose it. Now he had to face cares and obligations which had been unknown to him before; and the beginning of his cares lay in the stern discipline of the study of books. Yet once he had started he applied his mind and industry to it with such vigour that he had mastered more books in that short space than any child before or since. He also spent many hours playing stringed instruments of all kinds, persevering from morning to night until he became marvellously adept at them. He was learning the whole time, today one thing, tomorrow another, this year well, next year better.'

Tristan, of course, was a child-prodigy. All who met him were staggered by his easy command of innumerable languages, by his polished manners, by his superb musicianship and by his mastery of courtly pursuits like hunting and playing chess – not to mention his astonishing good looks. Perhaps Richard was not quite as accomplished as this. None the less we must always remember that he was not an ignorant or uncultivated soldier. Nor was he just a patron of troubadours. He was capable of composing his own songs and of writing verse in both French and Provençal. Moreover he enjoyed sacred music too. When the clerks of his royal chapel were singing in the choir, he would often walk among them, urging them with voice and hand to sing with greater gusto. He was sufficiently well educated in Latin to be able to crack a Latin joke at the expense of a less learned Archbishop of Canterbury.

But there were still more things which the youth had to learn. 'Besides all this Tristan learned to ride nimbly with shield and lance, to spur his mount skilfully on either flank, put it to the gallop with dash, wheel and give it free rein and urge it on with his knees, in strict accordance with the chivalric art. He often sought recreation in fencing, wrestling, running, jumping and throwing the javelin, and he did it to the utmost of his strength and skill.' In these subjects Richard was certainly in Tristan's class. The knightly art of fighting on horseback, particularly with lances, was an extremely difficult discipline to master – for horse as well as rider. The knight had

to swerve at the last moment to avoid a head-on collision with his
opponent, but at the same time he had to couch his lance to his
side as tightly as possible with his hand and under his arm so that
the lance blow was struck with all the weight and momentum of
his horse behind it, for if in swerving aside he moved his hand or
used his arm to thrust at his opponent then a blow delivered in this
manner would have no effect whatever. It was a technique which
required split-second timing and horsemanship of the highest order.
It also meant that well-trained war-horses were immensely valuable
assets. The poem which gives us the best insight into knightly and
aristocratic life *c.* 1200, *L'Histoire de Guillaume le Maréchal* (the
story of William Marshal), rarely fails to tell us how much a particular horse was worth: it could be as much as forty, fifty or even a
hundred *livres* – and this at a time when a serf could be bought for
ten *livres*. In the event of a surprise attack a knight was advised first
to mount and only then, if possible, to arm. His first obligation was
to save himself *and* his war-horse. (He would, of course, also have
other horses, for carrying his harness and baggage, for hunting and
everyday riding, and for mounting the servants who travelled with
him, a squire and a valet at the least.)

The best training in these disciplines took the form of war games
called tournaments, particularly since these were splendid social
occasions, enlivened by the presence of large numbers of ladies,
musicians and merchants bringing wares from all over the world.
But the twelfth-century tournament was very different from the
formalized jousting of the later Middle Ages which film-makers
have made so familiar to us. In war, skirmishes and battles were
won by knights who had learned to fight together as a unit, not by
displays of individual prowess. Therefore tournaments were mock-
battles contested by teams of knights and, as in war, the more
knights in your team the more likely you were to win. If one knight
became separated from the rest of his team he might find five or
six opponents all bearing down on him at once, and one of them
might strike him in the back. If thrown from his horse he would
not be given the opportunity to remount. All was fair in the tournament, as in war. It was thought extremely clever tactics when one
team pretended not to be taking part in a tournament, and only

joined in late in the day when all the other knights who had been fighting since soon after sunrise were exhausted. As in war, if you were captured you lost your horse and armour to the victorious knight and you might have to pay a ransom as well. Given the value of horses and armour this meant that a landless younger son could win fortune as well as fame if he became a tournament champion. The classic example of this was William Marshal, the fourth son of a Wiltshire baron, the story of whose successful career on the tournament field is told with loving detail in *L'Histoire de Guillaume le Maréchal*. Even foot-soldiers had a role to play. As in war, you could use them as a screen behind which your knights could withdraw and wait until they were ready to charge. In these circumstances tournaments were not confined within enclosed lists but ranged over several square miles of ground, taking in villages, woods and vineyards, all of which might suffer as much damage as in real war. When Richard was a young man there was reckoned to be a tournament about once a fortnight on the Continent; in England they were prohibited on the orders of Henry II. Tournaments were frowned upon by the church but in banning them Henry was not doing as he was told by the Pope; rather he was, as so often, following in the footsteps of his grandfather, Henry I. They were clearly a threat to public order. As can be imagined, they were very easily degenerated into hot-tempered battles fought in deadly earnest. Moreover, when barons and knights gathered together in arms, as though for war, who could tell what conspiracies and rebellions might not follow? But when Richard became king he encouraged tournaments in England. He knew their value as training for war and he did not fear rebellion.

The political and moral education of the boy and apprentice knight depended less upon the teaching of the church than upon the *chansons de geste* sung by minstrels. Their tales of legendary warriors and kings, Roland, Guillaume d'Orange, Arthur and Charlemagne, of their great conquests and their deeds of arms and chivalry, were meant to stir the hearts of all who listened and move them to live their own lives according to the pattern set by the heroes of the past. It was through the agency of the *chansons* that the young man might acquire a sense of honour and a sense of shame. Whereas the priests told him that he must die and would go either to heaven or to hell, the singers of songs told him that, though he must die, his name need not and that it was up to him whether he left behind a good or an evil reputation. A death-bed repentance and confession might gain him entrance into heaven; it might save his soul, but it could not save his reputation after a lifetime of dishonour. When William Marshal was dying a clerk tried to persuade him to sell about eighty fine robes in order to spend the money for the salvation of his soul. The old man was not persuaded. It had been his custom every year at Pentecost to distribute robes to the knights whom he maintained in his household; such acts of largesse were part of his duty as a good lord. He rounded angrily upon the clerk. 'Be quiet, you tiresome idiot, have you no sense of shame? Pentecost is at hand and my knights should have their new robes. This is the last time that I shall be able to supply them, yet you try to stop me.' Similarly when told that only if he returned all his tournament winnings would he get to heaven William replied in exasperation that it was impossible. 'If because of this the kingdom of God is closed to me, there is nothing I can do about it, for I can't return these things. I can only commend myself to God, repenting my sins. Unless the clergy want my complete damnation they can ask for no more. But their teaching must be false, or else no one would be saved.'

These ideals, knightly rather than clerical, were the ones which Richard learned to share, though at the end, as he lay dying, he was perhaps less certain of them than William Marshal. This is not to say that Richard was irreligious. We cannot, of course, look into his soul but on the basis of his ascertainable behaviour he grew up to be a conventionally pious man. He was assiduous in his attendance at Mass. In view of his delight in music and ceremony there is every reason to believe that he enjoyed the liturgy of the church. When he was king he was normally accompanied by the clerks of the royal chapel so he had plenty of opportunities to indulge in the pleasures of ritual. It was, after all, a ritual which exalted kings. Adam of Eynsham, the biographer of St Hugh of Lincoln, gives us a revealing description of Richard in the last summer of his life. Richard had ordered the confiscation of the estates of the see of Lincoln and Bishop Hugh decided to go himself to Normandy and protest. 'He found the King in the chapel of his new castle of the Rock of Andeli [that is, Château-Gaillard] hearing High Mass on the feast of St Augustine, and immediately greeted him. The King was on a royal throne near the entrance, and the two Bishops of Durham and Ely stood at his feet ... A good omen had encouraged Hugh for just as he reached the chapel steps he heard the choir in full voice chanting the words "Hail renowned bishop of Christ". When Richard did not respond to his greeting except by frowning and then turning away, Hugh remained undismayed. He said to him, "Lord King, kiss me." But Richard turned his head even further and looked the other way. Then the Bishop firmly gripped the King's tunic round his chest and shook it violently, saying again, "You owe me a kiss because I have come a long way to see you." The King answered, "You deserve no kiss from me." He shook him more vigorously than before, this time by his cloak, and said boldly, "I have every right to one"; adding, "Kiss me." Richard, overcome by his courage and determination, after a little while kissed him with a smile. Later on, in discussion with the members of his household, the King referred to Hugh. "If the other bishops were like him," he said, "no king or ruler would dare raise up his head against them." '

Like his father, who had appointed him bishop, Richard could only admire the courage and saintliness of Hugh of Lincoln. But the episode tells us more than perhaps Adam of Eynsham intended. It shows Richard enthroned amidst his choir and his bishops – in all there were two archbishops and five bishops present in his chapel on this occasion. The King was a central figure in the ritual of the church. Moreover the two bishops standing at the foot of the throne had both been appointed for administrative work done in the King's service. Before becoming Bishop of Durham in 1197, Master Philip of Poitiers had been a clerk of the King's chamber and his constant companion. He had gone with Richard on crusade and had shared with him the hazards of the perilous journey home. Master Eustace, consecrated Bishop of Ely in 1198, had been Vice-Chancellor and Keeper of the King's Seal since 1194. Both men were typical members of the new class of civil servants, who had been educated at university and styled themselves 'master'. For all his reverence for Hugh of Lincoln Richard had always been determined that other bishops should not be like him. He looked upon bishoprics as rewards which he could bestow upon clerks who served him loyally and efficiently. There was nothing remarkable about this point of view. Not only did nearly all princes think in the same way, but so did nearly all clerks. Very few men took clerical orders in the hope of devoting themselves to pastoral work at parish or diocesan level. Most of them looked forward to an administrative career in the service of a lord, whether pope, king, bishop or earl.

Ritually and administratively, then, Richard could see the value of churchmen. He was, of course, capable of being sarcastic at their expense. When Fulk of Neuilly, the most famous preacher of the time, accused him of having three wicked daughters, pride, avarice and sensuality, Richard amused his courtiers by offering to give his pride to the Templars, his avarice to the Cistercians, and his sensuality to bishops and abbots – reminding Fulk of the notorious weaknesses of some members of the church. But such remarks were commonplace and were made by ardent church reformers as often as by anyone else. Moreover, despite his comment on the Cistercians, Richard was a notably generous benefactor to them, as was pointed out by the chronicler from the Cistercian house at Coggeshall in Essex. Nor was the old order of the Benedictines made to feel left out in the cold. At St Alban's in the mid-thirteenth century there was a strong tradition of a close relationship between the abbey and the King. Richard also seems to have felt a special devotion for the shrine of Bury St Edmund's – he may well have been attracted by a cult which celebrated a king who died in the struggle against pagans.

Yet long before Richard's formal education had even started his future was being discussed. Like all royal children his chief function in his parents' eyes was to undertake the role of a pawn in the diplomatic game. Since diplomacy largely revolved around the family relationships of princely dynasties this meant that children had to expect to be betrothed early – and occasionally even married early. His elder brother, Henry, was betrothed in August 1158 to Margaret, Louis VII's first daughter by his second wife. At the time Henry was three years old while Margaret was still a baby. But she was old enough to be assigned a dowry, a stretch of land which lay

between the rivers Seine, Epte and Andelle, known as the Norman
Vexin. It was agreed that this would be handed over to the Angevins
when the marriage itself took place. Until that date Louis was to
retain the Norman Vexin while Margaret was to be kept in Henry's
custody. In September 1158 Henry travelled to Paris and then took
the little girl back to Normandy with him. The point of this
betrothal was that the castles of the Vexin controlled communications between Paris and Rouen. Long ago the Vexin had been
divided into two along the line of the River Epte: on the east bank
the French Vexin held by the King of France, on the west the Norman Vexin held by the Duke of Normandy. In 1145, however,
Count Geoffrey of Anjou and his son Henry had granted the Norman Vexin to Louis VII in return for his acquiescence in their conquest of Normandy. Now Henry II wanted it back. Possession of
its castles, Gisors, Neaufles, Dangu and a dozen others, was essential
if he was to sleep secure in Rouen.

   Richard's turn came a few months later. Early in 1159 Henry II
travelled south through Poitou and Saintonge until he came to Blaye
on the Gironde. There he met Raymond-Berengar IV, Count of Barcelona. Since Raymond-Berengar was married to the Queen of Aragon and ruled that kingdom in his wife's name, he might have taken
the title of king, but refused to do so, saying that it was better to
be known as the greatest count rather than the seventh greatest king.
Henry and he made a treaty of alliance, agreeing that Richard should
be betrothed to one of the Count's daughters and that, when
married, they should be granted the duchy of Aquitaine. The point
of this betrothal was that Henry was planning a campaign against
Count Raymond V of Toulouse and since the rich and powerful
Raymond-Berengar was already at odds with Toulouse he made a
natural and formidable ally. As Eleanor's husband Henry II had
taken over the old claim of the Dukes of Aquitaine to be lords of
Toulouse. Eleanor's grandfather, William IX of Aquitaine, had
married Philippa, the only child of Count William IV of Toulouse.
Philippa was ousted by her uncle, William IV's younger brother,
but in the eyes of her descendants she had been the rightful Countess of Toulouse and periodically they went to war to re-assert that
claim. Toulouse would be a rich prize and it would have been foolish

to allow the claim to drop. Traditionally looked upon as the capital of the former Visigothic kingdom of Aquitaine it seemed therefore to belong to Aquitaine. As the focus of roads linking the Atlantic ports of La Rochelle, Bordeaux and Bayonne with the flourishing maritime trade of the Mediterranean, Toulouse was an important commercial centre. Care was taken to ensure that the River Garonne remained open to shipping all the way from Bordeaux to Toulouse; swamps were drained and the forests lining the river banks were cleared. Thus financially and strategically his wife's claim made good political sense to Henry II, but naturally the present Count of Toulouse was not going to be dispossessed without a fight. As husband of Louis VII's sister, Constance, Raymond of Toulouse could count on help from his brother-in-law. The massive expedition launched in the summer of 1159 was the biggest military effort ever made by Henry II. Although he failed in his main aim of forcing the Count of Toulouse to submit he did succeed in capturing Cahors and the Quercy. As for Richard's betrothal nothing came of it. The girl whom he was to have married vanishes from the pages of history and we do not even know her name. But this short-lived diplomatic episode was not entirely without significance. It marked the beginning of Richard's association with Aquitaine.

In area the duchy of Aquitaine was larger than Henry's Norman and Angevin lands put together. As Counts of Poitou the Dukes had long ruled Poitou and Saintonge, and had been recognized as overlords by the Counts of Angoulême, La Marche and Périgord and by the Viscounts of Limoges. Then with the acquisition of Gascony in the mid-eleventh century they became rulers of Bordeaux and overlords of a number of counties and lordships extending from the mouth of the Garonne to the Pyrenees, in area about twice the size of Poitou. To the east lay border regions – Berry and Auvergne – where even the Duke's nominal suzerainty was at times doubtful. In Poitou the inhabitants spoke a northern French dialect; to the south, from Saintonge onwards, the vernacular was Limousin, a dialect of Provençal or Occitan, the language of troubadour poetry and very different from the French of the north, the Langue d'Œuil, as opposed to the Langue d'Oc of the south. Further south still towards Navarre, the inhabitants spoke Basque, a language which no one else could understand. According to an old story the Devil, intending to win the souls of the Basques, tried to learn their language, but after seven years of unremitting study had mastered only three words. At first, as Counts of Poitou, the Dukes had been chiefly involved in northern French politics but once they had also become Counts of Gascony their interests turned more and more to the south, towards Toulouse and towards Spain, where they took a leading part in the Holy War against the Moslems.

Richard, therefore, on his father's side an Angevin, was a southerner on his mother's. In his own lifetime the most vividly remembered of his maternal ancestors was his great-grandfather, Duke William IX (1071–1127). William was a crusader, much admired for his prowess, generosity and handsome appearance. But he was also a man whose attitude to life amused, astonished and alarmed his contemporaries. Above all he was the first known trou-badour and, as such, a key figure in the history of European litera-ture. In one of his songs he called himself a master of the art of love, good enough to be able to earn his living at it. No one could spend a night with him without wanting more. The content of the poem ought to be taken with several pinches of salt, partly because it belonged to the genre of boasting poem known as the *gap* which was a standard form of troubadour verse, and partly because William liked to mock himself as well as others. But there were people who took poems like this at face value and were shocked. They described him as the 'enemy of all chastity' and ascribed to him the intention of founding an abbey of prostitutes in which the offices of abbess, prioress and so on would be distributed according to the pro-fessional skill of the inmates. The real trouble with him, according to the Anglo-Norman chronicler William of Malmesbury, was that he took nothing seriously, that 'he turned everything into a joke and made his listeners laugh uncontrollably'. But as far as the church was concerned it was no joke when he refused to take excom-munication seriously. On one occasion he is alleged to have told a bald papal legate who had just excommunicated him for refusing to abandon his mistress that he would see the legate's hair in curlers before he gave her up. But the poems which he wrote are much more subtle than this obvious insult. Their craftsmanship makes it clear that he took the business of composing verse and music very seriously indeed. He wrote burlesque parodies and love lyrics, songs in which, as he himself put it, 'love, joy and youth were intermingled' (*totz mesclatz d'amor e de joy e de jouen*). And there was also the enigmatic poem *Farai un vers de dreyt nien* – 'I'll sing a song about nothing at all' – with verses like the following:

> I cannot tell when I am asleep
> Or awake – unless someone tells me so.
> My heart is on the point of breaking
> With a deep sorrow
> And I swear that this doesn't bother me
> In the slightest.
>
> I am sick and scared to death
> Though I only know about it from what men say.
> I'll look for a doctor who suits me
> But I don't know one
> And he'll be a good doctor if he can cure me
> When I am not ill.

In the past William IX has been portrayed as the genius who, single-handed, created a new art-form, the poetry of romantic and sexual love, *amour courtois* or (as it is usually translated) 'courtly love'. In fact he was commenting upon and sometimes parodying a form of love lyric which was already familiar and was composing for an audience which was sufficiently sophisticated to appreciate this approach. Among his successors as Duke of Aquitaine only Richard is known to have written verse and certainly neither of the two surviving poems attributed to him is of this quality. But one great poet is perhaps enough in any family, even the most civilized. For this is what William's descendants were: the most cultured princely family in twelfth-century Europe.

Because troubadour music and poetry were vital elements in the atmosphere which Richard breathed throughout his life it is important to understand just what courtly love was. The idea that the appearance of *amour courtois* in late eleventh-century Aquitaine was one of the great moments in the history of mankind was most powerfully expressed by C. S. Lewis in *The Allegory of Love*.

It seems to us natural that love should be the commonest theme of serious imaginative literature: but a glance at classical antiquity or at the Dark Ages at once shows us that what we took for 'nature' is really a special state of affairs, which will probably have an end, and which certainly had a beginning ... It seems – or it seemed to us till lately – a natural thing that love (under certain conditions) should be regarded as a noble and ennobling passion: it is only if we imagine ourselves trying to explain this doctrine to Aristotle, Virgil, St Paul, or the author of *Beowulf*, that we become aware how far from natural it is. Even our code of etiquette, with its rule that women always have precedence, is a legacy from courtly love, and is felt to be far from natural in modern Japan or India ... French poets, in the eleventh century, discovered or invented, or were the first to express, that romantic species of passion which English poets were still writing about in the nineteenth. They effected a change which has left no corner of our ethics, our imagination, or our daily life untouched, and they erected impassable barriers between us and the classical past or the Oriental present. Compared with this revolution the Renaissance is a mere ripple on the surface of literature.

These eloquent words contain an element of exaggeration. Frenchmen in the late eleventh century were not the first people to experience romantic passion; the emotion found expression in earlier poems in places as far apart as ancient Egypt and tenth-century Germany. But whereas such poems are rare in earlier periods, in twelfth-century Europe they multiply so explosively that the phenomenon cannot be explained merely as the reflection of a greater number of extant manuscripts. In the course of the eleventh and twelfth centuries aristocratic society – courtly society – came to look upon sexual love, its desires and its complications, as an absorbing and fashionable subject. It was part of a wider and profoundly important cultural movement – religious, theological and artistic as well as purely literary – whereby the problems of an individual's inner life, the reasonings of his mind, the demands of his heart, all came to be regarded as being as important as his external behaviour. So Peter Abelard could argue that those who crucified Christ had not sinned because they genuinely believed that they were acting rightly. On the cross Christ himself came to be portrayed as a man in agony rather than as a God in majesty. This emphasis on the human side of Christ's nature went hand in hand with an increasing veneration of his earthly mother. And in the poetry of the troubadours other women became the object of a cult of adoration, though here it was adoration expressed in purely physical terms.

The lover's certainty that his love was the source of everything good and worthwhile in his life – the belief which lay behind the radiantly lyrical love poems of Bernard de Ventadour, some of which were composed at the court of Henry II and Eleanor – was a belief which gave to woman, as man's partner and sometimes, in this context at least, the dominant partner, a place at the heart of things which had not been hers before. When a twelfth-century knight rode into a tournament or into battle he hoped to be worthy either his lineage or of his lady; earlier he had thought only of his ancestors. In the late twelfth-century romance *L'Escoufle* the good knight is '*toujours amoureux, ce qui le rendait hardi*'. He could dance as well as fight, and he could make polite conversation. 'We shall yet talk of this day in ladies' chambers,' said the Count of Soissons at the Battle of al-Mansurah. Not the kind of remark Roland would have made. Even at the most material level there were some differences in the status of women. In this new environment women were more frequently allowed to inherit property than they had been earlier, though inevitably the more they were heiresses the more those men who had power over them – uncles or guardians – regarded them as marketable assets. Marriage remained very much an institution whereby property was transferred from one family to another – just as Aquitaine was transferred first to the Capetians and then to the Angevins.

To Orderic Vitalis, an Anglo-Norman monk of the early twelfth century, the love poetry of Aquitaine and Provence seemed to be evidence of the moral corruption of the south. Orderic's attitude is hardly surprising. Moral corruption began with Eve and the church's attitude to passionate love was entirely hostile. Even in marriage it was sinful to seek pleasure in sex. To make matters worse it is clear that much troubadour poetry was concerned with adultery. In one poem William IX said that a closely guarded married woman was as bad a prospect as a millpond without fish. But since marriage was entered into for reasons of social, political and financial convenience it was hardly possible to celebrate love except outside it. In

practice, of course, twelfth-century society adopted a double standard on the subject. Men were expected to be unfaithful. One
chronicler noted with surprise that Count Baldwin of Hainault
loved his wife alone and observed that such behaviour was rarely
to be found in a man. On the other hand a woman's infidelity was
likely to produce a savage reaction. When Count Philip of Flanders
suspected that his wife had committed adultery with Gautier de
Fontaines he had the young man killed by hanging him upside down
in a cess-pit. And not even in the land of the troubadours were husbands more tolerant. When Aimar v, Viscount of Limoges, suspected that his wife and his uncle Archambaud of Comborn were
having an affair he went to war against his uncle and made his first
attack without warning.

It is not easy to understand why it should have been so but France
south of the Loire was undoubtedly the seedbed of the whole
'courtly love' movement. Ebles of Ventadour, the only other troubadour known from William ix's time, came from the Limousin,
and most of the outstanding song-writers of the next generation –
Cercamon, Marcabru, Jaufré Rudel, Bernard de Ventadour – lived
and worked within the borders of Aquitaine. When four Poitevin
knights were taken prisoner by Richard's Angevin grandfather
Count Geoffrey Plantagenet they won their release by composing
and singing a song in praise of their captor. In the history of European music the twelfth century is a key period of development, when
the unison of Gregorian chant gave ground before polyphony –
much to the disgust of conservative intellectuals like John of
Salisbury, who complained of 'the wanton and effeminate sound
produced by caressing, chiming and intertwining melodies, a
veritable harmony of sirens'. And in twelfth-century music there is
no place more famous than the abbey of St Martial's in Limoges.
As well as church music many of the earliest troubadour lyrics,
with their accompanying melodies, survive in manuscripts from St
Martial's.

In the visual arts Limoges was the great European centre of
enamel work. In sculpture there are the magnificent and intricately
carved façades of the church of Notre-Dame-la-Grande in Poitiers
and of the cathedral at Angoulême. Perhaps even more revealing

are the astonishing carvings which adorn many of the small Roman-esque churches of the Saintonge, for whereas the façades of impor-tant churches, under the patronage of princes like the Duke of Aquitaine or the Count of Angoulême, may well be the work of internationally famous masters, these village churches make plain the strength of a purely local tradition of superb craftsmanship.

The duchy of Aquitaine was not just the most civilized province in France, it was also a region of great wealth – it would have needed to be to support so much fine art. The learned English chronicler Ralph of Diss described its economy in glowing terms:

Aquitaine overflows with riches of many kinds, excelling other parts of the western world to such an extent that historians consider it to be one of the most fortunate and flourishing of the provinces of Gaul. Its fields are fertile, its vineyards productive and its forests teem with wild life. From the Pyrenees northwards the entire countryside is irrigated by the River Garonne and other streams; indeed it is from these life-giving waters [*aquae*] that the province takes its name.

Its main exports were salt and wine. Salt, one of the indispensable ingredients of medieval life, was produced along the whole length of the duchy's Atlantic coast. The main varieties were 'Bay Salt' from the Bay of Bourgneuf in the north in the marches between Poitou and Brittany, the salt of Brouage, panned on the sheltered shores behind the isles of Oléron and Ré, and, in the far south, the salt of Bayonne. However, for the twelfth century we are much better informed about the rapidly expanding wine trade. There is plenty of evidence for the planting of new vineyards in the Bordelais and even a Poitevin was prepared to admit that Bordeaux wine was of superb quality, but at this date by far the most important wine-exporting region was further north, in Aunis and Saintonge. A fine white wine was produced around Niort, St Jean d'Angély and La Rochelle and then shipped overseas from La Rochelle. This port, founded as late as 1130, very quickly came to enjoy all the character-istics of a boom town. Its modern quays were well suited to accom-modate the new large ships, known as cogs, which in the course of the second half of the twelfth century came to dominate the mari-time trade of the Baltic, North Sea and Channel coasts. With these ships the merchants of La Rochelle could compete in the markets of England and Flanders with wines produced nearer at hand in the Paris Basin and the Rhineland. So successfully did they break into the English market that they soon put the native vineyards out of business. After all, as one late twelfth-century writer put it, English wine could be drunk only with closed eyes and through clenched teeth.

This growing export trade was of great importance to the Duke of Aquitaine. By protecting the producers and merchants and by imposing tolls and customs dues he could profit from it – doubly so if he ruled over the English and Norman ports into which the wine was imported. These revenues, unknown and incalculable though they are, helped to make the Duke one of the greatest and most powerful princes in Western Europe. It is misleading to write of Aquitaine as though it were one vast feudal jungle where vassals rebelled against their lords, nephews fought against their uncles, and all done with a passionate ferocity which left little or no room for effective ducal government. Yet this still tends to be the way in which historians do in fact describe Aquitaine. It is easy enough to point to famous feuds such as that between Ebles II of Comborn (in the Limousin) and his uncle Bernard, during the course of which Ebles raped his aunt in front of witnesses and which ended when his uncle castrated and murdered him. But to generalize from such sensational particulars as these is to ignore both commonsense and political geography. It is as nonsensical as measuring the power of English kings solely in the light of unusual incidents occurring in the marches against Scotland. All princes had to face the problems posed by distant and turbulent borderlands. The relatively peaceful and well-governed 'home counties' of the Duke of Aquitaine, from Poitiers westwards to the sea at Talmont, then down the coast to Bordeaux and up the valley of the Garonne as far as Agen, comprised an area as large as midland and south-eastern England and included some of the most prosperous and commercially developed parts of the whole duchy. There was a special problem in the fact that castles held by the Lusignan family and particularly by the Counts of Angoulême could at times hinder land communications between the Duke's three administrative capitals, the old Roman

and episcopal cities of Poitiers, Saintes and Bordeaux. But this difficulty was not necessarily insurmountable and certainly does not
justify writing off the Duke as a political lightweight. By using his
superior financial resources Duke Guy-Geoffrey of Aquitaine had
outfought and outwitted all other rival claimants to Gascony. The
subsequent shift of focus southwards meant that his descendants
became yet more distant and therefore more insignificant-seeming
figures to those influential writers whose field of vision was restricted to the Anglo-Norman realm on either side of the Channel.

The marriage of Henry of Anjou to Eleanor and his accession,
two years later, to the throne of England had brought together under
a single sceptre peoples and provinces which hardly knew each
other. In the century since 1066 England and Normandy had
become two parts of a single political society, linked rather than
separated by the Channel, the main road of the Anglo-Norman
realm Men and women crossed easily from one side to the other;
many wealthy families held lands in both England and Normandy;
and even though sharp-eared language snobs were soon able to mock
French 'spoken after the manner of Marlborough', people at the
upper levels of society in fact spoke the same language, Norman
French, on both sides. But very few Englishmen came to know
Aquitaine; that is why Ralph of Diss took the trouble to include
a lengthy description of the duchy and its inhabitants in his
chronicle. Only those who were sufficiently moved by piety or curi-
osity to go on a pilgrimage to the celebrated shrine of Santiago de
Compostella, on roads which took them through Aquitaine, can
have learned anything at all about the land which was to be the chief
concern of Richard's life. The cult of *Santiago Matamoros*, St James
the slayer of Moors, was growing in popularity throughout the
twelfth century and, like the wine trade, it was beginning to forge
links between England and the south-west. Henry I's most lavish
monastic foundation, at Reading, where he was buried and where
Henry II, in 1156, buried his first-born son William, was dedicated
to St James. Although its collection of relics contained many choice
items, such as pieces of Aaron's rod and Christ's foreskin, the *pièce
de résistance* was undoubtedly the arm of St James, brought to England from Italy by Richard's grandmother, the Empress Matilda.

In 1173 an abbot of Reading became Archbishop of Bordeaux, and in 1181 Henry II endowed a hospital of St James for the benefit of poor pilgrims, also in Bordeaux.

By the mid-twelfth century pilgrims were sufficiently numerous to merit a guidebook. It was written by a clerk who knew Poitou well. He advised visitors what roads to take and pointed out the sights they should see on the way. Some of them can still be seen – for example, the church of St-Hilaire-le-Grand in Poitiers, or the lower church of St Eutropius, who was believed to be a descendant of Xerxes of Persia, in Saintes. Others have vanished, like the rich abbey of St Jean d'Angély where the head of St John the Baptist had been venerated ever since its miraculous discovery in the mid-eleventh century. In Blaye, on the northern bank of the Gironde, the pilgrim could look upon the tomb of Roland, the hero of the *Chanson de Roland*, the most famous of all the *chansons de geste*. In reality Roland had been killed in a Basque ambush at the Pass of Roncesvaux but in twelfth-century legend he died gloriously, fighting for Christendom in the great war against the infidel. The nearer the pilgrim approached the Pyrenees the deeper he penetrated a countryside where almost every landmark had some kind of association with Roland. In the abbey church of St Seurin at Bordeaux, for example, he could see Roland's horn, the sound of which might have summoned reinforcements to Roncesvalles but which Roland, more careful of his reputation than of his life, had refused to blow until it was too late. In this landscape, which Richard learned to know well, the idea of a holy war against the Saracens must have seemed very real and very close at hand.

The guidebook also provides useful information about the people who lived in the regions through which the pilgrim would have to pass. In Poitou they are tough and warlike, skilled with lances and bows and arrows, brave in the battle-line, swift in the chase, elegant in dress, handsome, articulate, generous and hospitable. In Saintonge, however, they speak in a rustic fashion. In the Bordelais the language is still worse. As for the Gascons, they are gossipy, licentious, and poorly dressed; although they eat and drink far too much they don't sit at table but squat around a fire; they all share the same cup and when they go to sleep they all share the same rotting straw, master and mistress, servants and all. The Basques and Navarrese are much like the Gascons – only worse. They all eat out of one big pot like pigs at a trough, and when they talk it sounds like a dog barking. When they want to warm themselves in front of a fire they are not ashamed to lift up their kilts and display their private parts. They treat their women like mules and they fornicate with animals; indeed in this respect they are so jealous that they go so far as to attach chastity belts to their mares and mules.

It is sadly obvious that as the author of the guidebook moved further south into regions more and more unfamiliar to him so his prejudices became more and more vitriolic. But for most Englishmen and Normans Poitou itself lay deep in the unfamiliar south. Even the pilgrims would have learned relatively little for they rarely strayed far from their fixed itinerary of shrines and hostels; like tourists they saw nothing except monuments and hotels. Thus Aquitaine remained a far-off, unknown country and its inhabitants were well known for their fickleness and treacherousness. No right-thinking Englishman would trust them an inch.

4

FAMILY CRISIS
1167-1174

ALTHOUGH Henry II suffered a partial setback in 1159 and never again mounted an expedition on the scale of the Toulouse campaign, he in no way altered his basic policy. Far from drawing in his horns and going on the defensive, he continued to seek out and exploit opportunities for further expansion. By November 1160 he had decided that Henry and Margaret were old enough to be married; Henry was now five and Margaret a couple of years younger. Immediately after the ceremony the castles of the Norman Vexin were handed over – much to King Louis's chagrin. Henry II's next targets were on his western frontiers. With the exception of the Celtic lands of Wales and Brittany, over which he exercised only a loose overlordship, he already controlled most of the seaboard of north-western Europe and he was determined to put an end to these exceptions. But in the early 1160s he had little success at bending the Welsh princes to his will, while one major invasion attempt in July 1165 was thwarted by atrocious summer weather. In Brittany by contrast matters went very much according to plan. In 1166 he marched on the Breton capital, Rennes, deposed Duke Conan and took over the duchy in the name of Conan's infant daughter and heiress Constance. The obvious thing to do with such an important heiress was to betroth her to one of his sons and the fact that he chose his third son, Geoffrey, shows that Richard was still marked out as the future Duke of Aquitaine.

Next year, in 1167, King Henry travelled south to spend Lent at one of his favourite monasteries, Grandmont in the Limousin. There he met his old enemy Raymond V of Toulouse, who had

recently divorced his wife, Louis VII's sister, and clearly needed
new friends if he was to bear the Capetian's displeasure with
equanimity. We are not told what precisely it was that was agreed
at Grandmont; we know only that Louis did not like it. Possibly
Count Raymond offered to do homage to Henry and to hold Toulouse as a fief of the duchy of Aquitaine. If so, Henry II had now
by diplomacy achieved cheaply that which eight years earlier he had
tried to do by the expensive means of war. Jacques Boussard, the
leading French historian of the Angevin Empire, felt confident
enough to write that Henry's authority now extended as far as the
Mediterranean! What is undoubtedly clear is that during these years
Henry's power was still steadily advancing, though most modern
writers tend to create the false impression of a king entirely preoccu-
pied with the awkward domestic problem of the quarrel with
Thomas Becket. In fact this was by no means the shatteringly important quarrel it appeared to be in hindsight to people living and
writing under the shadow of Becket's murder. It was, of course,
a nuisance and particularly so after 1166 when Becket took refuge
in the territory of King Louis, adding a further irritant to the permanently fragile relationship between the two kings. But Henry was
more concerned about the political repercussions of the advances
he was making on the Continent than about the troubles of the
church of Canterbury.

In the spring of 1167 he led an army into the Auvergne, right
on the eastern border of Aquitaine, in order to lay waste the land
of Count William of Auvergne, who seems to have dispossessed his
nephew the young Count. As ruler of Aquitaine Henry felt that it
was his duty to impose a settlement, but in recent years Louis VII
had been showing some interest in this region, which lay on the
route between Paris and Toulouse. He resented the assertion of
Aquitainian authority coming hard on the heels of the Grandmont
meeting and when Count William turned to him for help he
responded by raiding the Vexin to draw Henry back north. At the
same time as this threat Henry found himself faced with a revolt
of a section of the Breton nobility, alarmed by his high-handed
treatment of their duchy, and there were already hints of trouble
elsewhere in his dominions. In these circumstances it was not in

Henry's interest to press Louis too hard, for the Capetian might
well counter by lending support to disaffected elements within the
Angevin Empire. Moreover Henry was thinking more and more
about the future of his dynasty and his lands. He wanted to arrange
a family settlement, no easy matter with so many children and
such widespread territories to consider. But since any arrangement
would need the consent of Louis VII to be valid, he had somehow to
come to terms with the French King – despite Toulouse, despite
Auvergne, despite Becket. Knowing Louis's concern for the Holy
Land – in 1147 he had led the French army on the Second Crusade
– he put it about that all he really wanted to do was put his own
house in order, make proper provision for his children, and then
he would be off on crusade in his lord's company. The plan which
Henry still had in mind was for his eldest son to take all of those
lands which he himself had inherited from his father and mother,
i.e. Anjou, Maine, Normandy and England, while Richard should
have the land which he had acquired by virtue of his marriage to
Eleanor. It occurred to no one that the empire might survive as a
single political unit, or that it ought to do so. What mattered was
not the territorial integrity of the empire, but the just rights of each
member of the family.

But then, early in 1168, a new revolt broke out and became
entangled with the question of the family settlement. Since this time
it was a revolt in Aquitaine it was doubly significant for Richard's
future. What lay behind the rebellion is not at all clear, though
historians claim that it was a reaction to Henry's policy of central-
ization, breaking down the traditions of local autonomy and introducing more advanced Anglo-Norman methods of government. It
may be so, but convincing evidence for any such policy on Henry's
part is unfortunately lacking. The most that can be said with any
certainty is that the revolt was led by two families who were to
play a great part in the next generation of Aquitainian politics, two
families with whom Richard was to become very familiar: the house
of Lusignan and the house of Angoulême. The lands and castles
belonging to the Taillefer Counts of Angoulême and their vassals
at Jarnac, Bouteville, Archiac, Barbezieux and Montignac, as well
as Angoulême itself, lay across the roads which linked the centres

of ducal power at Poitiers and Saintes with Bordeaux. The lands
and castles belonging to the Lusignans and their vassals at Couhé,
Vouvant, Château-Larcher and Frontenay, as well as Lusignan
itself, lay across the roads which linked Poitiers with Saintes and
the new and thriving port of La Rochelle. The facts of political
geography are alone sufficient to suggest that there might be
many occasions when the Duke of Aquitaine found himself at odds
with the Taillefers and the Lusignans. Indeed feuds with these
families had been part of the staple political diet of the early twelfth-
century Dukes, though neither Eleanor's father nor grandfather can
be supposed to have been introducing 'Anglo-Norman methods of
government'.

In 1168 the Lusignans were nothing like as rich or powerful as
the Counts of Angoulême, who ruled what was in effect an independent principality in the heart of Aquitaine, and yet it was Lusignan
which seems to have been the storm centre of the revolt. This may
reflect King Henry's more immediate concern with rebels whose
main fortress was only fifteen miles south-west of Poitiers, or it may
be that Count William of Angoulême was overshadowed by the
more vigorous personality of the new head of the house of Lusignan,
Geoffrey de Lusignan. In 1168 Geoffrey stood on the threshold of
a long and turbulent career which was to earn him a great reputation
as a knight both in Europe and on crusade and to help lift his dynasty
out of the ranks of the barons of Poitou and place it firmly among
the leading princes of Christendom. At this date, however, the
Lusignans were no match for Henry II, now at the height of his
powers. They had to look on while he laid waste their estates
together with those of their supporters and captured and dismantled
the great castle of Lusignan itself. Only the fact that Henry had
so many other calls on his energy and resources enabled them to
survive. In March he was summoned north by the news that the
negotiations with Louis VII had reached a crucial stage. The French
King had provisionally agreed to a settlement and Henry's presence
was required to ratify it. The terms included clauses recognizing
Richard as Duke-designate of Aquitaine and arranging a betrothal
between him and Louis's daughter Alice. Nothing was said about
Toulouse, though the Capetian line on this was clear: the question

could only be settled by a judgement in the court of the feudal overlord, in other words in the court of King Louis.

Before going north to meet the French King, Henry had left Poitou in the hands of Queen Eleanor with an experienced commander, Earl Patrick of Salisbury, at her side as her military adviser. The rebels seized the chance to return to Lusignan in force and begin to rebuild it. When Henry heard of this he turned back again, deputing some of his officials to continue the discussions with Louis. The French King seems to have taken this as an insult and, if he had not already been in touch with the Poitevin rebels, he very soon was. He met their envoys at Bourges. An alliance was quickly forged. Both parties agreed not to make peace without the other's consent. Louis promised to help the Poitevins recover their losses, while they handed over hostages as a guarantee that they would keep their side of the bargain.

By early April Henry, concerned above all to secure his family settlement, was prepared to make restitution to the Poitevins in order to salvage it. But in the meantime Louis had taken a step back by withdrawing his consent to the betrothal of Richard and Alice. While these talks were continuing on the Norman border, a clash in Poitou between the men of Geoffrey de Lusignan and Earl Patrick resulted in the Earl's death. Making war in the twelfth century was rather like going on strike in the twentieth: it was a method of exerting economic and financial pressure on your opponent – it was not intended that it should end in his death. By devastating his fields, orchards and vineyards you hoped to force him to listen to a case which he was otherwise disposed to ignore; by military means he was to be compelled to come to terms. It was a regrettable side-effect of such disputes that the 'general public' suffered – villagers might see their homes and livelihoods destroyed, they might be hurt or occasionally even killed, but how else was their lord to be brought to reason or to arbitration except by ensuring that he could not collect his rents? If there were a powerful king he might find some other way of terminating disputes and for this reason the church – which was not supposed to engage in warfare – was generally in favour of a king who could provide strong government. The emergence of strong governments in European history is a movement labelled 'progress' – and 'progress' is obviously a good thing, if one has friends in the government. In the meantime, in places like Poitou, noblemen tried to settle their disputes by going to war. Yet, although making war was a fairly routine element in the life of an active nobleman, it was very rare indeed that one was killed; partly because, in the face of danger, a noble could don his expensive and effective armour, his helmet and coat of mail; and partly because his opponents did not try to kill him – if he should be so unfortunate as to be at their mercy they preferred to capture him and ransom him. This would bring financial pressure to bear on his friends and family, and besides it was profitable. But dead men paid no ransoms. In war it was only the poor who were expected to die and so the death of Earl Patrick came as a great shock to everyone. The Poitevins claimed that they had been attacked while peace talks were in progress and that though they had naturally defended themselves they had certainly not intended to kill the Earl. But the Earl's followers – and among them was his young nephew William Marshal – told a very different story. They said that he had been ambushed while unarmed and slain by a thrust in the back. William, though himself without a helmet, fought like a lion to avenge his uncle's death but was eventually overborne by weight of numbers as well as by another sword thrust from behind – and carried off into captivity. Years later that journey still remained vivid in his memory. Fearing King Henry's anger his captors kept under the cover of woodland, moving stealthily from one secret hide-out to another, dragging William along with his wound unbandaged and still bleeding. The whole episode left its mark on William's mind. For him the Poitevins were and always would be faithless traitors.

The death of Earl Patrick in these confused and possibly scandalous circumstances inevitably embittered relationships and made peace even harder to achieve. A further conference at La Ferté-Bernard in July 1168 met in an atmosphere of mutual suspicion and broke up with nothing achieved. For a future Duke of Aquitaine there was additional cause for disquiet in the presence of envoys from Gascony as well as from Poitou, Brittany, Wales and Scotland in the French camp. It seemed that both parts of his duchy were now in a state of unrest. Perhaps it was at this time that a clerk

associated with the rebel Poitevins produced a document designed
to show that Henry and Eleanor were within the prohibited degrees
of consanguinity and their marriage therefore invalid. The war went
on throughout the second half of 1168. As usual in his dealings with
Louis VII, Henry seems to have held the upper hand. He was much
richer than Louis, able – as the French king was not – to hire large
armies of mercenaries and to reduce his leading vassals, the Counts
of Flanders, Boulogne and Blois for example, to a position of neutrality by paying them substantial pensions. The contrast between
the two kings was ruefully noted by Louis himself in a remark he
made to Walter Map:

Your lord the King of England, who lacks nothing, has men, horses,
gold, silk, jewels, fruits, game and everything else. We in France have
nothing but bread and wine and gaiety.

Map adds that he made a note of this observation 'for it was merrily
said, and truly'.

Finally in January 1169 peace was made at Montmirail. Henry
II renewed his own homage to Louis and then watched his two elder
sons do homage: Henry for Normandy, Anjou and Maine, Richard
for Aquitaine. The betrothal of Richard and Alice was at last finalized; she was to come without a dowry. Where Richard was during
these years of military and diplomatic manœuvring we do not know,
but it is a reasonable guess that he was with his mother, since Aquitaine was her duchy and it was by her wish that it was to be made
over to him. His father too must have been well satisfied with the
Peace of Montmirail. In return for his family settlement he had
agreed to be reconciled to the Poitevin rebels and make good the
losses which they had suffered since the beginning of the war. But
this, of course, was a promise which Louis had no means of enforc-
ing. Whether he knew it or not the French King had effectively
abandoned his allies. Henry had set his house in order but had no
thoughts about setting off on crusade. Instead he was determined
to punish the rebels. In his own mind he was free to turn against
them, despite the terms agreed at Montmirail, because he and they
had not exchanged a kiss of peace. Louis VII, having given Henry
what he wanted, could do no more than bewail the fate of his friends.

The spring and early summer of 1169 Henry spent in the south, taking and demolishing many of the castles from which the rebels had defied his authority. The Counts of Angoulême and La Marche submitted, while, in a notorious incident, one of their allies, Robert de Seilhac, died – or so it was believed – as a result of the harsh treatment he received in Henry's prison. Despite the fact that Richard and his elder brother had performed homage to Louis VII for their lands it was obvious that their father had in no way relinquished control. But, like it or not, he nearly had to in August 1170, when he was very seriously ill. Believing that death was at hand he confirmed the territorial dispositions made at Montmirail and asked to be buried at the monastery of Grandmont in the Limousin, one of the monks of which had played an important part in the peace negotiations. On his recovery he made a pilgrimage to the shrine of Rocamadour in the Quercy. These and other indications – the marriage of his daughter Eleanor to Alfonso VIII of Castile, a projected campaign in the Auvergne, a claim that the archbishopric of Bourges rightfully belonged to the duchy of Aquitaine – show that the southern parts of his dominions continued to be very much in his mind in these months. Even after the murder of Thomas Becket in his own cathedral on 29 December 1170, there were churches in Aquitaine which still turned to Henry for help and protection. In March 1171 the monks of St Martial's, Limoges, though perhaps with some embarrassment, asked for, and were sent, aid in putting down a revolt of their townsmen at La Souterraine, a revolt which had the backing of Count Audebert of La Marche.

Soon after this incident Richard emerges from the obscurity which had surrounded his movements in the last two years since he knelt in homage at Montmirail. When he does emerge we see him in the company of his mother. Together he and Eleanor laid foundation stones for the monastery of St Augustine in Limoges in 1171. And at last, in June 1172, when he was fourteen years old, the great day came when Richard was formally installed as Duke of Aquitaine. In the abbey church of St Hilary in Poitiers where, four years earlier, Earl Patrick of Salisbury had been buried, he took his seat in the abbot's chair to receive from the hands of the Archbishop of Bordeaux and the Bishop of Poitiers the sacred lance and banner which were the insignia of the ducal office. But as Duke he was to be more than just the Count of Poitou. So Richard moved on to Limoges and there he was again proclaimed Duke in a ceremony witnessed by the Limousin chronicler Geoffrey·of Vigeois, who at that date was one of the monks of St Martial's. The climax of the ceremony came when the ring of St Valerie was slipped on to Richard's finger. In twelfth-century legend St Valerie was the martyred saint who personified Aquitaine and her story as told at Limoges – where she had lived and died and where her 'thousand-year-old' body was still preserved – was intended to show that Limoges was a more venerable city than Poitiers. Three years earlier Richard had performed homage to King Louis at Montmirail but now that he had worn the ring of St Valerie he could claim that he held his duchy in indissoluble union with the people of Aquitaine and the saints who watched over them. The two ceremonies at Poitiers and Limoges were a ritual expression of Aquitaine's *de facto* independence from the King of France. By the same token they might also be taken to mean that Richard's right to his duchy was independent of his father's will. But whatever the symbolic significance of these ceremonies may have been, it is clear that in practice Henry still retained the reins of power.

It must have been in these years that Henry II and Eleanor became increasingly estranged. Their last child, John, had been born in December 1167. The evidence, scrappy though it is, gives no hint of a meeting for more than two years, between the autumn of 1170 and the end of 1172 when they held their last Christmas court together at Chinon. Henry remained overall policy-maker but it looks as though Eleanor had been left to supervise the day-to-day running of her duchy and effectively in sole charge of her second son. In this period of her life the fifty-year-old duchess has been transformed from a tough old battleaxe into 'the presiding genius in a society of knights and troubadours'. But here again we enter the land of romance and legend. It has been said that at the court of Poitiers 'the gilded youth of Poitou and Aquitaine breathed an air that seemed to belong to some tale of chivalry'. Here there were music and dancing, tournaments and troubadours, talk of knight-errantry and courtly love. At the centre of this joyous court life stood the figure of Eleanor, 'dominating all around her by that intellectual radiance, that love of literature and fine language which was her hall-mark'. All very different, it is implied, from the sober court of Henry II where lawyers and administrators liked to spend their evenings discussing the wording of the latest royal writ.

Some literary historians have gone even further and have suggested that courtly love was much more than just a fashionable and pleasant way of passing time. They see it as a revolutionary and subversive moral doctrine. To glorify the love felt for another man's wife was to flout contemporary notions of obedience and authority, the authority of the church as well as the authority of the husband. By undermining these two bastions of a male world courtly love was, in effect, threatening the existence of the whole social order. The historians who have taken this line have identified Eleanor and her eldest daughter, Marie, Countess of Champagne (1140–98), as the outstanding patrons of this dangerous movement. The contemporary rumours that Eleanor had been an adulteress made it possible to believe that she preached what she practised. Marie is said to have been a frequent visitor to her mother's court at Poitiers and to have brought with her the greatest poet in France, Chrétien de Troyes. Among Chrétien's works was a romance, *Lancelot*, written at Marie's request, which took as its hero a man who had an illicit affair with the wife of his lord, King Arthur. In addition Eleanor and Marie appear to be central figures in a treatise entitled *De Amore* written by Andrew, a chaplain at the court of Champagne in the early 1180s.

This celebrated treatise, usually known as 'The Art of Courtly Love', lies at the origin of the legend of the Courts of Love, tribunals before which lovers were supposed to bring their quarrels in order to have them adjudicated by authorities in the art of love like Eleanor of Aquitaine and her daughter. One such dispute was settled by Marie with a verdict apparently asserting that true love cannot exist between man and wife. No one any longer seriously believes that Marie and Eleanor actually did preside over such tribunals. It is accepted that the Courts of Love were a fiction, an intellectual game. But it is still widely believed that it was a game which was avidly played at Poitiers whenever Marie, her chaplain Andrew, and

Chrétien de Troyes came to visit Eleanor. As a result of this belief Eleanor retains her place as the woman who, above all others, symbolizes the new social and cultural pattern of courtly love. She stands for the civilization of the South, of the *Midi*, the home of the troubadours, against the sterner, rougher, cruder world of the North, represented, in this image, by her husband, the King of the North Wind, whose authority she is subtly undermining and against whom she will soon break out in open rebellion. On this view, in the tension between Richard's parents there was not just the clash of temperaments, there was also the conflict of two cultures. It would be hard to imagine a more complex and bewildering environment for an adolescent to grow up in.

If it were true. The trouble is that the revised version of the legend of the Courts of Love is as ill-founded as the old one. Nowhere is there any evidence to show that the Countess Marie, Chrétien de Troyes and Andrew the Chaplain ever visited the court at Poitiers – or anywhere else, since Eleanor was certainly not continuously at Poitiers during these years. 'The Art of Courtly Love' was not written until about 1186, by which time Andrew had probably left Marie's service. The two verdicts which he attributes to Eleanor make it obvious that, in these passages at least, his intention was a satirical one. In the first case Eleanor gave a judicial decision condemning consanguineous marriages – of which she had made two. In the second case she judged the problem of a woman who had to choose between a mature knight of complete probity and a young man devoid of worth. According to Andrew, Eleanor's verdict was that a woman would act less wisely if she chose the less worthy one. Since Eleanor, at the age of thirty, had separated from a husband of her own age in order to marry a nineteen-year-old, Andrew's audience can hardly have missed the irony, particularly if – as seems possible – the book was written at the French royal court. The Countess Marie's denial of the existence of love in marriage is 'dated' to May 1174 – the one date in the whole book – when Eleanor was held in Chinon Castle, her husband's prisoner. The intellectual game was being played not by Eleanor in the years 1169–73 but by Andrew the Chaplain in the late 1180s. And if Andrew's approach was humorous and satirical can we afford to believe that the 'new concept' of love in adultery was ever at any time seriously advocated?

Exactly the same problem of irony is involved in evaluating Chrétien de Troyes' *Lancelot*. But the most serious fault with the modern legend of Eleanor of Aquitaine is the contrast drawn between her and her husband. Eleanor, it is true, was a patron of literature and art, but so were most princes and certainly Henry II was. Artists sought his favour more often than they sought his wife's, which is hardly surprising since he had more power and patronage to dispense. Yet even Bernard of Ventadour, the poet of lyrical love, composed for Henry more often than for Eleanor. But perhaps this too should not surprise us. Although the rumours of the Queen's supposed adulteries were real enough and, given the prevailing double standard in sexual matters, much more shocking than the stories of the King's mistresses, none the less if either of them ever had a romantic love affair it is likely to have been Henry rather than Eleanor. As late as 1191 the tomb of Rosamund Clifford – Henry's 'Fair Rosamund', who died in 1176 – was still covered in silk cloth and tended by the nuns of Godstow Priory in accordance with the terms of Henry's benefaction to their nunnery. The legend of Eleanor is doubly misleading. It does justice neither to Henry's interest in literature nor to Eleanor's own personality. For it is clear that she was an extraordinary woman; only not in the manner of legend. The legend must go – but at the same time we must be careful not to let the queen out with the asses' milk.

When Henry and Eleanor held their Christmas court at Chinon in 1172 whatever tensions there were between them remained hidden from public view. The King, now reconciled to the church and formally absolved from complicity in Becket's murder, pursued his old path of family politics and territorial expansion. Since 1171 he had been negotiating with Count Humbert of Maurienne. His youngest son John was to be betrothed to the Count's daughter and heiress presumptive. Since Count Humbert's lands controlled all the passes in the Western Alps it was a marriage which opened up intriguing, if uncertain, prospects, and Henry was willing to pay 5000 marks in order to secure it. In February 1173 he met Humbert at Montferrat in the Auvergne to finalize the details of the betrothal.

The occasion was made even more splendid by the presence of King Alfonso II of Aragon and Count Raymond V of Toulouse, who had asked him to act as an arbitrator in their long-standing quarrel. Just at the time when, in Rome, Pope Alexander III was preparing to canonize Thomas Becket it seemed that the prestige of Becket's old opponent was reaching still greater heights. To show the world how many princes felt it worth their while to dance attendance on him, Henry invited them and also the King of Navarre to a court he planned to hold in Limoges at the end of the month. There, on 25 February 1173, before them all, Count Raymond knelt and did homage for the county of Toulouse, first to Henry II, then to his eldest son Henry, and finally to Richard. The ceremony seemed designed to express the triumph of the united Angevin family over the old enemy of Toulouse. But beneath the splendid façade cracks were beginning to weaken the masonry.

It started when Count Humbert of Maurienne gave his daughter into Henry's custody and asked him what provision he was intending to make for her future husband. Five-year-old John was, of course, as yet John Lackland. In Kate Norgate's words, the question 'stirred up a trouble which was never again to be laid wholly to rest till the child who was its as yet innocent cause had broken his father's heart'. Henry replied that John would be given the three castles of Chinon, Loudun and Mirebeau. This proposal enraged young Henry. He had done homage for Normandy and Anjou at Montmirail and he had been crowned King of England in 1170. Yet he had never been assigned any lands from which he might maintain himself and his Queen in their proper estate. He was now eighteen years old and wanted to be master in his own household. In November 1172 he had met his father-in-law on the Norman border and it was believed that Louis VII had urged him to demand what was rightfully his. The Young King, as he was called, must have known that it would not be easy to persuade his father to give up any of his power and revenues. The Old King, after all, was not yet forty. The proposal to transfer Chinon, Loudun and Mirebeau to a mere child was surely just a trick giving Henry II an excuse to keep these three important castles in his own hands for many years to come. Young Henry, as Count of Anjou, angrily refused to give his consent to the plan. Instead he demanded that at least part of his inheritance should be handed over to him at once: either England or Normandy or Anjou. The Old King would not do it and from then on he and his eldest son could not talk without quarrelling.

Henry II would need to have been an unusually stupid man not to realize that there were bound to be difficult moments in the relationship between him and his heir. But he is unlikely to have foreseen the next blow. Count Raymond came to him privately and told him that Eleanor and his other sons were also plotting against him. Hastily leaving Limoges on the pretext of a hunting party Henry gave instructions that his castles should be put in a state of war-readiness. He then headed north, taking his eldest son with him. But at Chinon, while his father slept, the Young King slipped away by night and fled to the court of King Louis. Amazingly, despite Count Raymond's warning, Henry II had left Richard and Geoffrey in their mother's care. Presumably he believed that though his wife might join in a little family intrigue against him, she would not want to carry her opposition to the point of war – particularly if that were to involve her in an alliance with her ex-husband. Whatever his calculations may have been, of one thing we can be sure: he was grievously mistaken. Eleanor sent Richard and Geoffrey to join their brother at the French King's court while she herself summoned the Poitevins to arms.

It was an astonishing decision. That a Queen should rebel against the King her husband was something so unbelievable that Henry had not been able to bring himself to take Count Raymond's warning sufficiently seriously. When Ralph of Diss searched back through ancient and modern history for parallels to the revolt of 1173–4 he found more than thirty examples of sons rebelling against their parents, including some from the recent history of both Anjou and Poitou, but he cites no case of a Queen rebelling against her husband. In a letter penned on behalf of the Archbishop of Rouen by a famous stylist, Peter of Blois, Eleanor was reminded that it was a wife's duty to submit, a reminder backed up by the threat of ecclesiastical sanctions. 'For we know that unless you return to your husband you will be the cause of a general ruin.' Twelfth-century English historians, writing during Eleanor's own lifetime, were understandably cautious when they came to analyse her role in the revolt. Roger of Howden seems to suggest that behind Eleanor there stood the figure of a man, her uncle, Ralph de Faye, the seneschal of Poitou. He was undoubtedly an influential counsellor. As early as 1166 John de Belmeis, Bishop of Poitiers, writing to Becket, said of Eleanor that 'all her trust is in Ralph de Faye'. He was involved in the most important questions of policy – negotiations for the marriage of royal children: Eleanor in 1170 and John in 1173. But in view of Eleanor of Aquitaine's masterful political activity in later years it seems superfluous to look for a power behind the throne. If the initiative did not come from their mother it is hard to see either Richard, at fifteen, or Geoffrey, at fourteen, being persuaded to rebel by a man behind the scenes.

It was her own decision, no one else's. But it has remained as puzzling to modern historians as it was shocking to contemporaries. Some writers have said that Eleanor was driven to violence by Henry's adulteries, culminating in his open attachment to Rosamund Clifford. This, again, is to give too much weight to later legends which attribute Rosamund's death to the fury of a jealous Queen who, according to one version, tore the King's mistress's eyes out or, according to another, gave her a choice between poison and the knife. More recently, it has been argued that her revolt was politically motivated, that it reflected her resentment at being reduced to insignificance by Henry II's own dominant personality. This is certainly a more plausible general background to the revolt but it does not explain why Eleanor rebelled in 1173 and not at any other time. Doubtless the timing of the revolt can be partly understood in terms of the flaring up of the Young King's dissatisfaction at Limoges. But he was a feckless young man and likely to be kept in a state of frustration for a long time to come. So why did Eleanor decide that this was the moment to precipitate a family crisis and begin what one contemporary poet called 'la guerre senz amur', the war without love? It may be that there is a clue to this in something else that happened at Limoges. The homage sworn by Raymond of Toulouse was a great triumph for Henry II, but did Eleanor see it in that light? As Duchess of Aquitaine she had inherited the ducal claim to Toulouse, but at Limoges Raymond had not only done homage to the Dukes of Aquitaine, he had also done homage to the Young King. Did this mean that Aquitaine was going to be permanently subordinated to the ruler of the Anglo-Norman realm? The possibility must have made Eleanor's ancestors turn in their graves. Nor can it have been pleasing to the Poitevin nobles. One of them Hugh of Chauvigny, is reported to have hated all Englishmen. The death of Earl Patrick of Salisbury was still an episode which aroused harsh feelings on both sides.

The list of Eleanor's vassals who followed her into rebellion is headed by Count William of Angoulême, Geoffrey and Guy of Lusignan and their cousin Geoffrey de Rancon, lord of Taillebourg, and by William, called 'the archbishop', lord of Parthenay. Since Ralph de Faye was a member of the house of the Viscounts of Châtellerault this means that with the one exception of the Viscount of Thouars – who had earlier suffered badly as the result of a quarrel with Eleanor – she had been joined by all the leading barons of Poitou and the Angoumois. But equally striking is the fact that the rest of Aquitaine, including regions as turbulent as La Marche, the Limousin and the whole of Gascony, took virtually no part in the revolt. In the Limousin we know that the lords were caught up again in yet another round of the long-drawn-out feud between Viscount Aimar v and his uncles. It is probable that elsewhere, too, local interests took priority over the problems of the Angevin family.

Meanwhile Richard and his brothers had attended a great court held by Louis VII at Paris in the spring of 1173. There they had sworn not to make peace with their father except with the consent of the King and barons of France. For Richard this was the year when he came to man's estate, for it was about this time that Louis VII knighted him. A formidable coalition of princes was assembled, William, King of the Scots, and the Counts of Flanders, Boulogne and Blois, all ready to invade Henry's territories and counting upon the support of rebels scattered throughout his dominions. But in this, the great crisis of his reign, the Old King remained supremely cool, waiting for his enemies to show their hand before committing his own forces in sudden and decisive pounces. Above all he used his immense cash resources to hire large numbers of mercenaries.

These soldiers were generally known as Brabançons, but sometimes as Navarrese or Basques or Germans, not so much to indicate their precise place of origin as to express the fact that they were foreigners and spoke a language which was not understood. As professional soldiers they had a great reputation for ruthlessness both in battle and in ravaging the countryside. With this fearsome military instrument at his disposal Henry waited for the invasion.

In July 1173 Richard and his brothers took part in an attack on eastern Normandy made under the command of Philip of Flanders. At the siege of Drincourt, however, Philip's brother, Matthew of Boulogne, was wounded by a crossbow bolt. When he died a few days later Philip called off the invasion. If this was Richard's first experience of war it bore an ironical similarity to his last. Other attacks also petered out and by the autumn King Louis and the Angevin princes were sufficiently depressed to put out peace feelers. At a conference at Gisors Henry offered terms to his sons. To Richard he offered half the revenues of Aquitaine and control of four castles; similar proposals were put to Henry and Geoffrey. He was willing to submit these terms to arbitrators to vary as they thought fit, but only on condition that he was to retain full power and jurisdiction. He was prepared to bargain about money, but not about power. On Louis VII's advice the three brothers rejected these proposals. The war continued.

Early in November Henry led his Brabançons in a thrust to the south of Chinon, threatening the lands of Ralph de Faye. He captured the castles of La Haye, Preuilly and Champigny. It was probably this advance which persuaded Eleanor that the time had come to join her sons. Disguised in male clothing she made her way eastwards, but was arrested – some said betrayed – and sent to her husband. It may well have been the news of his mother's fate which stirred Richard to take his first independent political action. Up to this point, still only sixteen years old, he had remained very much a background figure, drawn along in the wake of his elder brother, and both of them overshadowed by their protector, King Louis of France. But with his mother arrested it was now up to him to take charge of the rebellion in Poitou.

His first move was to threaten La Rochelle. But the town

remained steadfastly loyal to the Old King and shut its gates against him. Its citizens presumably believed that their interests would be better served if Henry won, for he stood for the preservation of a single sovereign authority ruling in Poitou, England and Normandy, in other words over both ends of La Rochelle's trade, over wine-growers and wine-drinkers. But there were many who were jealous of the new town's phenomenal rise and who looked upon it as a sink of iniquity where the *nouveaux riches* wallowed in the luxury obtained from trade. If La Rochelle was against Richard then Saintes was for him. When, in 1150, the citizens of La Rochelle had asked the Bishop of Saintes for permission to build a new parish church to accommodate the growing number of worshippers, they had met with a refusal. In the end they had to go over the Bishop's head, obtaining the authorization they wanted from the Pope. The old episcopal city of the Saintonge, proud of its venerable past, its Capitol, its amphitheatre and its Roman walls, looked askance at the bustling intruder and feared that La Rochelle's gain would be its loss. So successfully indeed did the Bishops of Saintes oppose the claims of their rival that it was not until the seventeenth century that La Rochelle was allowed to have a cathedral of its own. In these circumstances it was only appropriate that in 1174, while his father occupied Poitiers, Richard should set up his headquarters in Saintes and turn the cathedral into an arms depot.

In seeing the importance of La Rochelle Richard had shown a good, if over-ambitious, grasp of strategy, but he was still no match for his father. It was not just that the Old King possessed the greater resources – which he did – he was also able to overwhelm his enemies by sheer speed of movement. He arrived at Saintes while Richard thought he was still celebrating Whitsun at Poitiers and took the city gates by storm. Richard and a few followers escaped downstream to Geoffrey de Rancon's castle at Taillebourg while the bulk of his troops were driven back into the cathedral, where they held out for a few days. In the interests of speed and surprise Henry had brought no artillery train with him from Poitiers so Richard was quite safe in the great fortress of Taillebourg, but he had lost his military stores as well as the services of the sixty knights and four hundred archers captured in Saintes. As a result during the rest of the summer he could make little headway against the officials whom Henry left in charge of Aquitaine when he once again turned his attention to the north. Richard struggled stubbornly on, but the effective end of the civil war came on 13 July when William the Lion, King of Scots, was captured at Alnwick, just one day after – as numerous chroniclers pointed out – Henry had done public penance for those hasty words which had led to Becket's murder.

The continuing resistance of the young Duke of Aquitaine delayed the progress of peace talks between the Kings of England and France but on 8 September they were able to agree to a truce until Michaelmas (29 September), the terms of which specifically excluded Richard. Free from all other threats of war Henry could concentrate on subduing Richard. As his father approached, Richard retreated steadily, never once daring to stand his ground against him. Angered when he heard that Louis and the Young King had deserted him, the news none the less convinced him that the cause was lost. On 23 September he entered his father's presence. Weeping, he threw himself flat on his face at Henry's feet and begged forgiveness. His father raised him up and gave him the kiss of peace. Thus everything went smoothly when the peace conference reconvened at Michaelmas at Montlouis, between Tours and Amboise. Like his brothers Richard agreed to accept rather less than he had been offered the previous autumn: half the revenues of Aquitaine, but this time only two residences, and apparently unfortified ones. Financially Henry treated his sons generously but he retained full power throughout his dominions. Moreover the Treaty of Montlouis said not one word about Eleanor. Her rebellion had been the most damaging of all blows to the Old King's cause and pride; and she would be punished accordingly. She was to remain Henry's captive for as long as he chose.

5

DUKE OF AQUITAINE
1174-1183

ELEANOR apart, for the rest of the King's subjects the Treaty of Montlouis meant, by and large, a return to the *status quo* as it was fifteen days before the outbreak of war. Loyal barons who had lost lands and castles had them restored. Most of Henry's prisoners were freed without ransom and given their lands back. But however much he desired peace and, with peace, an opportunity to make good war's heavy drain on his financial resources, there were limits to Henry's clemency. Rebels might get their lands back but all fortifications which they had raised since the beginning of the war were to be demolished. In the coming months and years the question of castles was to remain in the forefront of everyone's mind. The end result of Henry's policy was that ruined castles were to be seen throughout his dominions, visible reminders of the Old King's power and the penalties meted out to rebellious lords.

But it was not just a question of punishment; for those who had fought on the winning side there were rewards to reap. The town of La Rochelle was granted a 'commune', in other words it was given rights of self-government and allowed to elect a mayor instead of having to put up with being ruled by an official imposed upon it from above. In addition, in 1174 Henry abolished the right of wreck in England, Poitou and Gascony. This was the customary right to seize wrecked ships and their cargoes enjoyed by people living on the coast and which was believed to lead to the abuse of 'wrecking'. A privilege detested by merchants everywhere, it was particularly frustrating to those who had to round the dangerous coastline of Brittany with ships full of wine. Not only was there a relatively high chance of being wrecked, there was also a good chance of saving the cargo, since the huge tuns of wine could float and might drift ashore with some 200 gallons unharmed inside each one. Yet when Henry abolished the right of wreck throughout his dominions he made an exception of Brittany. It seems that many Breton lords relied heavily upon the profits of wreck to boost their incomes, and to abolish it might have caused yet another rebellion in an area where Angevin control was still fairly fragile. The upshot of this conflict of interests was a compromise. Merchants could buy safe-conducts and licences exempting them from the right of wreck from the Duke of Brittany. Since the first office known to sell these safe-conducts was at La Rochelle, the port that dominated the wine trade, it seems likely that a lobby of La Rochelle merchants played an influential role in shaping these developments.

The Old King and his sons celebrated Christmas 1174 together at Argentan. Then he sent Richard to Aquitaine with orders which went beyond the terms of the Treaty of Montlouis. Most castles, it is true, were to be reduced to the state they were in fifteen days before the outbreak of war; but others were to be razed to the ground. To Henry it may well have seemed a sensible way of killing two birds with one stone – chastising rebels and at the same time providing his warlike second son with useful experience. But perhaps the irony of the situation also appealed to him. The Poitevin barons must have felt the way Henry Morgan's old associates were to feel when he was appointed Governor of Jamaica with orders to stamp out piracy. To help Richard carry out this task Henry gave him full control over the armed forces of Aquitaine and instructed local officials to put their revenues at his disposal. Henry himself marched into Anjou to carry out a similar policy and sent Geoffrey to do the same in Brittany. Both sons seem to have succeeded in carrying out their father's orders. Richard indeed made a considerable impression by capturing Castillon-sur-Agen in August 1175. It was a strongly-built castle on an excellent defensive site and the garrison of thirty knights was able to hold out against Richard's artillery train for nearly two months, but eventually its lord, Arnald de Boville, was forced to capitulate.

Despite these successes 1176 was not to be a year of peace in

Aquitaine. By the spring Richard found himself faced by a formidable coalition of enemies. At its head were the sons of the Count
of Angoulême, their half-brother Viscount Aimar of Limoges,
Viscount Raymond II of Turenne, whose sister had married Count
William of Angoulême, and the lords of Chabanais and Mastac. To
seek help against this league of nobles Richard went to see his father
in England in April 1176. What lay behind this new outbreak? A
few chroniclers report the events of the war but they do not say
what caused it. In so far as modern historians have tried to explain
it, it is simply as a continuation of the war of 1173–4. This, however,
it was not. Apart from the sons of the Count of Angoulême the rebels
of 1176 were an entirely different group from the rebels of 1173–4.
Whereas in the earlier revolt fighting had centred on the northern
parts of the duchy, Poitou and the Saintonge, in 1176 it was focused
further south and east, in the Angoumois and the Limousin. Indeed
when Richard marched against Angoulême he made this move after
taking counsel with the barons of Poitou. We must look elsewhere
for an explanation.

Norman and English chroniclers also report another event,
apparently unconnected with the war, an event which occurred not
in 'turbulent Aquitaine' but far away in the quiet countryside of
Surrey. Shortly before Christmas 1175 Reginald, Earl of Cornwall,
an illegitimate son of Henry I, died at Chertsey and was buried in
Reading Abbey, his father's foundation. He left no son, just three
daughters. According to Anglo-Norman custom the estate should
have been divided between the daughters. But Henry II took into
his own hands the county of Cornwall and all the Earl's estates in
England, Wales and Normandy and kept them to provide for his
youngest son John, allowing only a small portion to go to Reginald's
daughters. The Earl had ruled Cornwall almost as an independent
principality, separate from the royal administration of the English
shires, and Henry was doubtless glad of the opportunity to integrate
it into his system of government – especially since at this period
production of tin from the Cornish mines was booming. With the
twelfth-century expansion of the European economy there was an
increasing demand for tin for domestic use in pewter and for ecclesiastical use in bell-metal. All this concerns Aquitaine because Earl

Reginald's eldest daughter, Sarah, had been given in marriage to Aimar of Limoges while he was a minor in Henry II's custody. For the Viscount it was an illustrious connection; in Limoges men saw Earl Reginald as a great and influential figure, a man who had helped Henry II to the English throne. And when it became clear that the Earl would have no sons, it became a marriage which aroused high expectations – expectations which were disappointed when the King took Cornwall for himself. Up to this point Aimar had remained loyal to the Old King. He had helped to entertain Henry and a vast gathering of kings and nobles for seven days at Limoges in February 1173 and had held aloof from the revolts of 1168 and 1173-4. In 1176 he suddenly changed his line. He went over to opposition and pursued this new policy until his death in 1199. But it is certain that even in the thirteenth century the Viscounts did not forget their Cornish connection. In 1175-6 Henry II's obsessive concern for John, revealed again and again in the last sixteen years of his reign, drove Aimar of Limoges to rebellion.

When Richard went to England in April 1176 he clearly found his father ready and able to help. On his return to Aquitaine he was able to recruit mercenaries on a large scale. They were much needed since one of the leading rebels, Vulgrin of Angoulême, had not only put his castles in a state of readiness but was able to take the field with a force of Brabançons. Richard defeated them in a battle between St Maigrin and Bouteville towards the end of May. Vulgrin's castles still held out but Richard ignored them and turned against Viscount Aimar. Advancing into the Limousin he captured the castle of Aixe, thus prising open the approach to Limoges along the line of the River Vienne. Limoges, like many other towns in the twelfth century, was growing up around two distinct nuclei. On the one hand there was St Stephen's Cathedral and the bishop's palace; locally this centre was known as the city, the *civitas* or the *urbs*. On the other was the abbey of St Martial and the castle of the Viscount; this was called the citadel, the *castrum*. The citadel seems to have been the most populous part; here were the workshops which produced the famous Limoges enamels. Within the citadel there was constant bickering between abbot, Viscount and towns-people – grown so rich that they obeyed no one, remarked Geoffrey of Vigeois ruefully – and yet also a sense of being bound together in opposition to their neighbour, the bishop's city. The two main parts of Limoges were separated geographically and by the fact that each had its own enclosure. Whenever there was fighting around Limoges one permanent complicating factor was the rivalry between city and citadel. During the troubles of 1173–4 the inhabitants of the citadel seized the opportunity to turn their enclosure into a proper circuit of walls, a move which was probably aimed against the city rather than against ducal authority, though clearly it was taking advantage of the latter's temporary weakness.

In June 1176 Richard laid siege to Limoges; after a few days' resistance Aimar's citadel capitulated. By the end of the month the Duke was back in Poitiers, where he met his brother Henry. The Young King had been pressing for permission to go on a pilgrimage to Compostella but Henry II, believing that this was just an excuse to get away from his watchful eye, had instead ordered him to help suppress the rebellion in Aquitaine. After holding a council with the barons of Poitou, Richard and Henry marched into the county of Angoulême. Having cleared the field of Vulgrin's troops Richard now intended to strike at the Taillefer castles, presumably accepting the fact that this would drive Vulgrin's father, Count William, to take his son's part. Châteauneuf, the castle controlling the key bridge across the River Charente west of Angoulême, on the main road from Poitiers to Bordeaux, fell after a fortnight's siege. At this point Henry packed up and left. He had been a reluctant ally and may well have resented playing second fiddle to his younger brother. In any event he never had much stomach for serious campaigning. Undeterred by the Young King's defection, Richard pressed on. He captured Moulineuf after a siege of ten days and then turned to Angoulême itself. Here, gathered within its walls, were the enemies who had so far eluded his grasp: Count William of Angoulême and Vulgrin, Aimar of Limoges, the Viscount of Ventadour and the lord of Chabanais. Seemingly mustered for a last ditch stand they in fact conceded defeat after only six days. Count William surrendered all his chief castles, Bouteville, Archiac, Montignac, Lachaise and Merpins, as well as the town of Angoulême. Richard took hostages from them and then sent them and other members of their league to England to sue for mercy at his father's feet. Henry II received them at Winchester on 21 September, but postponed consideration of their case until he himself should come to Normandy. In the meantime he sent them back to his son in Aquitaine.

The Old King, like his eldest son, sometimes toyed with the idea of going to Compostella. Moreover in the years 1176–7 he was taking a keen interest in the competing politics of the Spanish kingdoms and he may well have instructed Richard to ensure that the great road south from Bordeaux to the Pyrenees was kept open for travellers of all sorts, pilgrims, traders and couriers. Richard and his Brabancons carried out this task with an efficiency which must have shattered many observers accustomed to a more leisurely way of doing things. He celebrated Christmas Day 1176 at Bordeaux. By 9 January 1177 he had besieged Dax, which had been held against him by the Viscount of Dax and Bigorre, and taken it; he had besieged Bayonne, which the Viscount of Bayonne had held against him, and taken it; he had marched right up to 'the Gate of Spain' at Cize and there he had captured and demolished the castle of St Pierre. This lightning campaign undertaken in the depths of winter while most people were still celebrating Christmas had the desired effect. The leaders of the Basque and Navarrese communities swore that they would keep the peace and allow pilgrims to pass unmolested. Then Richard returned to Poitiers and from there, on 2 February, he sent envoys to his father reporting his success and announcing that he had pacified all parts of Aquitaine.

It was an exaggeration. At the end of the campaign he had dismissed his Brabançons. No longer paid, they had to live somehow and since they could make a good, professional job of plundering and devastating this was always their preferred solution to the problem of unemployment. For several months, under the command of William le Clerc, a defrocked priest and a well-known captain of mercenaries, they wrought havoc in the Limousin. Eventually, stirred by the preaching of Abbot Isambert of St Martial's, the nobles and populace organized a militia to combat them. Carrying a cross brought back from Jerusalem before them, the 'army of peace' caught up with the Brabançons at Malemort, near Brive, and relieved their outraged feelings in an orgy of slaughter.

Some months earlier, while Richard was still in the foothills of the Pyrenees, a crisis had blown up in the rich, flat pasture land of western Berry, the most north-easterly part of Aquitaine. The Duke's position here was weak since he possessed no lands or castles of his own and he had to rely solely on his rights as the acknowledged overlord. Strategically it was an important area. From Bourges Capetian forces could launch a quick strike against Tours and Poitiers. For this reason Henry II was always on the look-out for excuses and opportunities to intervene in Berry. In 1170 he had made a bid to capture Bourges itself but withdrew when Louis VII came up with an army. Then, towards the end of 1176, Ralph of Déols, lord of Châteauroux, died, leaving a three-year-old daughter as his only child. Henry claimed custody of the child but her kinsmen fortified their castles and refused to hand her over. This was a rebuff which could not go unpunished, especially since the income of the lord of Déols was reputed to be equal to the ordinary revenues of Normandy. Henry was busy in England so he at once ordered his eldest son to take an army from Normandy and Anjou and occupy the lordship with all speed.

After some initial success, however, the Young King's campaign ground to a halt and Henry decided that he would have to take a hand himself. It was time to clarify the confused political situation in Berry. In June 1177 he sent envoys to Paris bearing demands which were clearly intended to bring matters to a head. Louis VII was to honour the agreements he had made concerning the marriages of his daughters Margaret and Alice. He was to hand over the French Vexin (as the remainder of Margaret's dowry) and endow Alice with Bourges. Louis responded to these totally unjustified demands by arguing that it was Henry who had broken the agreement by keeping Alice in his custody for far too long. In addition he persuaded a papal legate to publish the fact that he had been instructed by Pope Alexander III to lay all of Henry's dominions under an interdict unless the marriage was celebrated in the near future. For more than a year Alexander, at the French King's request, had been putting discreet pressure on Henry either to return Alice to her father or marry her to Richard. Now that the threat of interdict had been made public Henry began to negotiate more seriously. In August he crossed to Normandy in force and summoned his sons to a family conference. By September, after meetings with the legate and King Louis, a new agreement had been reached at Nonancourt. Problems relating to Châteauroux and other lands in dispute in Berry and Auvergne were referred to a panel of arbitrators; Richard was to marry Alice; finally both Louis and Henry agreed to go on crusade and, in the meantime, made a mutual non-aggression pact. In three ways these complex diplomatic manœuvrings had touched Richard closely: as Alice's husband-to-be; as overlord of western Berry and the Auvergne; and finally as a future crusader, for it was probably in Normandy in September 1177 that he first heard a papal legate preach of the perils facing the Christian Kingdom of Jerusalem. It may have been at this time that the name Saladin began to mean something to him.

After the sealing of the Treaty of Nonancourt it was time for Henry II to carry out the promise made at Winchester last September and deal with William and Vulgrin of Angoulême, Aimar of Limoges and the other defeated rebels. He sent Richard on ahead while he travelled south through Berry, where once again his eldest son was making heavy weather of the task assigned to him. The Old King was soon in possession of the heiress of Déols, and sent her to Chinon for safe-keeping; then he took his army to the Limousin. Richard and he spent about a month here 'punishing the rebels as each deserved'. What this vague phrase meant we are not told except in the cases of Aimar of Limoges and Raymond of Turenne. Their punishment was certainly a severe one. They both had to resign their chief fortress, Turenne and the citadel of Limoges, delivering them into the hands of Richard's officers. There is no direct evidence for Angoulême but we know that in 1199 Count Ademar was still trying to recover lands which had once been held by his father Count William and 1176–7 is the most likely date for their confiscation by the Angevins. The presence of Henry and his sons, together with their army, made a considerable impression on the Limousin, though it is also clear that in the months between June 1176 and October 1177 Richard had effectively wielded power in this region, quartering his Brabancons on monastic estates as he chose.

In mid-November Henry II returned to Berry for a fruitless conference with Louis VII at Gracay on the subject of their conflicting
claims to Auvergne. Since the barons of Auvergne are reported to
have stated that their province belonged of old to the duchy of Aquitaine, the Old King was being remarkably easy-going in allowing
the dispute to be referred to another commission of inquiry. This
suggests that he had bigger fish to fry – and indeed he had. He
hurried back to the Limousin and completed a piece of business,
negotiations for which must already have been in train. At his
favourite monastery of Grandmont, where in 1170 he had wanted
to be buried, he met Count Audebert of La Marche. La Marche
was a huge fief held of the Duke of Aquitaine, but the Counts had
always been more or less independent. Their possessions dominated
the roads leading north from Limoges to Poitou and Berry. Count
Audebert had taken part in the rebellion of 1168 and had encouraged
the revolt of the townspeople of La Souterraine in 1171, but he had
now decided to leave his native soil behind. His family life had ended
in disaster. He had suspected his wife of having a lover, had killed
the man on Easter Day and repudiated his wife. When, later on,
his only son died it was taken to be a sign that he had killed the
supposed lover unjustly. Apart from a daughter who was believed
to be barren he had no other near kin living and in a state of acute
depression he determined to sell up and go to the Holy Land. For
Henry II this was an opportunity not to be missed, particularly convenient since he had just laid his hands on the lordship of Déols.
So in December 1177 in exchange for 15,000 *livres angevines* (roughly
£4000) and forty pack animals – clearly intended to be used for the
long pilgrimage to Jerusalem – Henry acquired the whole county
of La Marche. Since it was believed to be worth over £13,000 it
was an amazing bargain, but one which was available only to a pur-
chaser with immense cash reserves. It transformed the entire
structure of power in eastern Aquitaine. Inevitably it was a transaction which disturbed many of Audebert of La Marche's
neighbours, and especially his distant kinsmen, the Lusignans and
Taillefers. But there was nothing they could do. Henry took the
homage of the barons and knights of La Marche and then returned
to Angers to celebrate Christmas. It was one of the greatest feasts

of his reign. His sons were there and so was a concourse of knights so huge that it reminded men of his coronation. Unquestionably there was a great deal to celebrate.

For most of the next year, 1178, Richard's movements are veiled in obscurity. Only after his father's return to England in July do we possess any report of activity on his part. This 'unusual state of quiescence' was due, it has been suggested, to the restraint placed upon him by Henry's presence on the Continent. It is much more likely to be no more than a reflection of the fact that almost everything we know about Richard as Duke of Aquitaine comes from an English chronicler, Roger of Howden, and Roger only has information when he has access to the reports sent by Richard to his father, that is to say when Henry is in England. According to one such report Richard's chief concern in the autumn of 1178 was with his southern frontier. Arriving at Dax with a large army he found, to his great delight, that the townspeople had captured his old opponent, the Count of Bigorre, and held him in prison. But then Richard was persuaded to release him by Alfonso II, King of Aragon (1162–96). Apparently Alfonso came to visit Richard and agreed to stand surety for his friend's behaviour, guaranteeing that he would do nothing against the will of the Duke of Aquitaine or his father. As a further precaution Richard made the Count of Bigorre surrender Clermont and the castle of Montbron.

The description of the Count as Alfonso's 'friend' suggests that there was more to this incident than simply the curbing of an unruly vassal. Alfonso II, himself a troubadour and patron of troubadours, was in these years bidding fair to become 'Emperor of the Pyrenees'. In 1162 he had succeeded his father as ruler of Aragon and Barcelona. In 1170 he had persuaded Marie, Viscountess of Béarn, to do homage to him for all her lands – and this included some estates which, theoretically speaking, were within the duchy of Aquitaine. In 1173 she entered a nunnery, leaving Béarn to be governed in the name of her small son by a regent appointed by Alfonso II. In the last couple of years the pace of his advance had quickened. After a long struggle Raymond V of Toulouse had eventually, in 1176, resigned all his rights over Provence; and in 1177 Alfonso had taken over Roussillon. In March 1178 he had renewed an old alliance with

Castile – an aggressive alliance directed against the little mountain kingdom of Navarre. In addition he had, by virtue of a marriage alliance, attached the Count of Bigorre to his cause, and – as this incident reveals – Alfonso took the alliance seriously. With his influence spreading over the Pyrenees, – Béarn, Bigorre, Roussillon and Provence – Alfonso II was a formidable neighbour, a threat to the Dukes of Aquitaine as well as to the Kings of Navarre and Counts of Toulouse. There can be little doubt that when Richard led his army to Dax it was part of a campaign intended to counter the northward expansion of Aragon.

He then returned to hold his Christmas court at Saintes. By then it was clear that fresh trouble was brewing in the Angoumois. It looks as though Count William of Angoulême was already making his preparations for a pilgrimage to Jerusalem, leaving his eldest son Vulgrin as effective head of the family. Possibly Richard had summoned him to Saintes to do homage and Vulgrin had refused, not willing to accept the losses recently inflicted upon his family. His resistance was stiffened by an alliance with Geoffrey de Rancon. Geoffrey held large estates in Poitou and in the Saintonge – as well as an important fief, the lordship of Marcillac, as a vassal of the Counts of Angoulême. The Rancon family had participated in the revolts of 1168 and 1173–4 and, like the Taillefers, may well have been disturbed by the advance of Angevin power in the valley of the Charente, from Saintes eastwards through Cognac towards Angoulême. Geoffrey de Rancon's great castles at Taillebourg and Pons were well sited to disrupt communications between Bordeaux, Saintes and La Rochelle; and it was against one of these, Pons, that Richard launched his first attack early in 1179. But although he had mustered a large army the siege went badly for him. Evidently Geoffrey de Rancon had anticipated the attack and laid in plenty of supplies. By Easter week it was clear to Richard that he was making no headway against a well-conducted defence and that in terms of political psychology it was risky to stake his reputation on one big success. Leaving the larger part of his forces behind to maintain the blockade of Pons he marched north past Cognac and laid siege to Richemont. After three days the castle capitulated and was demolished. In the next three weeks the same treatment was handed out to four more castles: Genzac, Marcillac, Grouville and Anville. But then, instead of returning to the siege of Pons, he led his army in May 1179 to the enterprise which was to establish him once and for all as an acknowledged expert in the vital art of siege warfare: the capture of Taillebourg.

Taillebourg is situated on the right bank of the River Charente, perched on an outcrop of light-coloured rock. It still overlooks a bridge and in those days there was also a causeway to take the traveller over the marshy ground beyond. Since there were no fords and no other bridge, it controlled the only crossing of the Charente between Saintes and Tonnay-Charente. In contemporary opinion it was an impregnable fortress; indeed Richard himself had taken refuge there five years earlier when driven out of Saintes by his father. Protected on three sides by a sheer rock face and massively fortified on the fourth, its garrison had every reason to feel confident. No one – or so Ralph of Diss believed – had ever dared to attack it before. But Richard brought up siege machines and began to bombard the walls, concentrating on the fourth side where a small town nestled at the foot of the citadel. At the same time he set his troops to ravage the surrounding fields and vineyards. Partly out of over-confidence and partly as a result of the double pressure of having to sit still under a bombardment while their property was burned and looted under their noses, the garrison made a foray against Richard's camp, placed temptingly close to the walls. This was precisely what Richard was waiting for. His men counter-attacked. After a fierce struggle at the gates they were able to force their way in at the heels of the retreating defenders. The garrison withdrew into the citadel, leaving the town and the bulk of their supplies to be plundered at will. Soon afterwards the citadel itself capitulated. It had taken Richard only three days to capture Taillebourg. So great an impression did this make that Geoffrey de Rancon at once surrendered Pons. Richard then dismantled both castles. Having seen his ally overwhelmed in this startling fashion, Count Vulgrin decided that discretion was the better part of valour. He handed over the keys to Angoulême and Montignac and their walls too were razed to the ground. After an arduous five-year apprenticeship in the disciplines of war the twenty-one-year-old

Duke had produced his masterpiece. At the moment of crisis, in the hand-to-hand fighting at the gates of Taillebourg when the decision could have gone either way, Richard had thrown himself into the thick of the mêlée. When he took his news to his father in England he was given a conqueror's welcome. His demobilized Brabançons celebrated by sacking the suburbs of Bordeaux.

Although in their own eyes the rebels had simply been fighting for what was rightfully theirs, from the point of view of Henry II and Richard they were disturbers of the peace, and as princes maintaining the peace within their dominions, the Angevins could generally rely on the support of the church. Not always, of course, and at Limoges they had clearly bruised local pride. In 1178 the canons of St Stephen's had elected as bishop Sebrand Chabot, a man whom they knew would be unacceptable to the King. As a result they had been driven out of the city by Richard's agents and the cathedral was closed for twenty-one months. Normally, however, the church, in its desire for peace and undisturbed enjoyment of its own material wealth, could be relied upon to lend the weight of spiritual sanctions in support of the sword of power wielded by princes. Thus it may well be that the numerous nobles of Aquitaine who went on pilgrimage in the summer of 1179 did so as a penance imposed by the church. On the other hand they may also have been relieved to leave behind, for a while at least, the sight of their ruined castle-walls, a nagging reminder of the defeats they had suffered. Led by old Count William of Angoulême and his step-son Aimar of Limoges they left on 7 July, joining Audebert of La Marche on the road to Jerusalem. Barely a month later Count William died at Messina; and in the next year Audebert ended his days at Constantinople.

For a period of two years from the summer of 1179 to the summer of 1181 we know nothing of Richard's movements. In part this was due to Henry II's presence on the Continent from April 1180 to July 1181; in part it doubtless reflects the subdued mood of the Angoumois and the Limousin with so many of the wealthiest and most influential nobles away on pilgrimage. For Richard it seems to have been a period of reconciliation: with Sebrand Chabot, who was allowed to return to his see in April 1180, and with Aimar of

Limoges, who arrived back at Christmas of the same year. But by far the most important event of that year was the death of King Louis VII on 18 September and the accession of his son Philip II. Ever since the failure of the revolt of 1173-4 Louis had stopped giving aid and comfort to those who were discontented with Angevin rule. He had been a sick man, chiefly concerned to ensure the undisputed succession of his son and then end his days in peace. Philip was to be a very different kind of ruler. Although only fifteen at the time of his father's death he soon showed himself to be a cunning and unscrupulous politician. But if his reputation as one of the great Kings of French history is anything to go by, then the means he used were justified by the end, the destruction of the Angevin Empire. Later on a story was told of his early years as a young and untried king. At a council meeting of his barons one day he sat apart, chewing a hazel twig and apparently lost to the world. When challenged to say what was on his mind, he replied that he had been wondering whether it would ever be given to him to make France great again, as it had been in the days of Charlemagne. To fulfil this ambition he was prepared to go to any lengths, no matter how underhand or devious they might be. In the end he succeeded, largely because he outlived his enemies. But in the early stages of his reign, as he sought to establish himself in quarrels with some of his more powerful vassals, Philip relied heavily upon aid from Henry II and his sons, from the family which he was to do so much to tear apart. For the moment the Angevin dominions remained quiet and the new King of France was too busy elsewhere to go looking for trouble.

Richard's one recorded campaign in Aquitaine in 1181 took him to Gascony. It seems that the heir to the viscounty of Lomagne, south of Agen, refused to pay him homage. Richard's reply was to send an army to occupy Lectoure, the chief town of the viscounty, until in mid-August the recalcitrant heir came to heel, did homage and in return was dubbed a knight by his overlord. But shortly before this there occurred an event the consequences of which were to shatter the peace of Aquitaine. As usual it concerned a death and a disputed inheritance. On 29 June 1181 Count Vulgrin of Angoulême died. His only child was an infant daughter but he also had two adult brothers, William and Ademar, who clearly expected to obtain possession of the county and be the guardians of their niece. Richard had other ideas. Whenever possible he had been forcing the lords of Aquitaine to acknowledge that they held their 'honours', their counties, viscounties and other seigneuries, not as independent lordships but as fiefs, for which they owed the Duke homage. By doing homage a vassal accepted that his lord had certain rights over him: he might require service and, occasionally, he might intervene directly in the government of the fief. This was most likely to happen if a lordship was left without an adult male heir. Then the feudal overlord would seek custody of the heir or heiress, would wish to choose a wife or husband for them and, in the meantime, collect the profits which came from administering their estates. Just how extensive a lord's rights would be in these circumstances would depend partly upon local custom and partly upon the relative power of lord and vassal. Thus when Henry II, as overlord, claimed the wardship of the Déols heiress, her relatives put forward a counter-claim: the wardship more properly belonged to them, they said, as her kinsmen. At first they had been successful in maintaining their 'right' – even against the Young King – but when Henry II himself marched into Berry, the balance of power shifted abruptly. Henry took charge of the girl and then, making further use of his feudal right, gave her in marriage to an English noble, Baldwin de Redvers. Richard's predecessors had been able to exercise their feudal rights in some parts of their duchy, but not in others. The nobles of south-ern Gascony, of the Limousin, of western Berry, of La Marche and Angoulême had, on the whole, remained independent. In one well-remembered case Eleanor's father, Duke William X, had tried to insist that he should have the marriage of the probable heiress to the Viscount of Limoges, but the nobles of the Limousin, fearing 'the Poitevin yoke', successfully resisted this demand and she was given instead to a Count of Angoulême.

The marriage of Eleanor to Henry II transformed the situation. Able to call upon the financial and military resources of his whole empire, the new Duke was a political bulldozer possessed of a weight which could flatten opponents and their castles. In 1156 Henry II had taken young Aimar V of Limoges out of the custody of his uncles and had arranged his marriage to Sarah of Cornwall. But like all bulldozers he was ponderous and slow to turn. Despite his phenomenal energy the sheer size of his dominions inevitably meant that it could be months or even years before he was free to deal with a distant crisis or give his officials the support they needed against a major local potentate. After 1174, however, Henry hoped that the presence of his sons in different parts of the empire would in some measure provide the mobility, flexibility and speed of response which he alone could not give. Early in 1177, when commanding his eldest son to cope with the business of Déols, he said that he, when alone, had lost none of his rights and that it would be a disgrace if they were to lose anything now that there were several of them to rule. The Young King failed to live up to his father's hopes. He was generous, courteous and chivalrous. No one attended more tournaments than he did. Young knights loved him for he gave them pleasure and livelihood. But in politics and in real war he was a child, incapable of concentrating for long. Unable to see beyond the short-term gain he went from whim to whim, reacting without thought to whatever gossip he happened to have heard last. In the summer of 1177, when his wife was pregnant, she left him and returned to her father's court.

Richard by contrast may well have exceeded his father's expectations. During the years 1175 to 1179 the power of the Duke of Aquitaine had surged to a level never before attained. La Marche, Limoges and the lordships of the Pyrenees had been brought to recognize his authority. Even the most powerful of the Duke's vassals, the Counts of Angoulême, who for generations had been accustomed to act as though they were independent princes, had twice conceded defeat, in 1176 and 1179. The fact that Count Vulgrin, shortly before 1179, had married Elizabeth, daughter of Hugh, lord of Amboise, suggests that the marriage had been arranged to suit the Angevins, for Hugh was a trusted vassal. A connection like this, to a family from the Touraine, was an abrupt departure from the time-honoured pattern of Angoulême marriage alliances which linked the Counts to the lords of Périgord, the Limousin, La Marche and the Saintonge. It was Matilda, the only offspring of this marriage, who in 1181-2 became the unwitting cause of what the chronicler of the Limousin, Geoffrey de Vigeois, called 'a great calamity for our country'.

In Richard's view Matilda, Vulgrin's daughter, should inherit the county of Angoulême and he, as Duke and feudal overlord, should have custody of her. But the inheritance customs of western France held out far greater prospects to the brothers of the dead man than Richard was prepared to allow. A Duke of Aquitaine in the style of 1176 and 1179 was not going to have much time for customs which reflected the political realities of earlier days. Naturally this was not how Vulgrin's brothers, William and Ademar, saw it. They claimed the county and when driven out by Richard they fled to their half-brother, Aimar of Limoges. Here Richard had recently given offence by once again insisting that the walls of St Martial's should be pulled down. The rebels were soon joined by the Count of Périgord and the Viscounts of Ventadour, Comborn and Turenne, the most prominent members of that network of inter-marriage and cousinage which characterized Limousin and Angou-mois society. Richard's disregard for their cherished customs of inheritance threatened them all, directly or indirectly, and provided a cause to which all could rally in defence of the right order of their world.

The years 1182–3 were to be the make-or-break crisis of Richard's rule in Aquitaine, faced as he was by so many enemies. Charac-teristically he seized the initiative himself, launching a surprise attack on Puy-St-Front, the Count of Périgord's fortress at Péri-gueux, on 11 April 1182. He captured the citadel but he only had a few troops with him and it was clear he couldn't hold it for long, so he pushed on east past Excideuil into the Limousin, driving straight into the heartland of the rebel cause and devastating the country as he went. This aggressive move suggests that he had already asked for his father's help and was confident that it would soon be forthcoming. By mid-May the Old King had arrived. He summoned the leading rebels to a conference at Grandmont. Pre-sumably at this meeting he heard those charges against Richard which a little later were to reach the ears of some English chron-iclers. Gervase of Canterbury reports that 'the great nobles of Aquitaine hated him because of his great cruelty'. Ralph of Diss

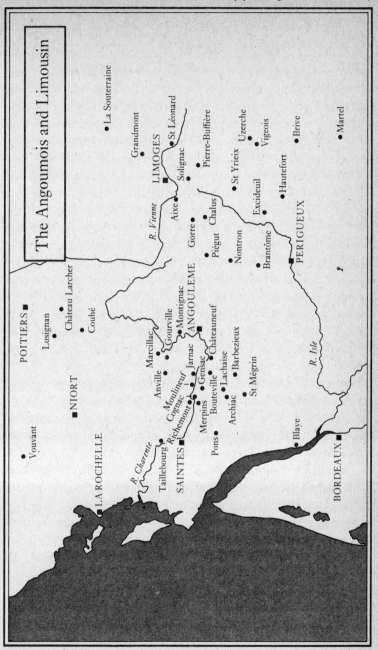

The Angoumois and Limousin

heard that he 'oppressed his subjects with unjustified demands and a régime of violence'. Roger of Howden, as usual, gives a more detailed account. 'He carried off his subjects' wives, daughters and kinswomen by force and made them his concubines; when he had sated his own lust on them he handed them down for his soldiers to enjoy. He afflicted his people with these and many other wrongs.' But Henry II was not impressed by complaints of this kind. He and Richard clearly shared the same view of an overlord's feudal rights. Henry sent a message to his eldest son to come and help and then he joined Richard in the business of subduing the Limousin. First they systematically attacked and occupied the chief strongholds held by Viscount Aimar and his vassals: Excideuil, St Yrieix and Pierre-Buffière. Then they turned on Count Élie of Périgord and laid siege to Puy-St-Front. Here, on 1 July, they were joined by the Young King and such was the overwhelming strength of their combined forces that both Aimar of Limoges and Elie of Périgord decided to sue for peace. Aimar promised to give no more help to his half-brothers of Angoulême and handed over his first- and third-born sons as hostages. Élie surrendered his fortress and Richard demolished its walls.

The events of the summer of 1182 show, beyond all doubt, that while they stood united the Angevins were masters of their huge dominions. A family of princes responding to their father's directives, and pulling together when any one of them was challenged, was an unbeatable instrument of government. But there were problems. What would happen when their father died? Would the Young King step into the Old King's shoes? Would he then command his younger brothers? Should they owe allegiance and obedience to him? Or would they go their separate ways, each ruling an independent principality? There could be little doubt that Richard and his elder brother would give very different answers to these questions. Yet somehow, against the pressure of these unavoidable and underlying tensions, Henry II had to find ways of preserving family unity, of upholding his system of government. The immediate problem was to satisfy his eldest son. As the one who might one day step into his father's shoes he was also the one who stood most in his father's shadow. Richard had Aquitaine; Geoffrey had

Brittany; but it was the Old King, not the young one, who held Anjou, England and Normandy. Though in time Henry would succeed to a far greater inheritance than either brother, he did not possess the patience to wait. He wanted to rule now – and in Aquitaine he thought he saw an opportunity. The rebels of 1182 had been defeated, but they had weighed up one of their conquerors – and they also saw an opportunity.

The Young King had passed through Limoges and St Yrieix on his way to join his father and brother at Puy-St-Front. At Limoges he had ostentatiously donated a cloak embroidered with the words *Henricus Rex* to the monks of St Martial's. On this and many other occasions he would have been able to gauge the strength of local feeling against Richard's imperious rule. A new field of activity seemed to be opening up for him if only he had the courage to grasp the nettle. But however frustrated he was, however jealous of his younger brother's reputation as a successful soldier, it cannot have been an easy decision. If he went to war against Richard, which side would their father take? As he edged ever closer to the point of no return, to an open commitment to the rebels, the Young King's life increasingly comes to bear the marks of a man tormented by uncertainty and doubt. He was not sure of the loyalty of his own household. The most famous knight in his following, William Marshal, was suspected of being Queen Margaret's lover. But the Young King was incapable of taking a firm line. He could neither put a stop to the gossip nor put William on trial. At Christmas William Marshal, loudly protesting his innocence, left his master's service and rode off in search of fresh tournaments. Some months earlier, in the autumn of 1182, young Henry had once again asked his father to give him a principality, Normandy, so that he could make proper provision for his own knights. When Henry II again refused, he stormed off to France, saying that he was going to go to Jerusalem. Eventually his father persuaded him to return to Normandy but not before Philip of France had learned something of his brother-in-law's troubles and half-formulated schemes.

As the Young King wavered between the three alternatives of remaining dutifully at his father's side, going to Jerusalem, or

marching into Aquitaine, he was certainly tempted by messages
from the rebels offering to recognize him as their Duke, but he may
also have been egged on by Geoffrey of Brittany. For Geoffrey,
although he seems to have taken no part in suppressing the revolt,
had also been in the Limousin during that summer. On the Feast
of St John (24 June) he had met his father at Grandmont 'together
with certain nobles' – as Geoffrey of Vigeois puts it. It would be
nice to know who these nobles were; or even to know whether the
chronicler's choice of phrase was due to ignorance or a desire for
brevity or for the sake of discretion. But, however innocent his presence at Grandmont may have been, we do know that by the winter
of early 1183 Geoffrey was playing a very devious game indeed. It
is not easy to see why. His eldest brother Henry had cause to feel
frustrated, but for a third son Geoffrey of Brittany was extremely
well endowed. Perhaps the answer is as simple as the one given by
some contemporary writers. 'Geoffrey, that son of perdition . . . that
son of iniquity' is how Roger of Howden sums up his character,
while Gerald of Wales gives a more elaborate description of a prince
'overflowing with words, smooth as oil, possessed, by his syrupy
and persuasive eloquence, of the power of dissolving the apparently
indissoluble, able to corrupt two kingdoms with his tongue, of tireless endeavour and a hypocrite in everything'. By the autumn of
1182 war had broken out again in Aquitaine. The Taillefer brothers
were still able to find support within the Angoumois, notably from
the lords of Archiac and Chalais. Encouraged by this, Viscount
Aimar decided to hire mercenaries in Gascony and denounce the
peace terms so recently agreed.

The Young King's opportunity was getting nearer, but if he were
to show his hand at last, he needed an excuse, a justification for
the war which would make sense in his father's eyes and just might
lead him to condone the attack on Richard. This justification was
provided by the castle of Clairvaux and it is clear that the scheme
very nearly worked. Richard had been rebuilding and strengthening Clairvaux and his motives for doing so have long puzzled
historians, since it was a step which could be interpreted as an
infringement of his elder brother's rights. Early in 1183 the
Limousin troubadour, Bertrand de Born, anxious to bring the

Young King into the rebel camp, composed a political song, a *sirventes*, which included the following lines:

Between Poitiers and l'Ile Bouchard and Mirebeau and Loudun and Chinon someone has dared to build a fair castle at Clairvaux, in the midst of the plain. I should not wish the young King to know about it or see, for he would not find it to his liking; but I fear, so white is the stone, that he cannot fail to see it from Mathefelon.

Despite its geographical inaccuracy the song, politically speaking, was right on target, designed as it was to show that the Duke of Aquitaine was building a castle right in the middle of the lands of the Count of Anjou. What was Richard doing? Was he strengthening his border where it faced the great Angevin arsenal and treasury at Chinon, which would one day come into the hands of his feckless elder brother? Possibly, but the site of Clairvaux suggests an explanation much nearer at hand. It lay only about six miles west of Châtellerault and documents from the 1130s indicate that the castellan of Clairvaux at that time was a vassal of the Viscount of Châtellerault. These Viscounts were among the most important barons of Poitou. Eleanor's father, Duke William X, had married one of their daughters; another member of the family had been William IX's most famous mistress. Their castle at Châtellerault controlled the strategically vital Tours–Poitiers road at the point where it crossed the River Vienne. In 1184 Richard returned to this area, founding a new town and castle at the bridge over the River Creuse at St Rémi de la Haye, about twelve miles on the other side of Châtellerault. This time it is clear that the new foundation was to the Viscount's detriment and was expected to anger him. All this suggests that when he started work on Clairvaux Richard anticipated the Viscount's hostility rather than his brother's. But the problem with Clairvaux was that although it lay in Poitou a Count of Anjou could claim to hold it. Like the more important castles of Loudun and Mirebeau it was one of the territorial gains made in the late tenth century at the expense of the Count of Poitou. Unlike these cherished Angevin possessions, however, Clairvaux had been held by relatively unimportant vassals and by the 1130s they seem to have become more closely attached to the Viscounts of

Châtellerault. If Richard had heard about the old Angevin claim when he began work on a castle within the political orbit of Châtellerault he probably thought it had long since lapsed. But some incidents in his later career suggest that he was inclined to act first and let his legal advisers sort out the formalities later. This trait of Richard's gave the Young King some reason to hope that he might be able to win over his father, Henry of Anjou, to an Angevin cause.

Towards the end of 1182 Richard was summoned from his war in the Angoumois to attend his father's Christmas court at Caen. It was intended as a splendid demonstration of the power and solidarity of the Angevin family, the greatest court ever held in Normandy. Besides all his sons Henry II was accompanied by a daughter, Matilda, and her husband, the greatest of the German princes, Henry the Lion, formerly Duke of Saxony and Bavaria, but now driven into exile and on his way to the shrine at Compostella. No Norman baron was to hold a court of his own that Christmas; they would all celebrate with the King. More than a thousand knights jostled in the ducal castle and halls of Caen. Among the knights who went with Richard was Bertrand de Born. The middle-aged troubadour was quarrelling with his brother Constantine over the family castle at Hautefort in the border lands between Périgord and the Limousin. Since the Duke supported Constantine's claim he may well have brought Bertrand to Normandy on the theory that it was safer than leaving him behind to foment trouble. In a courtly song Bertrand says that only the beauty of the Duchess Matilda prevented him from dying of boredom; her naked body would make night seem like day. Otherwise he found the Normans a dull crowd, unsophisticated and solemn. But it is highly unlikely that Bertrand found the trip as boring as his song implies. The Young King was there and the troubadour had high hopes of him. Someone had to overturn the present political arrangements in the Limousin if he was ever to lay his hands on Hautefort. In the next few weeks, as the Angevin court moved south from Caen, the tensions came to the surface and in Bertrand de Born the muddle, the bickering and the bitterness would have found a fascinated observer.

Henry II planned to provide a legal framework for the continuance of his empire by asking both Richard and Geoffrey to do homage to their elder brother; doubtless he also hoped that this clear recognition of his seniority would do something to allay the Young King's sense of frustration. Geoffrey agreed readily enough. Brittany had long since been in some way subject to Normandy. At Le Mans he performed the required homage. But Richard at first refused, arguing that he was as nobly born as his brother. Ten years after the court held at Limoges in 1173 Henry II had again raised the spectre of Aquitaine being permanently reduced to a subordinate role in the Angevin Empire. After a while the Old King persuaded Richard to change his mind. He agreed to do homage so long as it was spelt out that Aquitaine should belong to him and his heirs for ever. Now it was the Young King who drew back and, doubtless to their father's immense exasperation, refused to accept Richard's homage. Homage on these terms was totally incompatible with the engagements he had by now entered into with the rebels. But without some explanation his refusal to accept Richard's homage must have seemed incomprehensible and so, on 1 January 1183, the whole muddled story was blurted out. In the words of Roger of Howden, 'the young King, of his own accord and under no compulsion, laying his hands on the Holy Gospels in the presence of a large crowd of clerks and laymen, swore that from that day onward and for the rest of his life he would be loyal to King Henry, his father and his lord, and would serve him faithfully. Moreover since he did not wish to have preying on his mind any malice or grudge by reason of which his father might later be offended, he revealed that he had pledged himself to support the barons of Aquitaine against his brother Richard and said that he had done this because Richard had fortified the castle of Clairvaux though it really belonged to the Angevin patrimony which he should inherit from his father.'

The dispute over Clairvaux was easily solved. Grudgingly but fairly quickly Richard was induced to hand the castle over to his father. This done it soon became clear that Clairvaux had been no more than a pretext and that the real problems lay elsewhere. At Angers the Old King called Henry, Richard and Geoffrey together and compelled them to swear a compact of perpetual peace. But any oath of peace, if its terms were to be at all realistic, needed to include the Aquitainian rebels. So it was agreed that they would re-assemble to confirm their peace compact at Mirebeau and that the rebels would be invited to attend this meeting. Henry II sent Geoffrey to the Limousin to arrange a truce and to ensure that the discontented barons would come to the peace conference. Geoffrey, however, once on the loose, did nothing of the kind. Instead he joined the rebels. The Young King, who clearly knew what Geoffrey was plotting, then suggested that he should follow his brother, again supposedly as a peace-maker. Moreover he persuaded his father to agree that if the terms imposed on the rebels last summer were not acceptable to them now – as obviously they were not – then they would be granted a fresh hearing in the King's court. This, of course, was intolerable to Richard. He had resigned Clairvaux; he had agreed to do homage to his brother; and now it looked as though all the work of 1182 was going to be undone. As the news of the quarrel between the Old King's sons spread, those who had been defeated last year took fresh courage, while others like Geoffrey of Lusignan, who had previously been too cautious to join the revolt, now decided that their moment had come. Presumably some of those who were still loyal to Richard kept him informed of the deteriorating political situation, and of the contacts between his brothers and the rebels. While Henry II talked of peace and allowed first Geoffrey and then Henry to pull the wool over his eyes, Richard's duchy was slipping away from him. Finally he could contain his frustration no longer. After an angry scene with his father he left the court without permission and rode in haste to Poitou to fortify his castles and towns.

The Young King meanwhile had obtained Henry II's leave to go to the Limousin on his mission of peace. He sent his wife to the court of Philip Augustus and joined Geoffrey at Limoges early in February. There they were met by Viscount Aimar, who had with him a large force of Gascon *routiers* under a chief called William Arnald. The forbidding presence of these mercenaries was sufficient to persuade the inhabitants of the citadel that they too would be well advised to join the revolt. The abbot of St Martial's, the leader of the 1177 'crusade' against the Brabançons and well known for his loyalty to the Dukes of Aquitaine, took refuge in the abbey town of La Souterraine. A second contingent of *routiers* under William's uncle, Raymond le Brun, was making its way north to reinforce Aimar. Geoffrey had a fine company of knights with him at Limoges and had also mustered mercenaries in Brittany with orders to attack Poitou from the north-west. All in all the rebels had assembled a very considerable fighting force. But Richard was in no mood to sue for peace. He hunted down the Breton forces, executing all those who fell into his hands and organizing retaliatory raids on Geoffrey's estates. Then he seized the initiative in a dramatic fashion, just as he had in April 1182. At the head of a small cavalry force he rode almost non-stop for two days and nights and on 12 February he fell upon Aimar's *routiers* as they attacked the church of Gorre a dozen miles to the west of Limoges, believing him to be still somewhere beyond Poitiers. Aimar himself escaped. Richard's horses were too exhausted for a pursuit to be possible. But William Arnald was killed and many of his followers captured. Richard dragged his prisoners as far as Aixe, drowned some in the River Vienne, put others to the sword and blinded the rest. So far as churchmen like Geoffrey of Vigeois were concerned it was the fate which all *routiers* deserved.

By now Henry II himself was on his way to the Limousin, following his sons in the forlorn hope of finding a peace formula. Presumably he had already set in motion the machinery which next month would array a large army under his command, but when he approached Limoges he still had only a few men with him. In the citadel of St Martial everyone's nerves were on edge. As Henry II drew near, a watchman, mistaking the King's small band for a raiding party organized by the citizens of the episcopal city, sounded the alarm. The men of St Martial's swarmed out to drive off their enemies. In the confusion which reigned before one of the Englishmen in the citadel recognized the royal banner, one of Henry's household was wounded and the King himself had a narrow escape. Henry then withdrew to the relative safety of Richard's stronghold at Aixe. Here, that same evening, he was visited by the Young King, who tried to explain and excuse what had happened. But Henry was shocked and angry and would not listen, so his son went back

to his friends in Limoges. At Aimar's command the inhabitants of
St Martial's took an oath of allegiance to the Young King and then
prepared to stand siege. Since the citadel's walls had been razed
in 1181, ramparts of earth, stone and wood had to be erected from
the fabric of a number of churches which were hastily demolished
for the purpose. Not for another fortnight, however, did Henry and
Richard have a force sufficiently large to encircle St Martial's. For
the moment they had to be content to occupy the episcopal city
and from there keep a watchful eye on their enemies. The two
Henrys, father and son, spent these last two weeks of 'phoney' war in
a fruitless series of negotiations, emotional reconciliations, quarrels,
scuffles, promises made and broken. At times the Young King may
genuinely have regretted the path he had chosen but he was now
in too deep to be able to draw back. More of his allies had begun
to arrive on the scene. Philip of France had sent a force of Brabançons to help his brother-in-law, the opening shot in a campaign
which he was to wage for the next thirty years. They took St-
Léonard-de-Noblat by storm, massacred its inhabitants, and then
swept on past Limoges to capture and sack Brantôme. Yet more
mercenary bands, hired by Viscount Aimar and Raymond of
Turenne, were devastating the southern Limousin. Bertrand de
Born used the confusion to turn his brother out of Hautefort by
some treacherous means or other. The whole countryside was in
uproar.

When their main army arrived on 1 March Henry and Richard
made no attempt to chase the widely scattered bands of plundering
routiers. Instead they concentrated all their energies on subduing
the rebels' capital, the citadel of St Martial's. For both sides it was
to prove an arduous siege. Inside the citadel the Young King quickly
ran short of money. He and Aimar had engaged every *routier* chief
who offered his services, fearing that he would go over to Henry II
if they didn't. It was a sensible policy – if they could afford it.
But for obvious reasons his father had cut off the Young King's
allowance. He obtained a 'loan' from the burgesses, but this did
not last long. So he was driven to seize the chalices, plate and other
treasures which belonged to the shrine of St Martial. Having
emptied the citadel of gold and silver he left Limoges and went off

in search of new sources of pay for his mercenaries. He plundered Grandmont and then the abbey of La Couronne near Angoulême. But the citadel, under the command of Geoffrey of Brittany, Viscount Aimar and Geoffrey de Lusignan still held out. The besieging forces grew discouraged. Many of them were quartered in tents and they suffered badly from the cold, wet weather. Some left after only a fortnight and, as time went by, it became increasingly hard to maintain the blockade. Eventually in late April or early May Henry II decided to raise the siege.

We do not know where he went to next, nor whether Richard was still with him. The surviving chronicles of south-western France are poor indeed compared with the wealth of history written in England at this date, the golden age of medieval English historiography. But one thing is clear: although we know so little about it, this was a major crisis. Neighbouring princes were marching into Aquitaine in order to play their part in what was rapidly developing into a showdown on the scale of 1173-4.

On the Young King's side were Hugh, Duke of Burgundy, and Raymond, Count of Toulouse. For Raymond, whose county had been held as a fief of Aquitaine since 1173, the replacement of Richard by his elder brother held out the prospect of release from a galling sense of subordination. On the other hand Raymond's rival in the great struggle for Provence, Alfonso II of Aragon, came in on Richard's side. On balance, however, it looks as though by May 1183 Henry II and Richard were beginning to lose their grip on the war. At Limoges the Young King was free to go over to the attack. Although he was driven away by the defenders of the city of St Stephen's with derisive shouts of 'We do not want this man to reign over us', he was able to capture the castle of Aixe, which was so lightly garrisoned that it had clearly been abandoned by Henry and Richard.

Three days later, on 26 May, the Young King fell ill. For a little while longer his health held up sufficiently for him to plunder one more shrine, at Rocamadour, and then at Martel, on 11 June, he died. It was the end of the rebellion. Although his hesitations had alarmed some of them and although his acute shortage of money remained an embarrassment right up to the end, yet the rebels had committed themselves to him. Whatever the origin of the revolt, by early 1183 it had been transformed into a struggle to make him Duke of Aquitaine in place of the 'tyrannical' Richard. Owing to his lack of resources he had always been to some extent a figure-head, but he had become an indispensable one. He was the justifica-tion for the war, particularly in the eyes of neighbouring princes whose intervention might have been decisive but who were under-standably not that involved in the quarrel over the succession to Angoulême. As soon as they heard of his death, Hugh of Burgundy and Raymond of Toulouse returned home. Like the King in chess the Young King had possessed very little power of his own, yet with-out him it was impossible to carry on the game.

6

THE UNCERTAIN INHERITANCE
1183-1189

THE structure of Angevin rule in Aquitaine had been severely shaken by the Young King's intervention, but once he was gone it was not difficult to pick up the pieces. On hearing of his death Viscount Aimar and Geoffrey de Lusignan left Limoges in order to accompany his body as far as Grandmont. As the cortège approached Uzerche on its way north, the chronicler Geoffrey and a few monks from the priory of Vigeois, standing on a hill, watched it go by on the road below. It was, observed Geoffrey, a fine day – good campaigning weather. Henry II and Richard seized the opportunity to return to Limoges, to lay siege to Aixe and the citadel. On 24 June Aimar of Limoges surrendered. He promised to lend no more support to his half-brothers in Angoulême. The citadel's newly-built walls were razed to the ground. Then, while Henry II headed back to Anjou, Richard and Alfonso of Aragon besieged Bertrand de Born in Hautefort. The castle was believed to be impregnable but after seven days it was taken on 6 July and restored to Constantine de Born. Alfonso then returned to Barcelona, leaving Richard to devastate the estates of the Count of Périgord and his friends. Eventually all the rebels submitted and accepted peace terms. This normally meant that some of their castles were demolished and others retained in the King's hand. Count Geoffrey was punished by being deprived of all his fortresses in Brittany. But although Angevin rule in Aquitaine was fully restored, Richard's own position remained uncertain. The revolt had come close to success and it may well have shaken Henry II's confidence in his son's ability to rule Aquitaine. And if Richard were to resign the duchy then some interesting prospects would open up. For the moment, however, the Old King was content merely to resume control of those castles which he had granted to Richard before the outbreak of the war. Doubtless, at any rate for a while, his son could bear this loss of authority with patience in view of his new position as Henry's chief heir.

At Michaelmas 1183 Henry showed his hand. He summoned both Richard and John to Normandy and ordered Richard to hand over Aquitaine in return for John's homage. If Richard was to step into his dead brother's shoes then why should not John – for as yet John was still Lackland – step into Richard's shoes? It was an easy and natural solution. But this is not how it seemed to Richard. He had not worked and fought for eight years in order to give Aquitaine away to someone else. He asked for two or three days' grace so that he could consult with his friends and when this was granted, he took his leave. At nightfall he mounted and rode straight for Poitou, pausing only to send an envoy to his father with the message that he would never allow anyone to take his place as Duke of Aquitaine. To add to Henry's troubles he was constantly being pestered by King Philip's claim that now that the Young King was dead, his widow's marriage portion – Gisors and the other castles of the Norman Vexin – should be returned to France. Eventually at a conference held on the frontier between Gisors and Trie on 6 December 1183 Philip agreed to let Henry keep the Norman Vexin on condition that he paid Margaret an annual pension of 2700 *livres* and on the understanding that he granted it to whichever of his sons married Alice. Since Alice had long since been betrothed to Richard the studied vagueness of the phrase 'to whichever of his sons married her' suggests that Henry may have been toying with the idea of marrying her not to Richard but to John. In this event Philip might well have approved of any plan which would make proper provision for his half-sister and her husband, whether it was Aquitaine or even something more. At the same conference Henry II did homage to Philip for all his continental possessions. It looks as though he was deliberately emphasizing the legal basis of his right to order the affairs of Aquitaine.

Throughout the winter of 1183–4 the Old King continued his

efforts to prise Richard away from all or part of Aquitaine, but neither threats nor blandishments had any effect. At last, in a fit of anger, he gave John permission to invade the duchy and try to take it by force. Richard, of course, had been preparing for some such move. He had held his Christmas court at Talmont, north of La Rochelle, and distributed gifts on a lavish scale. But princely generosity could not buy everyone's loyalty. It was safer to hire soldiers as well and it is at this time that we first come across the name Mercadier, a name that from now on was to be closely linked with Richard's. In 1183 Mercadier was just the commander of yet another of the bands of *routiers* which were busily spreading havoc in the southern Limousin, but in the next fifteen years he became the most famous professional soldier in Europe. Instead of flitting from one employer to another he remained constant in Richard's service and was with him still at the end at Chalus. Perhaps this was because Richard paid better than all rival employers, but over so long an association other bonds must have developed. This is clear from words which Mercadier himself dictated in 1196: 'I fought for him strenuously and loyally. I never opposed his will but was prompt in obedience to his orders. In consequence of this service I gained his respect and was placed in command of his army.' He first appears acting under Richard's orders in February 1184 when he led a force which sacked Excideuil – a stroke directed against Aimar of Limoges, who was presumably hoping to profit from the quarrel between Henry II and his son.

In fact the expected invasion of Aquitaine did not materialize until some time after Henry had sailed to England in June. At the end of that month his officials were able to meet a Portuguese princess at La Rochelle and escort her safely across Poitou. This delay suggests that he had not intended his angry words to be taken literally, but at least one of his sons was clearly capable of making trouble, while claiming to be doing no more than carrying out his father's wishes. John was still only sixteen years old so it is probable that the real initiative for the invasion came from the unscrupulous Geoffrey, now apparently restored to his duchy; Richard and Geoffrey had been formally reconciled in the summer of 1183 but the memory of the struggle for Limoges obviously still rankled. The two younger brothers carried out raids in Poitou while Richard retaliated with counter-raids against Geoffrey's lands in Brittany. When news of this war reached Henry II in the autumn of 1184. he summoned all three to England. The fact that all three obeyed the summons shows that the Old King was still in effective control of the whole of his empire. In December Richard, Geoffrey and John were publicly reconciled at Westminster. It is clear that throughout the second half of 1184 Henry II had been seeking a solution to the problem of the succession. Immediately on his arrival in England he gave orders for Eleanor's release from custody. As a result she was present at the important council meetings at the end of the year and it would be surprising if her voice was not heard in the discussions about the future of Aquitaine – all the more so since she could be expected to have some influence over her children, and particularly over Richard. Henry's mind was still working on the possibility of marrying Alice of France to another of his sons. He welcomed an embassy from the Emperor, Frederick Barbarossa, and agreed to a proposal for a marriage alliance between Richard and one of the Emperor's daughters. The princess in question, however, died later that year. Henry kept Richard and John in England over Christmas, but sent Geoffrey to Normandy 'to hold it in custody'. Was this a veiled threat to Richard? A reminder that he should not take it for granted that he would in time succeed to England, Normandy and Anjou? If Richard insisted on keeping Aquitaine, would he have to give up his claim to inherit the rest? That Henry was now thinking of Richard's keeping his duchy is suggested by the plans he was making to install John as King of Ireland, but what price would the Old King demand in return for this concession? Richard was alarmed. Immediately after Christmas he obtained permission to return to Aquitaine and we next hear of him once again at war with Geoffrey.

Henry held Richard responsible for this further outbreak, which was in flagrant defiance of his recent ban. In April 1185 he crossed to Normandy and began to muster an army but he soon found a more effective means of dealing with his insubordinate but formidable son. He sent for Eleanor to join him in Normandy and when she arrived, a message went to Richard, requiring him to surrender

Aquitaine to his mother, the lawful duchess. In view of Richard's affection for his mother, this was a trump card. He laid down his arms, ordered his castellans to obey Eleanor's commands and returned, like a dutiful son, to his father's court. But for Richard too this was a triumph: the full rehabilitation of his mother to all her rights as Duchess of Aquitaine. It could only mean that his own future as Duke was doubly assured. In the meantime Henry, Eleanor and Richard acted as joint rulers. On occasions a fortunate, or bemused, beneficiary received no less than three charters each confirming him in the legitimate enjoyment of the same right. The real power in Aquitaine, in the sense of the power to appoint men or collect and transfer money, lay, of course, with Henry – as it always did when he was on the Continent and chose to exercise it. But, by the time he returned to England in April 1186, Richard's position as heir-apparent had been further strengthened. In the previous month Henry and Philip had held another conference at Gisors, confirming the settlement reached in December 1183, but this time, instead of promising that Alice would marry one of his sons, Henry agreed that she should be married to Richard. Geoffrey of Brittany had no illusions about the significance of this agreement. Any expectations he may have had of inheriting a larger share of the Angevin Empire were fading fast. His one hope now lay with Philip and he went to visit him in Paris, the traditional move for all discontented sons of Henry II. The rumour that he used his notoriously smooth tongue to get himself recognized as seneschal of France suggests that he was aiming at Anjou, since this was a title claimed by the Counts of Anjou.

While Geoffrey was intriguing against him in Paris, Richard was occupied with an invasion of Toulouse. His father had given him a plentiful supply of money and there was considerable justification for the war. Not only had Count Raymond v supported the Young King in 1183, but early in the next year his son Raymond vi had let some *routiers* into the Limousin. They had sacked Peyrat-le-Château and ravaged the surrounding countryside to the east of Limoges, possibly acting in collusion with Viscount Aimar, since it seems to have been in response to this act of aggression that Mercadier struck at Excideuil in February 1184. Unfortunately, later in the same year, some months after being hit on the head by a piece of falling masonry, Geoffrey of Vigeois died, and without his chronicle to guide us we are hopelessly ignorant of events in this part of the world. But it seems probable that in the period 1183-5 the Counts of Toulouse were able to recover much of the territory they had lost in 1159, above all Cahors and the Quercy. Richard's counter-attack in 1186 seems to have gone very well indeed. Count Raymond dared not risk battle against Richard's massive army; nor did the pleas for help which he sent to King Philip meet with any response. Presumably Philip judged that for the moment he had no means of putting pressure on either Henry or Richard which would be both legitimate and effective.

Once again it was an unexpected death which altered the situation. In a tournament at Paris in August 1186 Duke Geoffrey was trampled to death. Philip, as overlord of Brittany, at once claimed custody of Geoffrey's two daughters, and threatened to invade Normandy if Henry II did not hand them over. Having forced the Old King on to the defensive, Philip was able, in subsequent negotiations, to demand that Richard stop his harassment of Toulouse. In October the two Kings agreed on a truce until January 1187 but whether or not this was supposed to include the war in Toulouse is not clear. One indication that Richard was still maintaining a more aggressive attitude than his father lies in the fact that when the constable of Gisors killed a French knight in a skirmish which occurred after the truce had been made he thought it wiser to take refuge with Richard. By February 1187 at the latest, however, Richard had left the south and was in Normandy to welcome his father on his arrival from England. Two meetings with Philip during the spring resulted in the truce being prolonged until midsummer but otherwise served only to widen the gap between the two sides. In addition to demanding custody of Brittany, the King of France had yet again raised the question of Alice's marriage and the Norman Vexin. It looks as though the agreement of March 1186 had failed to make it clear beyond all possibility of argument whether or not the Angevins could keep the Vexin if Alice remained unmarried. Unquestionably, if either Richard or John had married her, it would have added plausibility to Philip's claim that this vital territory was his sister's marriage portion and, as such, might one day be returned to France. If, on the other hand, Henry II wished to maintain that the Vexin belonged of old to Normandy and was therefore his by hereditary right, it was safer not to confuse the issue by marrying Alice to one of his sons. Whatever the legal rights and wrongs, so long as the Angevins actually held Gisors they were clearly negotiating from a position of strength and could reasonably hope that one day the King of France would be forced to concede their case. The fate of Alice, more than twenty-five years in the King of England's custody without ever being married, has puzzled modern historians just as much as contemporary ones. Gossip said that the Old King had seduced her and Richard would not marry his father's mistress. It may be so, but diplomatic calculation also would have persuaded both of them that it was better if Alice did not marry an Angevin. Moreover, by simply keeping her in their power they were holding all their options open and preventing Philip from marrying her to someone else and so forging a new alliance. As a policy it was unscrupulous but probably effective, though certainly not without some disadvantages. For example, it meant that whenever the King of France wanted to stir up trouble, he always had a legitimate grievance to hand.

The early summer of 1187 was filled with the bustle of preparations for war. Since Philip was challenging Henry II's right to hold Alice, Brittany and the Vexin it was up to him to take the initiative. He could choose where to strike while Henry had to disperse his forces in an attempt to guard the whole of his long frontier. In June Philip made his move. He marched into Berry. By prior arrangement the lord of Issoudun and, further north in the Loire valley, the lord of Fréteval opened their castles to his troops. In Berry, where Angevin and Capetian possessions lay intermingled, it was hard to be loyal to one allegiance only. This was particularly true of the lord of Issoudun, since he was Robert of Dreux, King Philip's cousin. Richard and John barred any further advance by holding Châteauroux long enough to permit their father to come up with the main Angevin army and force Philip to raise the siege. But Philip, his prestige at stake in this first open challenge to the Angevin position, could not afford to retreat. Instead, on 23 June he drew up his forces in battle array. Henry II did likewise. The scene was all set for a pitched battle.

At the last minute both sides drew back. It would have been extraordinary had they chosen to fight. Pitched battles were rare; between kings they were very rare indeed. In his whole life Henry II never fought a battle; not did Philip until 1214 and although that battle, at Bouvines, turned out to be the victory which crowned his career he did his best to avoid it. Philip's reluctance to risk battle helps to explain why even so famous a soldier as Richard never fought a battle in Europe, with the possible exception of his 'battle' against Vulgrin of Angoulême's mercenaries in 1176 – but that was probably a slaughter rather than a battle. Warfare was not normally about battles. It was about laying waste enemy territory, about the pursuit of a retreating army, about sieges. Most battles indeed occurred as a result of sieges when, as at Châteauroux in June 1187, a besieging army found itself faced by a relieving army. But even in these circumstances a full-scale pitched battle between two more or less evenly matched armies, with well-armed knights and infantry on both sides, was an extraordinary event. Battles were, quite simply, far too risky. In the confusion of battle an accident might decide the issue one way or another and the fortunes of a single day might undo the patient work of months or years. Though comparatively few knights were actually killed in battle, the prince who committed his cause to battle was also putting himself in jeopardy, since it was always clear that the surest way to win a battle was to capture or kill the opposing commander, as Harold was killed at Hastings. Most of the time sensible princes deliberately took steps to avoid so chancy a business.

The armies arrayed in the fields outside Châteauroux contained many nobles who knew each other well, who had met at tournaments or on pilgrimages, who were cousins or neighbours. Even if, for once, the Kings had not been bluffing when they drew up their armies, these men were reluctant to attack each other. Moreover a papal legate had arrived, sent by Urban III with instructions to settle the quarrels of north-west Europe and prepare men for a crusade. With his moral support a group of nobles and clergy from both sides tried to work out peace terms. This proved to be impossible. For as long as there was an alternative neither Philip nor Henry was prepared to make any concession to the other, and there was, of course, an alternative: not peace, not war, but a truce. The requirements of the crusade and the tensions of being brought to the brink of battle both pointed to the need for a long, rather than a short, truce. Two years was the period finally agreed upon. The armies separated and Philip was left in possession of Issoudun and Fréteval.

But that day Philip gained something more significant than temporary control of a couple of lordships. When he went back to Paris Richard went with him. 'Philip so honoured him', wrote Roger of Howden, 'that every day they ate at the same table, shared the same dish and at night the bed did not separate them. Between the two of them there grew up so great an affection that King Henry was much alarmed and, afraid of what the future might hold in store, he decided to postpone his return to England until he knew what lay behind this sudden friendship.' This does not mean – as some modern writers have assumed – that Richard and Philip were having a homosexual affair. It was common for people of the same sex to share a bed. For example Henry II and William Marshal did so. The *jongleur* who reported this had no fears that his audience would misunderstand him. He meant to imply that the Old King trusted William, that they were close politically, not sexually. If men exchanged a kiss it was a gesture of friendship or of peace, not of erotic passion. It is an elementary mistake to take it for granted that an act which has one symbolic meaning for us today possessed that same meaning eight hundred years ago. When Richard and Philip rode to Paris together, it was an act not of sex but of political defiance – as Henry II knew only too well. Gestures of this kind were part of the vocabulary of politics; an astute politician like Philip used them to great effect. When Geoffrey of Brittany was buried it was said that Philip had been forcibly prevented from throwing himself into the grave to join his friend. Now in the summer of 1187 Henry sent messenger after messenger to Richard asking him to return and promising to grant him everything that was justly his. Feigning obedience, Richard left Paris but then turned and swooped on Chinon. He seized all the coin in the castle treasury and carried it off to spend on re-stocking and repairing the castles of Aquitaine.

Henry's response was to send yet more messengers and at long last he was able to persuade his son to come to see him. Richard admitted that he had listened to the advice of people who were deliberately trying to sow dissension between them. Then at Angers he did homage to his father, swearing on the Gospels that he would be faithful to him against all men.

What had caused this sudden breach between father and son? Why had Richard first of all defended Châteauroux against Philip and then ridden away in his company? Almost certainly the explanation lies in the highly charged atmosphere of a battlefield on the eve of battle. Richard seems to have played an important part in the peace and truce talks, and as he went to and fro between the armies his father may have begun to wonder just what these exchanges meant. Was his son willing to accept terms which he would find unacceptable? Possibly there were moments when Henry persuaded himself that he was being betrayed. Moreover, if Richard discussed peace on the assumption that he would be the heir to all his father's dominions then he may well have re-activated very real differences of opinion which had lain dormant since the spring of 1185. Those nerve-racking hours, with the armies drawn up in battle array in sight of each other, can hardly have been the best of times for a calm discussion of the problem of the succession. Presumably that is why Philip chose precisely that moment to raise again the spectre which was to haunt the Old King's last years.

At Châteauroux on 23 June 1187 Henry II and Philip had been confronted with the problem of whether or not to commit their forces to battle – the most difficult and terrible decision to face an army commander – and they had drawn back. A few days later, on the morning of 3 July, in a camp at Saffuriya in Galilee another king, the King of Jerusalem, after a night of doubt and conflicting advice, took the opposite decision. A powerful Muslim force was besieging his city of Tiberias and he gave the order to advance to its relief knowing full well that by leaving his camp he was risking battle. He did not reach Tiberias. Marching in fierce summer heat and unrelentingly harassed by Muslim mounted archers, the army was forced to halt at Hattin, in a waterless region, in the hope of being able to continue next day. The Christian soldiers spent a thirsty and sleepless night, their eyes smarting from the smoke which blew into their camp as the enemy systematically set fire to the dry scrub around them. When morning came the King, Guy of Lusignan, could see what he must have known already. His exhausted army was completely surrounded. Inspired by the presence of their most sacred relic, the Holy Cross, the Christian soldiers put up a tremendous fight. But the outcome of the battle was a foregone conclusion. On 4 July the army of Jerusalem was annihilated. Guy of Lusignan and the Holy Cross were captured. Those Templars and Hospitallers who survived the battle itself were executed immediately afterwards. As the elite troops of the Christian army these monk-knights could not be allowed to live to fight another day. With practically all its fighting men either killed or captured, the Kingdom of Jerusalem lay helpless at the feet of the invader. In an attempt to appease the wrath of God and save Jerusalem itself, the defenders of the Holy City indulged in extraordinary rituals of penance. Mothers shaved the heads of their daughters and then made them undress to take cold baths in public on the Hill of Calvary. It was in vain. On 2 October the Muslim army marched into the city. The al-Aqsa mosque was restored to Islam. But it is symptomatic of the greater tolerance of the Muslims that the Jewish community was allowed to return to Jerusalem and four Christian priests were allowed to hold services in the Church of the Holy Sepulchre. Ever since 1099, when the first crusaders captured the Holy City and massacred the people who lived there, Jews and Muslims alike, the Christians had always treated Jerusalem as though it belonged to them alone.

Guy of Lusignan had been beaten by a greater man. The Muslim leader was Al-Malik al-Nasir Salah ed-Din Yusuf; in the West he was known as Saladin. Whereas Guy had only arrived in the Middle East in 1180 and at the time of his defeat had been King of Jerusalem for less than a year, Saladin had ruled Egypt since 1169 and Syria since 1176. His legendary reputation in the Muslim world as the liberator of Jerusalem has at times obscured the fact that he was an ambitious, skilful and experienced statesman. He had received his political education in the household of Nur ed-Din, ruler of Syria from 1154 to 1174 and in those years the crusaders' greatest enemy.

From Nur ed-Din Saladin learned to appreciate the importance of *jihad*, the Holy War against the unbelievers, as the powerful religious force which alone was capable of uniting the divided Muslim world. Like Nur ed-Din, Saladin became the champion of Islamic ortho-doxy and unity, the patron and friend of poets and preachers whose eloquence was pressed into the service of the *jihad* – and its leader. Although as a general he may be faulted, in diplomatic skill and political understanding he towered head and shoulders above his Middle Eastern rivals, Muslim and Christian alike. No man knew better than he the value of a generous gesture. Guy of Lusignan was by no means the handsome fool he has often been made out to be, but his grip on the crown was precarious and the resources of his kingdom were depleted. Against the mighty Saladin he had very little chance.

By the end of 1187 only three coastal towns – Tyre, Tripoli and Antioch – were left in Christian hands. Inland a handful of castles still held out. Many garrisons had surrendered quickly because they knew they could rely on Saladin to keep his word to spare their lives. Outremer – 'the land beyond the sea' – was on the verge of extinction, less than a hundred years after the men of the First Cru-sade had called it into life. Since the failure of the Second Crusade in 1148 the young men of Western Europe had been reluctant to go east, but the news of the disaster at Hattin and the fall of Jerusa-lem changed all that. In the autumn Richard took the cross at Tours, in the new cathedral which was rising in place of the old one where, sixty years earlier, his great-grandfather, Fulk v of Anjou, had lain prostrate before the high altar to receive the cross on the way to becoming King of Jerusalem. Now another Angevin had responded to the call for help. North of the Alps he was the first prince to announce that he was going on crusade. He acted in haste, without seeking his father's permission. As for Philip, the prospect of seeing the man who was supposed to marry his sister go off on crusade for an indefinite period seems to have been too much for him. Imme-diately after Christmas, despite the truce, he gathered a large army and threatened to invade unless Henry either returned Gisors or forced Richard to marry Alice. The two Kings held another conference on the border between Gisors and Trie on 21 January 1188. But instead of talking about Gisors, they talked about Jerusalem. They listened to an impassioned sermon delivered by the Archbishop of Tyre and were moved to take the cross themselves. According to Roger of Howden, as they did so, the shape of a cross could be seen outlined in the sky above their heads.

As long ago as 1172 Henry II had promised to mount a crusade and ever since then he had done nothing about it – though he had given a good deal of financial aid to the stricken kingdom. Philip was as reluctant as Henry, but the two Kings were now swept along by the tide of public opinion. In every way possible preachers and troubadours stirred up enthusiasm. Men who did not take the cross received gifts of distaff and wool, implying that they were no better than women. According to Muslim reports, the preachers used visual aids: 'Among other things they made a picture showing the Messiah, and an Arab striking him, showing blood on the face of Christ – blessings on Him! – and they said to the crowds: "This is the Messiah, struck by Mahomet the prophet of the Muslims, who has wounded and killed him."' In another picture,

Jerusalem was painted showing the Church of the Resurrection with the Messiah's tomb. Above the tomb there was a horse, and mounted on it was a Saracen knight who was trampling the tomb, over which his horse was urinating. This picture was sent abroad to markets and meeting places. Priests carried it about, groaning 'Oh, the shame.' In this way they raised a huge army, God alone knows how many.

The rewards offered to those who took the cross were considerable. On the most mundane level, repayment of any debts they owed was postponed until their return; while they were on the crusade their property was taken under the protection of the church. More important, they were granted a plenary indulgence which freed them from the terrors of purgatory and hell, and held out to them the promise of eternal life in heaven. In the words of St Bernard of Clairvaux, the most successful saint of the twelfth century, they were being offered an amazing bargain:

O mighty soldier, O man of war, at last you have a cause for which you can fight without endangering your soul; a cause in which to win is glorious and for which to die is but gain. Are you a shrewd businessman, quick to see the profits of this world? If you are, I can offer you a bargain which you cannot afford to miss. Take the sign of the cross. At once you will have indulgence for all the sins which you confess with a contrite heart. The cross is cheap and if you wear it with humility you will find that you have obtained the Kingdom of Heaven.

Unlike his father, Richard was genuinely committed to the crusading cause. He was a soldier and no war could bring greater prestige than the war against the Saracens, the war in the Holy Land, the emotional centre of the Christian world. On this battle-ground no act of bravery, no deed of chivalry, would go unrecorded. But it would be a mistake to think that Richard was indifferent to the attractions of a plenary indulgence. While at Messina, *en route* for the Holy Land, he seems to have been overcome by a sense of the wickedness of his life. He summoned all the archbishops and bishops who were with him in Sicily and flung himself to the ground at their feet. Then, naked and holding three scourges in his hands, he confessed his sins. What these sins were Roger of Howden does not tell us and any guess is bound to be a subjective one, reflecting upon ourselves and upon our age rather than upon Richard's behaviour. For example the German scholar who wrote a monumental life of Philip Augustus in six volumes and, in the process, came to study Richard's career with great thoroughness, believed that 'he had abandoned himself entirely to the pleasures of Messina where the women seemed very seductive to warriors from the North'. Whatever his sins it is clear that a man subject to such fits of remorse would have been well aware that a crusade was a religious act as well as a great military adventure. At Beaulieu Abbey near Loches he would have seen the piece of stone from the Holy Sepulchre which his notoriously savage ancestor Count Fulk the Black was believed to have bitten off while kneeling down to pray there on one of his three pilgrimages to Jerusalem. And to a penitent soldier a crusade was even better than an unarmed pilgrimage. As the troubadour Pous de Capdeuil put it, 'What more can kings desire than the right to save themselves from hell-fire by mighty deeds of arms?'

Crusades required organization as well as enthusiasm. At the conference on 21 January it had been agreed that the men of the King of France should wear red crosses, the men of the King of England white crosses and the men of the Count of Flanders green crosses. Later that month other decrees were issued at Le Mans, where Richard had joined his father and a host of barons from Anjou, Maine and Touraine. These included arrangements for the collection of a crusading tax known as the Saladin Tithe, details of the financial privileges to be enjoyed by the crusaders and a set of rules of conduct which they were supposed to observe. They were not to swear or gamble, and the only women who were to be allowed on crusade were washerwomen of good character (for crusaders were supposed to be neatly, though not ostentatiously dressed). According to Roger of Howden the fact that crusaders were exempted from paying the Saladin Tithe meant that the publication of the edict of Le Mans was followed by a great rush to take the cross.

Many contemporaries believed that Richard was unwilling to wait until the two Kings had completed their long-drawn-out preparations. He wanted to go on crusade at once, but his father would not let him. It is by no means certain that this is true. Later on Richard was to show beyond all doubt that he recognized the value of careful and methodical preparation. But what is unquestionably true is that he spent much of 1188 not on the way to the Holy Land but in the castles and camps of south-western France, and that widespread rumour said that his enemies were bribed and incited into action by his own father, determined to keep Richard back until they could go together. The rumours must have reached Richard's ears – indeed they may have been primarily intended for him. They possessed a certain plausibility in as much as Richard could not have gone on crusade without first ensuring that his position as his father's heir was fully and publicly recognized in the most formal manner possible, while everything about Henry's policy in the last four years indicated that he was reluctant to make any such announcement.

Even while Richard was attending the crusading conference at Le Mans a rebellion broke out in Aquitaine. According to one account the signal for revolt was given when Geoffrey de Lusignan killed one of the Duke's closest advisers. He was then joined by his old associates, Ademar of Angoulême and Geoffrey de Rancon, and together they ravaged some of Richard's lands. Ademar had become the undisputed head of the Taillefer family after the death of his brother William a few years earlier. It looks as though Richard had some time ago given up his insistence that Angoulême should be inherited by Vulgrin's daughter Matilda. None the less old grievances like the Taillefer claim to La Marche were still outstanding and Richard may have added new ones by demanding a high price in return for agreeing to recognize Ademar as Count. We only possess one piece of information with which to lend precision to the general statement that Richard went through the rebels' lands with fire and sword, capturing and demolishing their fortresses, and this suggests that Geoffrey de Rancon's castle of Taillebourg was once again at the centre of events. As in 1179, however, it fell before Richard's onslaught. The rebels were forced to sue for peace – and they received it, but only on condition that they too took the cross. In the case of Geoffrey de Lusignan at least, this enforced vow was speedily fulfilled, since he reached Outremer at some date during the summer of 1188.

No sooner was this revolt put down than Richard became involved in a new war with Count Raymond of Toulouse. The two of them had been at daggers drawn ever since 1183, and in recent months, as incident followed incident, tension had been building up to a new peak. Raymond was accused of arresting some Aquitainian merchants as they crossed his lands and then either imprisoning, blinding, castrating or killing them. In the course of one of Richard's retaliatory raids he captured an important man, Peter Seillan, a member of the family which governed the city of Toulouse on the Count's behalf and one of his closest advisers. Since Richard held Seillan responsible for much of the trouble he refused to release him, either for a ransom or in exchange for prisoners taken by Count Raymond, even though these now included two of King Henry's household knights, who had apparently wandered into the territory of Toulouse on their way back from the shrine of Compostella. But Raymond was equally intransigent: he refused to free the pilgrims except in return for Peter Seillan. King Philip travelled south in an attempt to make peace but faced with such

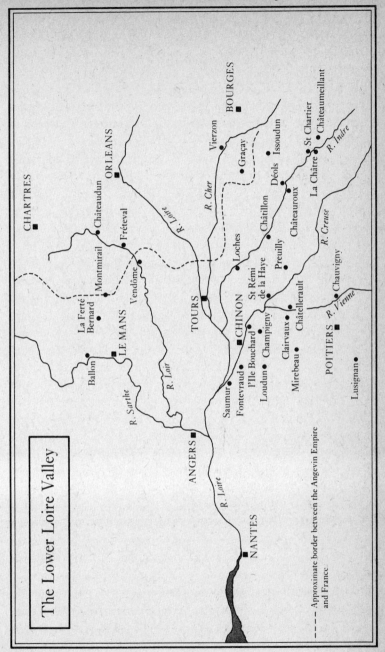

The Lower Loire Valley

CHARTRES

ORLEANS

BOURGES

Châteaudun

Montmirail
Fréteval

Vierzon

Graçay

Déols Issoudun

St Chartier
La Châtre   Châteaumeillant

R. Indre

R. Loire

R. Cher

Vendôme

Châtillon

Châteauroux

La Ferté
Bernard

Montmirail

Loches

Preuilly

R. Creuse

LE MANS

TOURS

CHINON

St Rémi
de la Haye

Châtellerault

Chauvigny

Ballon

R. Sarthe

R. Loir

Saumur

Fontevraud

l'Ile Bouchard

Loudun   Champigny

Clairvaux

Mirebeau

POITIERS

R. Vienne

Lusignan

ANGERS

R. Loire

NANTES

- - - - Approximate border between the Angevin Empire
and France

stubbornness on both sides he was forced to return with nothing accomplished. His irritation at this failure to control his warring vassals was further increased in the spring of 1188 when Richard, no longer distracted by rebellion, launched his Brabançons in a massive attack on Toulouse. This time it was not a question of skirmishing along the border, but of a major re-occupation of territory lost since 1183. Within a short space of time Richard had captured no less than seventeen castles and with garrisons installed in Cahors and Moissac was firmly in control of the Quercy. As his army approached close to the walls of Toulouse itself the townspeople seized the opportunity to emancipate themselves from comital authority. With his whole political position in western Toulouse crumbling, Raymond again appealed for help to his overlord, King Philip, and this time his appeal was answered.

Arguing that Richard's attack on Toulouse was a breach of the truce of 1187 – which Richard denied – Philip invaded Berry for the second time in twelve months, though he first took care to ascertain that Henry II disclaimed any responsibility for his son's actions and was therefore unlikely to move swiftly to his assistance. He took with him a full train of siege artillery with sappers and engineers. On 16 June he captured Châteauroux and this time it fell into his lap so easily that men talked of treason. A few ducal castles held out, but apart from these the whole of Berry was prepared to recognize Philip's authority. Further north, and a few miles west of Fréteval, which Philip had held since last June, the lord of Vendôme switched his allegiance to France. Richard hurried back to the defence of his north-eastern frontier. His father, shaken by the speed of the collapse and alarmed by the imminent threat to Loches and other key castles in the Angevin heartland, hastily mustered an army in England. It included a large force of Welsh infantry – soldiers who were soon to win a fearsome reputation for themselves. Narrowly escaping shipwreck in a tremendous storm in the Channel Henry reached Normandy on 11 July. On learning of Henry's movements Philip withdrew from Berry in order to defend his border with Normandy. Thus Richard was free to recover much of the lost terrain unhindered by the presence of a hostile field army. But the central fortress of Châteauroux itself, under the command of Philip's most famous knight, William des Barres, resisted all his efforts to capture it. Indeed in one mêlée outside the gates Richard was thrown from his horse and rescued only by the strong arm of a sturdy butcher. In the meantime, however, Henry II had made no attempt to invade France; not relishing the prospect of another confrontation like that at Châteauroux in 1187, he preferred to keep his army encamped within Normandy. This enabled Philip to seize the initiative again. Leaving his Norman border in the capable hands of his cousin, the warlike Bishop of Beauvais, he advanced westwards from Vendôme, along the valley of the Loire. But he was checked at Trou. Although he captured some knights and burned down the town, he was unable to take the castle. A castle garrison was sometimes glad to see their town reduced to ashes, reckoning that it simplified the task of defence. Richard at once countered Philip's thrust by moving into the Loire valley himself. He captured Les Roches, a fortress halfway between Trou and Vendôme. Philip then returned to Paris, while Richard, keeping abreast of him, rode on to Normandy.

Only after his son's arrival at his camp did Henry II rouse himself from the passivity of the last month. He had done little except reiterate his protests against Philip's invasion of his dominions. But the King of France had shown a contemptuous disregard for Henry's complaints. At the end of a conference at Gisors in mid-August he had hewn down the famous elm tree which marked the border and was the traditional meeting place of Kings of France and Dukes of Normandy. In his view peace conferences were a waste of time; the old elm had outlived its usefulness. Clearly if Henry's protests were to be taken seriously he would have to match his words with deeds. On 30 August 1188 the Angevin army crossed the border near Pacy-sur-Eure and marched towards Mantes, where Philip was believed to be staying. Richard was involved in a skirmish with some French knights, among them his old opponent William des Barres, who recognized him by the lion on his shield. What really happened is anyone's guess but afterwards each accused the other of cheating. Richard claimed that William des Barres surrendered to him and was released on parole while he went in pursuit of more victims. This was standard practice, both in tournaments and in war, but the French knight, he said, broke parole and escaped on a squire's rouncy. William claimed that Richard cheated by plunging his sword into William's horse when he found that he could not win by fair means. Despite the conflicting accounts it is clear that Richard had the upper hand and that William des Barres lost his valuable war-horse. Clashes like this one, between individual knights or groups of knights, often seem to be the main ingredient of medieval war as described by contemporary chroniclers. It made good sense, of course, for the writers to celebrate the deeds of prowess of their aristocratic patrons. But such knightly combats, whether chivalrously conducted or not, were in fact only a very small part of war. As Henry's army advanced towards Mantes it burned and looted everything which lay in its path. What this meant is made crystal clear by the description of an army on the march in the *Chanson des Lorrains*:

The march begins. Out in front are the scouts and incendiaries. After them come the foragers whose job it is to collect the spoils and carry them in the great baggage train. Soon all is in tumult. The peasants, having just come out to the fields, turn back, uttering loud cries. The shepherds gather their flocks and drive them towards the neighbouring woods in the hope of saving them. The incendiaries set the villages on fire and the foragers visit and sack them. The terrified inhabitants are either burned or led away with their hands tied to be held for ransom. Everywhere bells ring the alarm; a surge of fear sweeps over the countryside. Wherever you look you can see helmets glinting in the sun, pennons waving in the breeze, the whole plain covered with horsemen. Money, cattle, mules and sheep are all seized. The smoke billows and spreads, flames crackle. Peasants and shepherds scatter in all directions.

This was the classic method of waging war. 'This is how war is begun: such is my advice,' said Count Philip of Flanders in 1174. 'First destroy the land.' That evening, on 30 August 1188, Henry's army returned to Ivry loaded down with plunder. Next day, having seen his father stirred into action at last, Richard headed back to Berry, burning Vendôme on the way.

The war continued into the autumn but increasingly half-heartedly on both sides. The needs of harvest and vintage, the expense of keeping large numbers of men in arms and the reluctance of some of the leading French nobles to fight against princes who, like themselves, had taken the cross, all combined to persuade Philip, despite his dramatic gesture at Gisors, to ask for another peace conference. Richard and the two Kings met on 7 October at Châtillon-sur-Indre, on the border between Touraine and Berry. There is no doubt that Philip had an advantage on occasions like this since he alone represented France while the Angevins were represented by two princes whose interests diverged somewhat and whose differences could be, and were, skilfully exploited by the Capetian King. Philip consistently offered to return his conquests in Berry on condition that Richard's conquests in Toulouse were handed back to Count Raymond. While both Angevins would naturally have liked to get their own way in both regions it is likely that the Quercy meant more to Richard than it did to Henry. At Châtillon the Old King was apparently willing to accept the proposed exchange and this might explain why Richard rounded on Philip, calling him a 'vile recreant'. Philip, however, seems to have overplayed his hand, demanding that Henry surrender Pacy-sur-Eure as security while the exchange was being carried out and causing the English King to break off the conference in indignation.

So far as Richard was concerned if his father was eventually going to insist that he give up his conquests then it was at least possible that he would get better terms if he approached Philip directly and offered to abide by the judgement of the French court. Philip would doubtless be gratified by an explicit recognition of his position as overlord of Aquitaine and Toulouse and might well concede something in return. This, at any rate, was the offer which Richard made to the King of France while the latter was disbanding his mercenaries at Bourges. Although Richard claimed that he took this initiative in the hope of bringing about peace so that the crusade could get under way, his father objected strongly, presumably on the grounds that the general position of the Angevins would be weakened if they admitted the principle that their disputes could be settled in their overlord's court. This was the beginning of the final breach between Henry and his son. Once Richard had begun to negotiate directly with Philip it was relatively easy for the King of France to play upon his fears, and above all on the fear engendered by the common gossip that the Old King wanted to disinherit him and confer the crown upon John. Why had John not taken the cross? Soon Richard and Philip were in agreement and, at the Duke's insistence, a fresh peace conference was arranged. In order to have peace and Philip's support in his bid to be recognized, once and for all, as heir to the throne, it seems that Richard was at long last ready to marry Alice.

The three men met at Bonsmoulins on 18 November. Henry II was understandably disconcerted when Richard and Philip arrived together. The atmosphere was very tense. On the first day of the conference all parties were able to keep a grip on themselves and talk calmly. On the second the strain began to tell. Some sharp words were exchanged. By the third day they were quarrelling openly and at times so fiercely that the knights standing around went for their swords. Philip had opened the proceedings by again suggesting an exchange of conquests, but Richard opposed this, arguing that this would mean that he gave up lands, including the Quercy, which brought him an annual revenue of a thousand marks or more, in return for estates in Berry which, though they were fiefs belonging to Aquitaine, were in fact held by other lords and so were of very little direct financial benefit to him. It is possible that this difference of opinion was pre-arranged and intended simply to minimize the extent of the co-operation between Richard and Philip as a preliminary to the new proposal which the King of France now made and which clearly had been worked out between them. Philip offered to return all his gains of the last year on one condition: that Henry gave Alice in marriage to Richard and made his barons, both in England and on the Continent, swear an oath of fealty to Richard as heir. But the Old King rejected this, saying that he refused to act under pressure of this kind. Finally Richard, in the hearing of all, asked his father if he would recognize him as his heir. This blunt and simple question was the crux. Henry remained silent. 'Now at last', said Richard, 'I must believe what I had always thought was impossible.' Then he turned to Philip and, going on his knees before him, did homage for Normandy, Aquitaine, Anjou, Maine, Berry and his conquests in Toulouse. Saving only the fealty which he owed to his father he swore allegiance to Philip against all men. In other words, in return for this act of homage, the King of France was prepared to restore all of his gains while permitting Richard to keep all of his. After this shattering dénouement there seemed little more that could be done at Bonsmoulins. The Kings agreed to meet again in mid-January 1189 and made a truce to last until then.

It may be that Henry II was not plotting to make John his heir. Certainly, so far as we can see, he took no steps to promote the interests of his younger son, apart from not insisting that he take the cross. It is not hard to imagine that the Old King was obsessed by the problems that had arisen after he had recognized young Henry as his heir and was determined not to make the same mistake again. But in fact it would not have been the same mistake. Richard was not Henry. In character he was very different from his dead elder brother. He was now thirty-one years old and a soldier and politician of great experience. When entrusted with government he did not make a mess of it; if deprived of his rights he would make a much more serious opponent than the Young King. In Philip of France moreover he had – as Henry II was well aware – an ally vastly different from the Louis VII of the 1170s. The costs of treating Richard in this fashion were far greater than the gains to be made from keeping him in suspense about his future. In W. L. Warren's words, 'Henry had adopted the tactic of trying to discipline Richard by keeping him in uncertainty and had then become caught in the toils of his own deviousness.' The tactic worked for a while but it was madness to remain obstinately wedded to it while his son's frustration increased and while men pressed for an end to political uncertainty in order to permit the launching of the crusade.

At last the Old King's touch had deserted him. As he kept the last Christmas of his life at Saumur, he can hardly have failed to see how many of his barons stayed away, a sure sign that they were preparing to transfer their allegiance to Richard and Philip. In these cheerless circumstances Henry fell ill and was unable to attend the peace talks in January 1189. But his enemies believed that the sickness was just another of his delaying tactics and so they renewed the war as soon as the truce expired. They were at once joined by the Bretons rising in rebellion against the King who had done much to limit their independence. Henry sent envoy after envoy to

Richard in the hope of calling him back to his side, but not even when he used an ambassador as distinguished as the Archbishop of Canterbury was his son to be persuaded. Quite simply Richard no longer believed anything his father said. Henry also sent messengers separately to Philip, presumably in the hope of driving a wedge between the allies, but Richard had instructed one of his most trusted advisers, his chancellor William Longchamp, to remain at the French court and look after his interests.

Not until after Easter was King Henry well enough to attend a conference, but even then nothing was achieved. Eventually a papal legate, John of Anagni, arrived in northern France on a peace-making mission and he was able to obtain an undertaking from both Kings that they would abide by the decisions of an arbitration panel consisting of himself and four Archbishops, Rheims, Bourges, Rouen and Canterbury. At Whitsun they all assembled at La Ferté-Bernard in Maine, twenty-five miles north-east of Le Mans. Both sides came fully armed and on their guard. There Philip and Richard laid down three conditions upon which they were prepared to make peace. Alice should be married to Richard. Henry should acknowledge Richard as his heir. John should take the cross. Richard indeed added that there was no way that he would go to Jerusalem unless his younger brother went with him. Henry rejected these terms and made a counter-proposal, that Alice should marry John, which he must have known would be unacceptable. John of Anagni threatened to lay an interdict on France if Philip did not come to terms with Henry, but Philip was unmoved and observed that the legate's money bags were obviously full of English silver. With that the conference came to an end and Henry withdrew to Le Mans.

But Philip and Richard did not withdraw to the frontier. Instead they launched a successful surprise attack on La Ferté-Bernard. Then, in quick succession, other castles to the north-east of Le Mans – Montfort, Maletable, Beaumont and Ballon – were handed over to Richard. On 12 June, after a feint in the direction of Tours, Richard and Philip suddenly swooped on Le Mans itself. Henry II fled northwards towards Normandy, abandoning the town in which he was born. Hard on his heels came the pursuit, and at the head of the pursuers was Richard. They caught up with Henry's rearguard, which was under William Marshal's command and, in William's opinion, would have overwhelmed them had not William himself saved the day. He turned and rode straight at Richard. Because they had both anticipated, not a fight, but a long, hard ride neither of them was wearing a hauberk and as William levelled his lance Richard suddenly saw the danger he was in. 'By God's legs' – one of his favourite oaths – 'do not kill me, Marshal. That would be wrong, I am unarmed.' 'No, let the Devil kill you,' retorted William, 'for I won't.' Then, adjusting his aim, he ran his lance through Richard's horse. The story of the Lionheart's narrow escape was told by William Marshal himself and since William never suffered from modesty it may have been improved in the telling. But that something like this happened is very probable. Within a few weeks Richard was loading Marshal with honours, lands and responsibility and an incident such as this, combining skill at arms with sound political common sense, could well have impressed him. At all events the pursuit came to a sudden halt and Henry was able to make good his escape in peace.

But the Old King was far from being at peace. Instead of pushing on to Normandy to muster an army and then return to Maine in force, he switched direction and went home to die. With just a handful of followers he rode to Chinon, the castle of his ancestors, and stayed there, ill and exhausted, while Richard and Philip overran Maine and Touraine. On 3 July Tours itself, the strategic key to the whole empire, fell. Next day Henry, though in such agony that he could hardly sit on his horse, met Philip and Richard at Ballon and there agreed to the terms which they dictated. He would pay Philip 20,000 marks and in all things submit to his judgement. Alice was to be handed over to a guardian nominated by Richard, who would marry her after his return from crusade. Henry's subjects, both in England and on the Continent, were to swear allegiance to Richard. The starting date of the crusade was fixed for Lent 1190 when both Kings and Richard were to muster at Vézelay. If Henry failed to abide by these terms his barons were to transfer their allegiance to Philip and Richard. According to Gerald of Wales, who gives the most vivid, if not the most reliable, account of these days, Henry was then required to give Richard the kiss of peace. As he pretended to do so he hissed in his son's ear, 'God grant that I may not die until I have had my revenge on you.'

The conference over, Henry was carried back to Chinon on a litter and there, on 6 July 1189, he died. He had not obtained his revenge. Indeed his last hours had been made even more bitter by the news that John had deserted him. The news of the fall of Le Mans had convinced him that his father's ship was sinking. From Chinon Henry's body was carried to Fontevraud and laid in the abbey church. When Richard arrived at Fontevraud he strode directly into the church, saying nothing. Without showing any sign of emotion he stood for a while at the head of the bier. Then he turned away. He was king now and there was work to be done.

PREPARING THE
CRUSADE
1189-1190

As Richard turned away from his father's body he called over two of the dead King's most loyal followers: William Marshal and Maurice of Craon. 'So, Marshal, the other day you tried to kill me and would have done so had I not turned your lance aside.' This accusation wounded William's knightly pride and he replied indignantly that had he wanted to kill Richard nothing could have stopped him. 'Marshal, you are pardoned. I bear you no malice.' Indeed far from punishing William and the others who had stayed with the Old King until the end and who on this account had awaited his son's arrival in the abbey church with some trepidation, Richard praised and rewarded them. The men whom Richard punished were those who had decided to desert his father when the Old King's cause seemed lost. But to those who remained loyal he confirmed the gifts which his father had promised. To William Marshal, for example, he granted the hand of Isabel de Clare, heiress to the lordship of Striguil in the marches of Wales, to the county of Pembroke and to the immense lordship of Leinster in Ireland. William rushed to Dieppe, fell off a gang plank in his haste to get aboard ship, and married the girl as soon as he was in London. Richard's well-calculated act of generosity had, in effect, made him a millionaire overnight. In the ability of kings to bestow gifts on this scale lay much of their power; in the careful management of the vast system of patronage lay an essential part of the art of kingship.

Among the other promises made by Henry II to those who were still with him was the gift of the hand of the widowed heiress of Déols and Châteauroux to Baldwin of Béthune. But Châteauroux had actually been in the possession of the Old King's enemies since June 1188 and it was of vital strategic importance in the defence of Aquitaine. For this reason Richard had already promised the heiress to one of his most accomplished and trusted knights, Andrew de Chauveny. Baldwin, however, was a knight well known for his prowess and sense of honour. Fifteen years later, when John had lost Normandy and a group of English landowners who had held estates in Normandy requested permission to perform homage to Philip for their Norman lands, he asked Baldwin for his advice. The petitioners had told John that though their bodies might be with the King of France their hearts would be with him. Baldwin made short work of this argument. 'If their bodies are against me and their hearts for me and those hearts whose bodies are against me were to come into my hands, I would throw them down the privy.' Richard in 1189 could ill afford to lose a man of this calibre, so Baldwin was assured that he would be given adequate compensation for the loss of Châteauroux. In due course he too married a rich widow and, in consequence, became Count of Aumâle. Both Andrew de Chauveny and Baldwin of Béthune went on crusade as two of Richard's closest companions-in-arms, and Baldwin was to serve his King as a hostage in Germany. When Richard returned to England in 1194 he said that he owed more to Baldwin than to any other man. Knights like William Marshal, Baldwin of Béthune and Maurice de Craon were to be celebrated in the song and verse of minstrels for the way in which they approached contemporary ideals of courtly and chivalrous excellence. It was such men as this that Richard drew to his side.

Doubtless strategic considerations also lay behind another marriage which Richard arranged in July 1189, between his niece Matilda and Geoffrey, son and heir of the Count of Perche. This alliance strengthened his border in a vital area, on the north-eastern edge of Maine, in other words precisely where he and Philip had broken through a few weeks earlier. The same train of thought would have forced Richard to concern himself with the defence of Tours, since the fall of this city on 3 July had been the final blow which had brought Henry II to his knees. The position at Tours was extremely complicated. Although it lay within the Angevin dominions, the two main churches there, the cathedral and the abbey of St Martin, each possessing its separate urban settlement, were both closely attached by tradition and privilege to the French crown. The Kings of France cherished this special relationship and found it useful. In 1167, for example, when he was at war with Henry II, Louis VII had written to the abbot and treasurer of St Martin's:

We wish to be informed about the King of England's intentions. Will he be advancing into Poitou or returning to the Norman sea-coast? If you are certain about this send us the information by letter to be returned with our sergeants. If the matter is uncertain, send such rumours as you have through one of them and retain the other until you are able to give us further information.

In the light of letters like this it is hardly surprising that Richard felt that something had to be done about Tours. Still in July 1189 he met Philip in the chapter house of St Martin's and they came to an arrangement which was designed to remove the causes of friction between the abbey and the Counts of Anjou. From Philip's point of view the agreement would prevent the abbey's wealth in men and money being used in a war against him; from Richard's point of view harmonious relations with the church would make it less likely to operate as an espionage centre on behalf of the Kings of France. The problem of Tours was, however, far from being solved in 1189.

From the Loire valley Richard went to Normandy. At Rouen on 20 July he was girded with the ducal sword and received an oath of fealty from the clergy and people of the duchy. Two days later he rode out of the great border castle of Gisors for another conference with King Philip and – according to Philip's historian, Rigord of St Denis – as he did so, the wooden bridge collapsed under him, tumbling the new Duke and his horse into the ditch. For Rigord it was clearly meant as an omen that Gisors would not for much longer be prepared to accept Richard as its lord. Once again the King of France claimed the Norman Vexin, but dropped his demand for the time being when Richard expressed his willingness to marry Alice. In addition to the 20,000 marks promised by Henry II, Richard agreed to pay 4000 marks as a contribution to his ally's costs in the recent campaign. In return Philip restored the lands which he had conquered, including Châteauroux, but excluding Graçay and Issoudun. Apart from this territorial loss and the concession of more or less non-existent rights in the Auvergne, Richard had inherited the whole of the Angevin continental empire – and in November 1188 at Bonsmoulins he had not rated Graçay and Issoudun very highly. While Andrew de Chauveny held Châteauroux the frontier in Berry would be in safe hands. After all the doubts of Henry's last years and after the chaos of the last few weeks, Richard must have felt reasonably satisfied with this outcome. He was free to look forward to the crusade.

But first he had to take possession of England. There was no great hurry to do this; his succession to the throne was now beyond all question. In the end it had turned out to be the first time for centuries that a son had been his father's undisputed heir. From Fontevraud Richard had sent orders that his mother should be released from the strict surveillance under which she had again been placed by Henry, probably towards the end of 1188. Once free, her main task was to ensure that Richard would be welcomed as a prince who restored justice after the arbitrary and oppressive rule of the Old King. Confiscated estates were restored. The prisons were emptied. Those who were in gaol by due process of law were required to find sureties that they would stand trial, but those who had been imprisoned merely because the King or his judges had ordered it were freed unconditionally. Eleanor wrote that she knew from her own experience how delightful it was to be released from confinement. According to one chronicler, William of Newburgh, the only result was that evil-doers were free to transgress more confidently in the future, but it is clear that it was a political gesture which achieved its purpose. Henry II had been a great king but his popularity had waned considerably towards the end of his reign – partly as a result of the Saladin Tithe, for although it was acknowledged that this was taxation in a good cause, the careful assessment and unprecedently high rate created widespread resentment. Thus when Richard landed at Portsmouth on 13 August 1189 he was greeted with enthusiasm. People found it all too easy to believe that a new king meant a fresh start and an easier life. Even the laments composed upon the death of Henry were transformed into songs of welcome. In a contrived piece of theatre Richard enacted the part assigned to him by his own propaganda by arriving in England with one of the Old King's most unpopular ministers, Stephen of Tours, the *parvenu* and unchivalrous seneschal of Anjou, in tow and ostentatiously loaded down with chains. Such, it was implied, was to be the fate of all those powerful men, headed by the justiciar Ranulf Glanville, who had dominated Henry II's administration and had enriched themselves at the subjects' expense.

> *Redit aetas aurea*
> *Mundus renovatur*
> *Dives nunc deprimitur*
> *Pauper exaltatur.*

> The age of gold returns
> The world's reform draws nigh
> The rich man now cast down
> The pauper raised on high.

On Sunday 13 September he was crowned in Westminster Abbey. In Roger of Howden's description of the ceremony we have the first detailed account of a coronation in English history. At the heart of the coronation service lay not the crowning of the new ruler but his anointing. All his clothes were stripped off except his breeches and his shirt, which was bare to the chest. Baldwin, the Archbishop of Canterbury, then anointed him with holy oil on his head, chest and hands. (Until Victoria all subsequent monarchs were anointed in the same way. She was anointed only on the head and hands.) It was this act which was believed to confer upon the new ruler the divine sanction for his kingship.

> Not all the water in the rough rude sea
> Can wash the balm from an anointed King.

After the anointing Richard was dressed in ceremonial robes and then crowned. In later coronation services it was the Archbishop who took the crown from the altar in order to place it on the King's head, but in 1189 Richard himself picked up the crown and handed it to the Archbishop. Whether or not this was an innovation it was a characteristic gesture of self-help. He then mounted the throne and sat there while Mass was celebrated.

After the service came the coronation banquet. The clergy, in due order of rank, dined at his table, while the laity, earls, barons and knights, had separate tables. They all feasted splendidly. Some idea of the scale of the occasion may be gathered from the fact that at least 1770 pitchers, 900 cups and 5050 dishes had been bought in preparation for it. It was just the kind of pageantry in which Richard, unlike his father, delighted. But two groups were barred from attending the coronation: women and Jews. The exclusion of women has been used as supporting evidence for the theory that Richard was a homosexual who preferred to turn his coronation banquet into a bachelor party. Unfortunately for this theory what little evidence we do have for earlier coronations from the tenth to the twelfth centuries makes it perfectly plain that women always were excluded. Indeed one mid-twelfth century writer, Geoffrey of Monmouth, believed that this was a tradition which went back to the Trojans and the earliest days of British history. So the argument from the 'bachelor party' would have more force if it were used to suggest that the early medieval kings of England were all, without exception, homosexual.

The exclusion of the Jews had more serious consequences. While the feasting went on inside the palace, a riot developed outside. Some Jews, bringing gifts for the new King, had tried to enter, but the Christian crowd at the gates would not have this. They fell upon the Jews, killing some and wounding others. The trouble then spread to the city of London, where it continued throughout the night. Jews were killed, their houses plundered and burned down. Richard was furious because the Jews were under his special protection – not because he was unusually tolerant but because, like all kings of the time, he regarded them as a source of revenue. Despite his efforts to prevent them there were more anti-Jewish riots in the next few months: at Lynn, Norwich, Lincoln, Stamford and elsewhere. Men were full of the crusading spirit. They longed to see Jerusalem and the Holy Cross, and they looked with anger upon the descendants of the people who had clamoured for the crucifixion of Christ. Besides, going on crusade was an expensive business and the loot taken from Jews could help many a poor but pious man on his way. This wave of popular anti-Semitism reached its height at York in March 1190. About one hundred and fifty Jews managed to escape the mob and take refuge in the castle. But urged on by a fanatical hermit the mob proceeded to besiege the place. When the Jews realized that they could not hold out much longer most of them committed suicide, having first killed their wives and children. The rest, relying on the besiegers' promises that they would be spared if they accepted Christian baptism, came out of the castle and were promptly massacred.

By this time Richard had already left the country. In the words of Sellar and Yeatman in *1066 and All That*, 'Whenever he returned to England he always set out again immediately for the Mediterranean and was therefore known as Richard Gare de Lyon.' He had, in fact, come to England not, as men hoped, to reform the state of the kingdom but to organize a crusade and raise the money to pay for it. In terms of troops, war equipment and money Richard was to outshine all the other leaders of the crusade. In consequence he played the commanding role; the Third Crusade was very much *his* crusade. This was not just because he ruled over large territories; it was also because among these territories were some where the administrative system was particularly well-developed. Above all this is true of England, and the surviving records of government finance, notably the rolls of the court of the exchequer, commonly known as Pipe Rolls, give some indication – though certainly an incomplete one – of the massive scale of Richard's preparations. His officials went from port to port commandeering the biggest and best ships they could find. All the details we have about this operation come from England – the Cinque Ports alone supplied at least thirty-three ships – but it is clear that Normandy, Brittany and Aquitaine were also required to contribute. It seems that the normal arrangement was for Richard to pay two-thirds of the cost of a ship, leaving the remaining one-third as a crusading obligation imposed upon others. The King also paid the wages of the crews, at the rate of 2d a day for sailors and 4d for the steersmen. In the financial year beginning at Michaelmas 1189 Henry of Cornhill, who dealt with more naval business than any other senior royal official, spent over £5000 on ships and wages. In addition the ships had to be provisioned and laden with war supplies – 50,000 horse-shoes from the iron-works of the Forest of Dean, for example. As the ruler of a sea-borne empire he was to be the first crusader King to equip and take his own fleet to Outremer.

All this had to be paid for. One of his first actions on arriving in England had been to send officials to all the royal treasuries to count and take into safe-keeping the silver accumulated by his father. According to Roger of Howden this amounted to over 100,000 marks. This was a massive sum, though one quickly diminished by the payment of the 24,000 marks owed to Philip. Various ways of raising more money were open to Richard. He might have imposed a tax but this would have had several disadvantages. By 1162 the traditional English tax, the Danegeld, was bringing in so little that Henry decided not to levy it again. On the other hand the new crusading tax, the Saladin Tithe of 1188, based upon a revolutionary method of assessing wealth, being both novel and effective– it brought in £60,000 compared with the £3000 of the 1162 geld – was also highly unpopular. It was very doubtful whether Richard could successfully impose another tax to pay for the same crusade which the Saladin Tithe had been designed to finance. Equally serious was the fact that the proceeds of a tax would be a long time coming in and that it would require a considerable administrative effort, one which was possibly out of proportion to the results achieved in terms of yield. Other methods seemed more promising. At this time the country's wealth was concentrated in the hands of a relatively small number of people, all of them closely bound to the King by legal and political ties. In consequence it paid the King to concentrate on them, to exploit their relationship with him rather than try to impose a widespread public tax. One opportunity of this kind had occurred in August when the Bishop of Ely died intestate, for this meant that the King was entitled to seize the Bishop's moveable wealth: 3000 marks in coin, as well as gold and silver plate, precious cloth, grain, horses and other livestock. This is the kind of action Gerald of Wales had in mind when he pointed out that the Angevins relied more upon irregular profits

than upon a steady income. 'The King is like a robber permanently
on the prowl, always probing, always searching for the weak spot
where there is something for him to steal.'

After his coronation Richard set systematically to work. In Roger
of Howden's words, 'he put up for sale everything he had – offices,
lordships, earldoms, sheriffdoms, castles, towns, lands, the lot.'
What this sweeping phrase meant in practice can best be seen in
the case of the sheriffs. The sheriff, the crown's chief agent in each
county, was an unpaid official who was appointed and could be removed at the King's will. Twice a year he had to render an account
at the exchequer but this apart he was given almost a free hand to
wield power in his shire and power, naturally, meant profit. To be
appointed sheriff was, in a twentieth-century phrase, to be 'given
a licence to print money'. When Richard came to the throne there
were thirty-one sheriffs but only seven of them survived in office.
In East Anglia they carried on much as before; everywhere else there
was replacement and re-shuffling, and every transaction brought in
money. In Worcestershire, for example, Robert Marmion was removed and fined £1000, presumably for misconduct. It may be an
indication of the scale of profits which could be made by an unscrupulous sheriff that Marmion was able to pay 700 marks within
a year. He was succeeded by William Beauchamp, who offered 100
marks for the job. Besides raising money these manœuvres also had
the effect of cutting the Glanville family connection down to size,
for at the end of Henry II's reign, the justiciar and his kinsmen had
seemed to be all-powerful in England. Ranulf Glanville himself
relinquished the sheriffdom of Yorkshire and, according to Richard
of Devizes, had to pay a fine of £15,000. The level of the fine is,
of course, related to his position as chief justiciar rather than to his
local authority as sheriff, but it is noteworthy that his steward,
Reiner, who acted as his deputy in Yorkshire, was fined 1000 marks.
The new sheriff was John Marshal, William's brother. Ranulf Glanville's son-in-law was removed and fined more than 1000 marks.
His replacement was William Longchamp's brother. The new
King's own men were taking over the administration but, as in the
case of the Marshal family, they were very often men whose faces
had been familiar at the Old King's court. It ought not to be argued

– though it commonly *is* argued – that Richard 'by discharging almost all the experienced sheriffs and substituting new men in their stead' had taken a step towards destroying 'the firm and orderly government that his father had imposed'. Indeed all the evidence points in the other direction. Even when Richard was hundreds of miles away the Pipe Rolls show that the country's financial and judicial machinery continued to operate as usual – if anything, with increasing thoroughness.

Other privileges, places and offices of profit were treated in a similar fashion. Thus in a series of massive bargains Godfrey de Luci, Bishop of Winchester – the richest see in England – bought the sheriffdom of Hampshire with custody of Winchester and Porchester castles, paid £3000 for two manors claimed by the church of Winchester and offered 1000 marks to have possession of his own inheritance. It is hard to see why financial transactions of this kind should be called 'the reckless expedients of a negligent king'. Nor are they evidence to prove that Richard was uninterested in administrative problems and lacked his father's supposed genius for solving them. The general post of sheriffs in 1189 was very similar to Henry's own clean sweep in 1170. That offices as well as titles, charters and privileges should be bought and sold was all perfectly usual. It was simply that those transactions which were normally spread over several years were now concentrated into a few hectic months in order to meet the demands of an overriding need: the crusade. By these methods Richard raised enormous sums of money fast. Few people complained; most of them, after all, were buying something which they wanted at prices they were prepared to pay.

The difficulties which arose in Richard's absence were not administrative but political. The absence of an effective and legitimate ruler, whether it was because the King was a child, or mad, or feeble-minded, or in prison, or on crusade, always created severe problems for the political and social system. They were not necessarily insoluble. During the absence of Louis VII and Eleanor on the Second Crusade, Suger of St Denis had governed France well, though it is worth noting that even he had to face an opposition movement led by the King's brother, Robert of Dreux. It was easy enough for Richard to foresee that his brothers might prove troublesome while he was away, particularly since he had no legitimate children and, like Robert of Dreux in 1147, they might well hope to inherit the crown. His half-brother, Geoffrey, presented the lesser problem. Geoffrey, one of Henry II's illegitimate children, had had a chequered career. In 1172, on his father's orders, he had been elected Bishop of Lincoln, but being only twenty years old at the time he was sent to Tours to complete his studies. He resolutely refused to be consecrated, and when in 1181 the Pope eventually told him that he must either be consecrated or resign, he resigned. Henry then appointed him chancellor and he served his father faithfully, being one of the few to stay with the Old King until the bitter end. 'This is my true son; the others are the bastards.' There had been several occasions when Henry II had cause to make this declaration.

On his deathbed Henry promised Geoffrey either the bishopric of Winchester or the archbishopric of York. But ecclesiastical office held little attraction for Richard's half-brother. As he himself said, he preferred horses and dogs to books and priests. Moreover others said that he was hoping for higher things. It was reported that he had once put the lid of a golden bowl on his head and asked his friends whether a crown wouldn't suit him. After all William the Conqueror had started life as William the Bastard. That there was some substance to these rumours is indicated by the obstinacy with which he had set his face against ordination, since once he was a priest he would be ineligible for all secular office including the office of kingship. Moreover it was clear that Richard was well aware of Geoffrey's ambitions, for he leapt at the chance to shunt his half-brother aside while simultaneously respecting the wishes of a dying man. In July 1189 he ordered the canons of York to elect his half-brother as Archbishop. Some of them objected on the grounds that the warlike Geoffrey was a man of blood, conceived in adultery and born of a whore. He was none the less elected and the validity of the election was confirmed, at Richard's request, by a papal legate. On 23 September, though still loudly proclaiming his reluctance, Geoffrey was ordained a priest.

John was to pose a more serious problem. In another act of filial piety Richard confirmed all the gifts which his father had promised to John: lands to the value of £4000 a year in England, the county of Mortain in Normandy and the hand of the heiress to the earldom of Gloucester. Since Henry – as so often – had not gone beyond the stage of promises it was up to Richard to decide upon the composition of John's £4000 worth of English land. He gave him a solid block of territory in the south-west, the counties of Cornwall, Devon, Dorset and Somerset, and two more counties in the Midlands, Nottingham and Derby. Of all Richard's actions during his visit to England this is the one which has been most generally and most severely criticized. 'At no time since the conquest has a subject been allowed to exercise control over so vast a territory.' It has been described as 'a most imprudent and dangerous act, producing disastrous results'. But criticism of this type is very wide of the mark. John was not simply a subject. He was an Angevin prince. Why was he not ruling Anjou? Or Aquitaine, or Brittany, or Normandy, or England? Far from being treated with lavish generosity he had, in fact, been pensioned off with the wealth appropriate to his status but with very little power. It is significant that he was not given custody of the most important castles in his counties. That he would make trouble as soon as Richard was at a safe distance was all too likely, but what alternative was there? If Richard were to insist upon his going on crusade as well, he would be putting the whole future of the Angevin dynasty at risk. What would happen if neither of them came back from Outremer? The nearest heir was a two-year-old boy, Arthur, the posthumous son of Geoffrey of Brittany. If he were called upon to rule there would be chaos and only one certain outcome: the rapid break-up of the Angevin Empire. Rather than risk this it was safer to leave John in Europe. The combined power, influence and political skill of their mother and the ministers whom Richard appointed should be sufficient to keep him in check. And, though not without some alarms, this is how it turned out.

On 12 December 1189 Richard sailed from Dover. As chief justiciar he nominated Hugh du Puiset, a man with thirty-five years' experience of ruling the bishopric and palatinate of Durham. The chancellor was William Longchamp, a Norman who had been a clerk in Henry II's chancery before entering Richard's service. He was now Bishop of Ely and the King's most trusted civil servant as well as being a man of considerable culture and learning, the author of a treatise on civil law. Unfortunately the two men found it impossible to work together, so in March 1190 Richard altered the arrangement, limiting Bishop Hugh's authority to the lands north of the Humber and appointing Longchamp as justiciar for the rest of England. Even this apparently clear division of authority failed, however, to prevent tension. Hugh was gradually out-manœuvred and by June Longchamp was clearly supreme: as chancellor, justiciar and papal legate he held a more powerful combination of offices than any earlier royal servant.

By this time, of course, Richard had turned his attention to making arrangements for the government of his continental dominions while he was away. Yet without exception modern historians have based their opinions of Richard's administrative and governmental skill upon the arrangements which he made in England, as though England was the only part of the Angevin Empire which mattered. This is obviously nonsense and, if we take into account all of his territories, then it is doubly clear that the arrangements which he made held up remarkably well under the prolonged strain of his crusade and imprisonment. The first task was to ensure the security of his borders. On 30 December 1189 and again on 16 March 1190 he met Philip in conference near Nonancourt. The two Kings swore to protect the goods of all crusaders and to act in good faith towards one another. The King of France would help the King of England to defend his land exactly as he would want to see Paris defended if it were besieged; the King of England would help the King of France to defend his land just as he would wish to defend Rouen if it were besieged. The barons of both Kings swore to remain true to their allegiance and to keep the peace while their lords were abroad. By the time of the second conference it was clear that the crusade preparations were behind schedule, so their departure date was postponed until 24 June. No sooner had they taken this decision than news arrived that Isabella of Hainault, Philip's Queen, had died in childbirth on the day before. This was further reason to delay the departure, though there were some who took it as a sign that God was becoming impatient. Fortunately the survival of the Kingdom of Jerusalem did not depend upon the Kings of England

and France alone. Ever since September 1189 a steady stream of crusaders had been arriving in the Holy Land. Most important of all, the old Emperor, Frederick Barbarossa, though the last of the kings to take the cross, had been the first to set off. He left Regensburg in May 1189 and, following the Danube route, had made slow but steady progress. By Easter 1190 he had crossed the Bosphorus and was now in Asia Minor.

During the first six months of 1190 Richard toured his dominions. As seneschal of Normandy he re-appointed William FitzRalf, a well-tried servant who had held the office since 1180 and was to retain it until his death in 1200. In Anjou the position is less clear. Stephen of Tours had been replaced by Payn de Rochefort, but by May 1190 Stephen was back at Richard's court and he may have received his old office back for the period of the King's absence. Whoever the seneschal was, it is at least clear that there was no sign of trouble in Anjou while Richard was away. In Aquitaine two seneschals were appointed: in Poitou, Peter Bertin, formerly provost of Benon, and a man with long experience in the service of the Duke; in Gascony Élie de la Celle, a member of a distinguished administrative family. (Possibly this was the model which Richard had in mind when he divided England into the lands north and south of the Humber with a justiciar in charge of each part, but whereas in England the experiment failed through the personal animosities of Hugh du Puiset and William Longchamp, in Aquitaine there were no such problems.) Given the turbulent reputation of the province very few difficulties actually arose there and those that did were efficiently coped with by Richard's seneschals.

During May and early June Richard was in the far south. He visited Bayonne and hanged the lord of the Pyrenean castle of Chis for the crime of highway robbery. Though many of this lord's victims had been pilgrims on their way to Compostella it is hard to believe that it was devotion to the cult of St James alone which brought Richard into the Pyrenees. In view of the humiliating defeats which he had recently inflicted on Raymond of Toulouse he could hardly expect the south-eastern frontier of Aquitaine to remain at peace for long after his departure on crusade. The obvious answer was to renew and strengthen the alliance with the great

enemy of Toulouse, King Alfonso II of Aragon – the alliance which
had served Richard well in the crisis of 1183, and which had enabled
him to recover the homage of Béarn by February 1187 at the latest.
With this alliance came the friendship of King Sancho VI of
Navarre, since at this date Navarre and Aragon were drawing
together in opposition to King Alfonso VIII of Castile, and were
soon to make a formal treaty. It is against this background that we
must see Richard's marriage to Sancho VI's daughter, Berengaria
of Navarre.

The circumstances of their wedding were, to say the least, odd.
Richard was to spend the winter of 1190-1 in Sicily on his way to
Outremer. Berengaria arrived at his court at Messina at the end
of March 1191 and they were eventually married in Cyprus in St
George's Chapel, Limassol, on 12 May. On the face of it Sancho
of Navarre seems to have been extraordinarily rash to send his
daughter so far in search of a husband who was himself moving
eastwards, all the more so since it was only in March 1191 that Philip
finally agreed to release Richard from his promise to marry Alice,
and Berengaria had probably left home in November or December
1190. It would be strange indeed if Sancho had regarded a crusader
betrothed to someone else as the ideal husband for his daughter.
He must surely have demanded far-reaching assurances and with
the best will in the world, the negotiations which preceded Berengaria's departure from Navarre must have been complex and prolonged. The question is: who conducted these negotiations and
when did they begin? Because Berengaria was taken to Sicily by
Eleanor of Aquitaine, historians have tended to assume that it was
Eleanor who conducted the negotiations and that she did so during
the summer and autumn of 1190, when Richard had already
embarked on the first stage of his journey to Outremer: thus the
oft-repeated charge against Richard, that he went on crusade still
unmarried and without giving a thought to the problem of an heir.
But there are, in fact, indications which point to a much earlier date.
The soldiers in Richard's crusading army seem to have believed that
he had formed an attachment to Berengaria while he was still Count
of Poitou. This may well be an over-romantic view. In one of the
sirventes of Bertrand de Born, however, there are some lines which

refer to Richard's perjury in becoming betrothed to the King of Navarre's daughter. Although it is never easy to date these poems the most probable date for this one is 1188, since it also contains references to attacks on Angoulême and Toulouse. Yet even if Richard and Sancho VI had come to terms in 1188 it is clear that by the end of the year the arrangement must have fallen through. When Richard and Philip rode together to the conference at Bons-moulins in November Richard was once again willing – in public at least – to marry Alice of France, and he repeated this promise in July 1189.

But at Candlemas 1190 (2 February) Richard held court at La Réole on the banks of the Garonne. The court was attended by many of the greater lords of Gascony, archbishops, bishops, abbots as well as secular magnates like the Counts of Béarn and Armagnac. It is possible that they had come simply to welcome their lord for the first time since he had become Duke of Normandy and King of England, yet the presence of Henry, son of Henry the Lion, Duke of Saxony, at La Réole suggests that important questions of foreign policy may also have been on the agenda. A very similar court had assembled twenty years earlier at Bordeaux to settle the marriage between Richard's sister Eleanor and young Alfonso VIII of Castile. All these are no more than straws in the wind. Much more striking is the evidence which shows that, from La Réole, Richard sent a writ to England summoning Archbishop Baldwin of Canterbury and some other bishops to a council meeting in Normandy in mid-March, or rather to an important family conference, for as well as the bishops – whose advice on questions of marriage law would doubtless be useful – Richard also summoned his brothers John and Geoffrey, his mother Eleanor and Alice, the sister of the King of France. The question of Richard's betrothal to Alice must have been discussed at this meeting though the chroniclers tell us nothing about it. Of its nature this was confidential business. The chroniclers, however, say that both John and Geoffrey were forced to take an oath not to enter England within the next three years, so clearly family politics were very much in Richard's mind. A few days after presiding over this conference he met King Philip. Again we do not know what they said to each other, only that the crusade was postponed. It was all very awkward. Whatever the date of Bertrand de Born's poem may be, what it does show beyond all doubt is that Philip would be disgraced if his sister was discarded and humiliated in this fashion and he did nothing to avenge her honour. If Richard were determined not to marry her – and obviously he was so determined, since otherwise he would have married her before he went away on crusade – could he afford to say this openly? Or would that destroy the fragile peace between the kingdoms and cause further interminable delays? Perhaps only when he and Philip were already on crusade could he marry someone else without inviting an immediate attack upon his lands. But it cannot have been easy to persuade Sancho of Navarre to send his daughter to be married somewhere abroad in these ambiguous and hazardous circumstances, especially if Richard had once before offered marriage and then withdrawn it. In February and March 1190 Richard may well have found that he needed more time to complete such intricate negotiations. Probably it was not until May and early June, when he visited Bayonne and was close to the Navarrese border, that he had the opportunity for a face-to-face meeting with Sancho and was at last able to bring the matter to a satisfactory conclusion. It was a splendid match for the daughter of a minor Spanish king – if it had not been, it is hard to imagine how Sancho could ever have agreed to such an extraordinary arrangement. But it was also a useful diplomatic marriage for Richard. It helped to secure his distant southern frontier and it provided his seneschals in Aquitaine with an ally upon whom they could call for reinforcements should there be a rebellion in his absence. Now at last Richard was ready to go. But far from him going on crusade without a thought for the problem of the succession it rather looks as though the opposite was the case: that he had postponed his departure until most of the problems surrounding his marriage had been resolved. He then waited in Sicily until Philip had yielded and until Berengaria had arrived. Richard was by no means just a fanatical crusader who neglected everything else.

From Bayonne he returned to Anjou. There, at Chinon, he issued disciplinary regulations for the sailors of the crusading fleet, the main part of which was now about to sail to its first rendezvous near Lisbon at the mouth of the Tagus. The ordinance makes interesting reading: 'Any man who kills another shall be bound to the dead man and, if at sea, be thrown overboard, if on land, buried with him. If it be proved by lawful witnesses that any man has drawn his knife against another, his hand shall be cut off. If any man shall punch another without drawing blood he shall be dipped in the sea [keel-hauled?] three times. Abusive or blasphemous language shall be punished by fines varying according to the number of offences. A convicted thief shall be shaved like a champion, tarred and feathered and put ashore at the first opportunity.'

Richard then went on to Tours, where he received the staff and scrip which were the traditional attributes of the pilgrim. According to Roger of Howden, when he leaned on it, the staff broke. Undaunted by this omen he rode out of Angevin territory and joined forces with Philip of France at Vézelay on 2 July. There the two Kings concluded a vitally important agreement. They were going to war to win land and plunder as well as glory and they decided that the spoils of conquest should be divided equally between them. Then, on 4 July 1190, the third anniversary of the battle of Hattin, their armies began to move off. Richard's crusade had begun.

SICILY AND CYPRUS
1190-1191

How many crusaders were there with Richard and Philip as they rode out of Vézelay? Unfortunately there is no way of obtaining an accurate assessment of their numbers. One writer says that the army was a hundred thousand strong, but this is certainly a wild exaggeration, implying only that the army was a very large one. We have to remember that in Richard's day this meant no more than a few thousand men. When an eye-witness describes the camp of the two Kings at Vézelay as a veritable city of tents and pavilions, we have to remember that most cities contained only a few thousand inhabitants. To us, then, the army would have seemed a small one – and yet there are indications that it was as large as a twelfth-century army could possibly be. The problems involved in feeding thousands of men and horses imposed an upper limit on the size of armies. It has been calculated, for example, that if an army 60,000 strong took with it provisions to last for one month, it would need about 11,000 carts. If these carts were stretched out in single file this would mean a supply train well over a hundred miles long. Such a wagon train would be hopelessly vulnerable to enemy raids – and it would be several days before a commander at the head of the column even knew of an attack on the rear. On the other hand, if the army tried to do without a supply train and live off the country it was limited by the amount of food which the surrounding area could produce – an amount presumably related to that region's normal population. Moreover the medieval farmer's grain yields per acre were at best only one-quarter or one-fifth of the yields obtained in the early twentieth century. In these circumstances 6000 rather than 60,000 was about the maximum size of any twelfth-century army which intended to stay in the field for long. It is significant that when Richard and Philip reached Lyons they decided to separate because the countryside could not support their joint army.

Fortunately for the historian, the army was accompanied by two men who left behind detailed accounts of the crusade. Even more fortunate is the fact that the two men had very different points of view; we are thus often permitted to see the same events from different angles and can obtain some kind of perspective. One of them was Roger of Howden. As befits a royal clerk his chronicle is sober and reliable. He was very well-informed. Copies of official documents, treaties and the like, often came into his hands, and he liked to insert them into his chronicle. Thus he kept what almost deserves to be called the official diary of the crusade, at any rate up until August 1191 when he returned home, probably in the company of King Philip of France. But Roger of Howden's chronicle is not as dry as most official histories. He was a keen sightseer and liked to jot down quick descriptions of the places he had visited – of Marseilles for example:

It is a city situated twenty miles from the mouth of the Rhône and is subject to the King of Aragon. Here can be found the relics of St Lazarus, the brother of St Mary Magdalene and of Martha. After Jesus raised him from the dead he became Bishop of Marseilles. The city possesses a fine harbour, almost completely enclosed by high hills, but capable of holding many large ships. On one side of the harbour is the cathedral close; on the other the great abbey of St Victor where a hundred Benedictine monks serve God. Here, so they say, are preserved one hundred and forty bodies of the Innocents who were slaughtered for Christ; also the relics of St Victor and his companions, the rods with which Our Lord was scourged, the jaw-bone of St Lazarus and one of the ribs of St Lawrence the Martyr.

Moreover Roger knew that his readers were interested in anything that seemed curious or wonderful. Here, for instance, is a characteristic passage:

In the sea around Sardinia and Corsica some very strange fish may be found. They can leap into the air and fly for about a furlong before

diving back into the water. A man [Roger himself perhaps] happened
to be sitting at table on board ship when suddenly one of these flying
fish landed on the table right in front of him, so he can vouch for the
fact that these odd creatures really do exist. This same area is also in-
habited by certain birds of prey which hunt these fish and feed upon
them.

The second of our two informants was a Norman minstrel named
Ambroise. He composed a long poem called the *Estoire de la Guerre
Sainte*, 'History of the Holy War'. Ambroise saw things from the point
of view of the ordinary soldier. He shows us their dogged courage,
and their sufferings; he records their dreams and disappointments.
Whereas Howden takes us close to the council chamber and shows
us king and counts at work, Ambroise takes us into the tents of
the poor soldiers and tells us what they thought of the decisions
taken by their commanding officers.

At Lyons the crusading army encountered its first setback. The
rear of Richard's army was delayed for three days when the wooden
bridge over the Rhône collapsed under the weight of those trying
to cross. A hundred or so fell into the river. Mercifully, however,
only two were drowned – or rather, as Ambroise in characteristically
pious phrases, put it:

> I mean but two discovered were,
> To be more certain none would dare,
> The water there so fiercely surges
> That little which falls in emerges.
> If these be dead in the world's sight
> They stand before God clean and bright:
> 'Twas on His path they set their feet;
> They shall have mercy, as is meet.

Not until Richard had organized the building of a bridge of boats
could the rest of his army get across. Philip meanwhile was on his
way to Genoa. For 5850 marks he had hired a Genoese fleet to convey his army to Outremer. They were to provide transport for 650
knights and 1300 squires with their horses; there was to be food
and fodder for eight months, wine for four months. If the Genoese

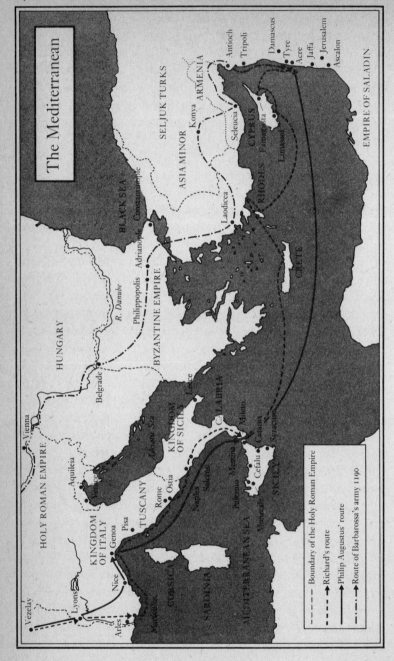

The Mediterranean

ships had a similar capacity to those in Richard's fleet then twenty-five ships should have been sufficient to carry the whole of Philip's force.

On 31 July Richard reached Marseilles, where he expected to find his huge fleet of over one hundred ships waiting for him. But on this day the fleet was still only approaching the Straits of Gibraltar. The main flotilla, sixty-three ships under the command of Robert de Sablé and Richard Canvill, had reached the Tagus safely but then, while waiting for the arrival of the thirty ships of William de Fors of Oleron's squadron, crews and passengers visited Lisbon and ran riot. In an excess of religious zeal they attacked the city's Muslim and Jewish population, burned down their houses and plundered their property. But there was no element of religious discrimination in the freedom with which they raped women and stripped vineyards bare of fruit. Eventually the exasperated King of Portugal shut the gates of Lisbon, trapping several hundred drunken men inside the city and throwing them into gaol. By the time that this had been sorted out and the overdue squadron arrived, it was already 24 July and a further two days passed before the whole fleet was ready to start coasting around Spain. The upshot of it all was that by the time they reached Marseilles – three weeks late on 22 August – they found Richard already gone. After waiting a week he had divided the force which had marched from Vézelay into two. One contingent, led by Archbishop Baldwin of Canterbury, Ranulf Glanville and Glanville's nephew, Hubert Walter, the recently elected Bishop of Salisbury, sailed directly to Outremer – presumably in hired ships – and arrived at Tyre on 16 September. The second contingent, Richard's own company, embarked in ten large ships (known as busses) and twenty galleys, also hired, and then coasted eastwards in a more leisurely fashion. He visited Genoa, where Philip was lying ill in a house near the church of St Lawrence; according to an English chronicler the French King suffered from sea-sickness. Richard spent five days at Portofino and while he was there the two Kings had the first of their many disagreements. Philip sent a message, asking Richard for the loan of five galleys. Richard offered three, which Philip refused. It was a small matter, but it boded ill for the future of the crusade.

Richard sailed on down the coast of Italy, occasionally going ashore to stretch his legs. But although he landed at the mouth of the Tiber, only a few miles from Rome, he did not bother to visit the Pope, Clement III. Indeed a cardinal who was sent to meet him was told in no uncertain terms just what the King thought of the greed of the papacy. Apparently it had cost Richard 1500 marks to persuade the Pope to make William Longchamp legate for the English church. The gospel preached in Rome was the gospel according to the mark of silver – or so contemporary satirists insisted. It was not that Richard was in too much of a hurry to visit Rome; he made this plain by staying ten days at Naples and five days at Salerno, mostly doing some sightseeing but perhaps also talking to the doctors of Salerno, the principal medical school of western Europe. Judging by the number of doctors who attended him at one time or another Richard took good care of his health, although it was a subject on which contemporaries speculated wildly. Some said he suffered from a feverish ague and as a result trembled so much that he wanted to make the whole world tremble before him. Others said that he had over a hundred ulcers in his body through which corrupt humours drained. Still others said that he was wasted away by premature and excessive soldiering. About the only thing we can be reasonably sure of is that, like his father, he had a tendency to put on weight.

While Richard was at Salerno, he heard the news for which he had been waiting. His fleet, after putting into Marseilles for a week's re-fitting, had been sighted and was now approaching Messina. So he pushed on and crossed the Straits of Messina on 22 September. Earlier that day he had had a narrow escape. Passing through a small village on an overland journey from Mileto with just one companion he heard the cry of a hawk coming from one of the houses. Believing that only noblemen had the right to own hawks he pushed his way in and seized the bird. He was at once surrounded by a crowd of angry villagers and when he refused to give it back they attacked him with sticks and stones. One man drew a knife and Richard struck him a blow with the flat of his sword only to see the blade snap. So the crusader King was reduced to pelting villagers with anything he could lay his hands on in order to make his escape from

a very awkward corner. Next day he made up for the petty absurdity
of this occasion by the grandeur of his entry into Messina. He
assembled the whole of his fleet and then, in a galley at its head,
he sailed into the harbour. An eye-witness described the
scene:

The populace rushed out eagerly to behold him, crowding along
the shore. And lo, on the horizon they saw a fleet of innumerable
galleys, filling the Straits, and then, still far off, they could hear the shrill
sound of trumpets. As the galleys came nearer they could see that they
were painted in different colours and hung with shields glittering in the
sun. They could make out standards and pennons fixed to spearheads
and fluttering in the breeze. Around the ships the sea boiled as the
oarsmen drove them onwards. Then, with trumpet peals ringing in their
ears, the onlookers beheld what they had been waiting for: the King of
England, magnificently dressed and standing on a raised platform, so that
he could see and be seen.

The pomp and noisy splendour of his arrival stood in deliberate
contrast to the quiet way in which Philip had slipped into the town
a week earlier. After disembarking, Richard conferred with Philip,
who at once announced his intention of leaving for the Holy Land
that same day. But no sooner had he left the harbour than the wind
shifted and, much to his dismay, Philip was forced to return to Messina and to further meetings with the King of England. Philip lodged
in a palace in the city, while Richard and his army camped outside
the walls.

Entirely by chance, they had arrived in Sicily at a critical moment
in the history of this fascinating country. The twelfth century had
been a golden age for the kingdom of Sicily – a kingdom which included much of southern Italy as well as the island itself. It was
a fertile and prosperous land where the greedy goats had not yet
done their work of destruction. Besides corn – for Sicily was still
one of the great granaries of the Mediterranean world – there were
oranges and lemons, cotton and sugar-cane in abundance. It was
a land to tempt a conqueror and had already been conquered several
times in its turbulent history, most recently by the Normans –
cousins of the men who conquered England – in the decades between
1060 and 1090. But the most remarkable thing about Sicily was

neither its wealth nor its highly developed system of government, but the diversity of its population. Greek, Arab and Norman lived side by side, each with their own language and religion. The court at Palermo spoke Norman French and issued decrees in Latin, Greek and Arabic. Yet these very different communities lived together fairly well. The Muslim traveller Ibn Jubayr remarked on the absence of discontent among the island's Muslim population and noted with interest that Christian women were beginning to follow Arab fashions: they wore veils when they went out of doors and they never stopped talking. The blend of different cultures produced a unique civilization. At Palermo, Monreale and Cefalù the visitor can still see superb examples of its art and architecture.

But in 1190 Sicily stood on the eve of another conquest. Its trouble had been brought about by a dispute over the succession to the throne following the death of King William II in 1189. He had no children and his heir was his thirty-five-year-old aunt, Constance. But she was married to a German, Henry of Hohenstaufen, Frederick Barbarossa's eldest surviving son and heir. No one in Sicily wanted a German king and Pope Clement III had a terrifying vision of what would happen to the papacy if it came to be completely surrounded by the territories of one overmighty ruler. So Pope and Sicilian barons conspired together against Constance and her German husband. The crown passed to Tancred of Lecce, an illegitimate cousin of William II. He was, in the most literal sense of the words, an ugly little bastard, whose enemies never tired of poking fun at his dwarfish figure. He looked, so it was said, like a monkey with a crown on its head. His hold on the throne was anything but secure. He faced a revolt on the island, while on the mainland rebel barons joined forces with an invading German army. No sooner had he overcome these threats than he was faced by the problem of having an enormous army of crusaders encamped within his unsettled kingdom. They were supposed to be going to Jerusalem but who could tell what damage they might do *en route*? Only a few years later, in 1204, a crusading army sacked the greatest city in the Christian world, Constantinople, and with that blow destroyed the Byzantine Empire. According to one of the most distinguished of English medieval historians, Sir Maurice Powicke, 'the

thought of Richard before Constantinople makes the heart leap'.
For Tancred the sight of Richard before Messina was enough to
make his heart sink. There were family matters on which Tancred
and Richard were far from seeing eye to eye. King William II had
been married to Richard's sister Joan. When he died a dower should
have been assigned to his widow. But Tancred did not trust her.
He kept her in close confinement and withheld the dower. Clearly
Richard was not going to stand for this. Immediately after his
arrival, he sent envoys to Palermo, and Tancred agreed to release
Joan. She reached Messina on 28 September and when Philip saw
her he looked so cheerful that in no time at all it was rumoured
that he was going to marry her. But Richard was less pleased.
Although Tancred had given some money to Joan he was still holding on to her dower. Moreover William II, in his will, had left a
large legacy, including money, gold plate and war galleys, to his
father-in-law, Henry II. As it happened, however, Henry died a few
months before William, so Tancred regarded this part of the will
as null and void. Richard took a different view. The bequest had
been intended to help finance Henry's crusade. Now here was
Richard, Henry's heir and a crusader. Naturally he claimed the
money and the galleys.

To add to the complications the crusaders and the – mainly Greek
– population of Messina soon took a violent dislike to each other.
According to Ambroise the latter were to blame.

> For the townsfolk, rabble, and the scum
> Of the city – bastard Greeks were some,
> And some of them Saracen-born –
> Did heap upon our pilgrims scorn
> Fingers to eyes, they mocked at us,
> Calling us dogs malodorous.
> They did us foulness every day:
> Sometimes our pilgrims they did slay,
> And their corpses in the privies threw.
> And this was proven to be true.

On the other hand Ambroise did admit that the 'pilgrims' were
anxious to make friends with the women of Messina, though he adds

that they had no intention of seducing them – they merely wanted
to irritate their husbands. Almost certainly it was rising food prices
which lay behind all this trouble. The presence of a large army
stretched the resources of the region, and prices went up in response
to the increased demand. But this is not how the crusaders saw it.
They put the blame on the greed of the local shopkeepers. Soon
the crusaders and the Griffons – as the Greeks were called by the
men of the west – were virtually at war. Tension mounted further
when, on 2 October, Richard occupied the Greek monastery of St
Saviour's and turned it into a supply-dump, unloading the stores
from his ships. To the worried Sicilians this looked like the first
move in an armed take-over of the whole island. Next day fighting
broke out and Richard found he was unable to put a stop to it.
Alarmed by the prospect of losing control of the situation he invited
King Philip and the Sicilian governors of Messina to a conference
in his lodgings on 4 October. But while they were trying to reach
agreement, presumably on the problems of food prices and army
discipline, a confused clamour of shouts and the clash of arms
brought their discussion to an abrupt end. The lodging of one of
the barons of Aquitaine, Hugh of Lusignan, was being attacked.
Richard at once left the conference and ordered his men to arm
themselves. He was now determined to settle the matter by force.
Rather than allow this kind of rioting to go on indefinitely he would
seize control of Messina. King Philip had tried to make peace
between the two sides and he would have no part in so drastic a
step. The enthusiasts in the Angevin camp suspected him of having
gone over to the Sicilians and believed that he prevented Richard's
galleys from attacking the city from the sea. But on the landward
side, where Richard was directing operations, the Angevins had
better luck. The gates of the city were broken down and the troops
stormed in with Richard at their head. Many were killed in the street
fighting, including twenty-five of the King's own household troop.
But it was all over so quickly that, in Ambroise's words, it would
have taken longer for a priest to say Matins than it took the
King of England to capture Messina. After the fighting came the
plundering – the normal reward for those who risked their lives in
an assault.

1 Richard's first Great Seal (reverse).

2 His second Great Seal (obverse).

3 The Great Seal of Philip Augustus, who ascended the French throne in 1180.

4 Geoffrey of Anjou, Richard's
paternal grandfather, who was
buried in Le Mans Cathedral.

5 Adenez, King of the Minstrels, presenting a poem to the Queen of France.
From a thirteenth-century manuscript.

6 A knight charging with his lance, while protected by his shield, depicted in the *Roman de Girard de Roussillon*, early thirteenth century.

7 Château Gaillard and the Seine valley, Les Andelys.

8 The army of Emperor Henry VI attacking Naples, 1191.

9 Crusaders attacking a town by breaking down the gates with an axe, from the thirteenth-century *Les Histoires d'Outremer*.

10 The French King carrying out the maritime blockade and land assault on Acre in 1191.

11 Krak des Chevaliers, the great Crusader fortress, was constructed between 1140 and 1200.

12 A battle scene from the *Roman de Girard de Roussillon*.

13 The castle of Chinon in Touraine.

14 The remains of Chalus-Chabrol.

15 Effigies of Eleanor of Aquitaine and Richard I in Fontevraud Abbey.

16 Victorian statue of Richard I in Westminster Palace Yard by Marochetti, Prince Albert's favourite sculptor.

17 Romantic portrayal of Richard on his death-bed forgiving the crossbowman who has wounded him. Bas relief by Marochetti.

> And ye may know of surety
> That much was lost of property
> When they successfully attacked
> The town. It speedily was sacked;
> Their galleys were destroyed and burned,
> Which were not poor or to be spurned.
> And there were women taken, fair
> And excellent and debonair.

When King Philip saw Richard's banners waving above the walls and towers of Messina, he was furious. He demanded that they should be taken down and his own hoisted up in their place. This was not just an empty dispute about whose flags should wave over the town. To plant a banner in a captured town was to stake a claim to a share of the town, to share in its government and to share in its plunder. If Richard was claiming that Messina was now his, to do with as he liked by virtue of the right of conquest, then Philip was reminding him of the agreement they had made at Vézelay. Richard finally allowed his banner to be hauled down and replaced by the standards of the Templars and Hospitallers in whose custody Messina should remain until Tancred had met his terms. Ambroise believed that it was this quarrel over the banners

> Which in the French King did create
> Envy that time will ne'er abate.
> And herewith was the warring born
> Whereby was Normandy sore torn.

But though he gave way on the legal formalities, Richard made sure that he still kept control of the situation. He took hostages from the wealthier citizens of Messina and began to build a wooden castle on a hill overlooking the town. He called the castle 'Mategriffon', meaning 'Kill the Greeks'.

If he were to recover Messina Tancred had very little choice. By 6 October his council had agreed terms with Richard. Tancred would pay an additional 20,000 ounces of gold in lieu of Joan's dower. In addition, a marriage was arranged between one of his daughters and Richard's nephew, Arthur of Brittany, whom

Richard designated as his heir should he die without issue. Richard received another 20,000 ounces of gold, which he was supposed to settle upon Tancred's daughter when the marriage took place. In return Richard acknowledged that his claim on Tancred had been met in full and promised that for as long as he was in Sicily he would give Tancred military aid against any invader. Here, at least, Tancred had gained something, an ally against Henry of Hohenstaufen, now King Henry VI of Germany. He had earlier tried to persuade Philip to agree to a similar marriage alliance, but the French King had refused to be drawn into a treaty which would jeopardize his friendship with Henry VI. Since Richard, like his father, maintained close family and political ties with Henry the Lion, the Duke who was the chief German opponent of the Hohenstaufen in the 1180s and 1190s, he, rather than Philip, was Tancred's natural ally. 40,000 ounces of gold was a heavy price to pay for the temporary assistance of a crusading army; the diplomatic asset of Richard's friendship was perhaps more valuable. When Henry VI entered Italy next year his projected invasion of Sicily was thrown into disarray by a revolt in Germany organized by Henry the Lion's son, Henry – the same prince who had attended Richard's court at La Réole in Gascony in February 1190. So far as Richard was concerned the immediate advantages of the treaty were obvious, particularly since Joan was willing to see her 20,000 spent in the service of the crusade. In the long term it was unlikely that anything would come of the marriage arranged between his nephew and Tancred's daughter since most diplomatic betrothals of this kind did not, in fact, lead to a wedding – and it was all the more unlikely when, as in this case, the future bridegroom was only three years old. Moreover, when he designated Arthur as his heir presumptive, Richard was probably already aware of Berengaria's imminent departure from Navarre. He did not expect to die without issue.

On 8 October, in an effort to prevent further disturbances, the three Kings fixed the price of bread at a penny a loaf, stabilized the price of wine, and laid down that no merchant should make a profit of more than ten per cent on a deal. Whether or not this price freeze was rigidly enforced, the crusaders were in fact able to spend a further six months in Sicily without there being any more serious trouble. Another cause of dissension, this time within the army, was gambling and the debts which some soldiers were running up. It was decided that the moratorium on repayment of their debts which all crusaders enjoyed should apply only to those debts contracted before the start of the crusade and not during it. Philip and Richard banned all gambling by ordinary soldiers and sailors except when their officers were present. Soldiers who disobeyed this order were to be stripped naked and whipped through the army on three successive days, while sailors were to be keel-hauled three days running. Knights and clergy, however, could play for up to twenty shillings a day, on pain of a fine if they exceeded this limit. Kings were specifically permitted to gamble away as much as they pleased. A financial and disciplinary committee was established to enforce these regulations and to control the army's common chest, the fund which took over and administered half the possessions of those who died while on crusade. Among its members were the Masters of the Temple and the Hospital, Duke Hugh of Burgundy, Robert de Sablé and Andrew de Chauveny.

By mid-October it was too late in the year to sail safely to the Holy Land, so the two Kings decided to winter in Sicily. In his treaty with Tancred Richard spoke of being held up by 'rough winds, waves and weather'. But if he was impatient to be on his way he gave little sign of it – unlike many of the ordinary crusaders. They

> said it was wrong
> To linger. They made loud laments
> Because it cost them much expense.

Richard calmed their complaints by a generous distribution of gifts. Philip too was able to lavish substantial cash sums upon his followers, since Richard had given him a share – probably a third – of the 40,000 ounces he had received from Tancred. So the time passed quietly and pleasantly enough. The presence of the crusading army no longer posed a threat to Tancred and this persuaded some Sicilian rebels to submit. Richard celebrated Christmas in magnificent style in his castle of Mategriffon. King Philip was his guest and all who were there marvelled at the splendour of the gold and silver plate, at the variety and abundance of meat and drink.

But the winter closure of the sea-lanes meant that the Christian army in the Holy Land, hemmed in by Saladin, was running dangerously short of provisions. They had to contend not only with Muslim attacks but also with the threat of starvation and the diseases associated with malnutrition. Whenever a horse was killed it was at once surrounded by a crowd of jostling soldiers, each fighting to obtain a piece of the flesh; nothing was wasted, they ate head, intestines and all. Men were seen down on their hands and knees, eating grass. It was estimated that with a fast, direct passage a ship sailing from Marseilles could reach the Holy Land in fifteen days – though the average journey time was more than twice that. Meanwhile Richard's immense supply of stores was under guard in the monastery of St Saviour's and his ships were beached and undergoing repairs. The trip from Marseilles to Outremer took him twelve months.

While he was in Sicily Richard heard strange stories about a Cistercian abbot who lived as a hermit in Calabria and who was supposed to have the gift of prophecy. This man was called Joachim of Fiore. He believed that he had discovered the concealed meaning of the Bible, and especially of the Book of Revelation. This discovery led him to see a pattern in history, a pattern which enabled him to predict the future of the world. Richard was intrigued and asked Joachim to come and talk to him. Joachim came and expounded that prophetic system of thought which has been described as the most influential one known to Europe before the appearance of Marxism. Joachim divided world history into three ages: the Age of the Father, the Age of the Son and the Age of the Spirit. The Third Age was to be the culmination of human history, a time of love, joy and freedom when God would be in the hearts of all men. The Empire and the church of Rome would have withered away. In their place there would be a community of saints who had no bodily needs; therefore there would be no wealth, no property, no work. Complicated calculations had revealed to Joachim that the Third Age was nigh. It would come some time between 1200 and

1260. What particularly interested Richard was Joachim's identifi-
cation of Saladin as the sixth of the seven great persecutors of the
church in the Second Age. Joachim prophesied that Saladin would
soon be driven out of the Kingdom of Jerusalem and killed; that
the infidels would be slaughtered and the Christians would return
once more to the Holy Land. 'And God', he said, 'has decreed that
all these things will be done through you. Persevere in the enterprise
you have begun and He will give you victory over your enemies
and glorify your name for evermore.' Even without Joachim and
his prophecies Richard and his followers were confident that their
crusade would be a success, but to listen to these fervent words was
doubtless reassuring.

Yet it was salutary to be reminded that Saladin's defeat did not
mean the end of all their troubles. After Saladin would come the
seventh persecutor, Antichrist, who would rule for three-and-a-half
years. According to Joachim Antichrist had already been born at
Rome, was now fifteen years old and would be elected Pope before
revealing his true self to the world. This prophecy made Richard
question the abbot's calculations. Perhaps the present Pope,
Clement III, whom he disliked, was Antichrist. Indeed Richard had
theories of his own. In his view Antichrist was to be born in Egypt
or Antioch and would rule the Holy Land. After his death there
would be a period of sixty days during which people whom Antichrist had seduced would be given the opportunity to repent of their
sins. Joachim, however, stood fast to his calculations and in no way
altered his system to take account of Richard's prejudices or ideas.
He should stick to soldiering and leave the interpretation of the
Bible to those who were experts. On the whole the churchmen in
Richard's entourage seem to have been interested, rather than
impressed, by Joachim's ideas. Most of them, after all, were practical down-to-earth men chosen by a king who wanted bishops who
knew how to command men and supply armies. None the less Joa-
chimite patterns of thought were to remain influential. For centuries
the lunatic fringe among European intellectuals was to find the
peculiar logic of Joachim's vision irresistibly attractive. In particular the idea of a Third Age, to be reached after a period of violent
upheaval, was to have a permanent appeal.

By February 1191 the army in Sicily was getting impatient. Building siege-machines, though useful preparatory work, was not what they had left home for. Only Richard's generosity in distributing gifts to all and sundry held the troops together. But the enforced idleness was getting on Richard's nerves too. In this restless atmosphere it was easy for a trivial incident to be blown up out of all proportion. One day when Richard was out riding with knights from his and Philip's household, they met a peasant with a supply of canes. At once they took the canes and arranged an impromptu tournament. Richard clashed with his former opponent, William des Barres, and as old antagonisms came to the surface the knightly contest quickly degenerated into a brawl in which no one else was allowed to intervene. Richard tried to throw William to the ground but he hung on grimly to his horse's neck and could not be shifted. Finding himself unable to win, Richard completely lost his temper and ordered William never to show his face in his presence again; from now on he would look upon him as an enemy. Richard indeed forced Philip to send William away and not until the eve of the French King's departure from Sicily did he relent and allow William to return to his lord's – and the crusade's – service. Even then Richard gave way only after Philip and all the leading men in the army had gone down on their knees before him.

Meanwhile, however, Richard and Philip were at odds over a matter far more serious than the consequences of William des Barres's skill with a cane. This was the question of Richard's marriage. By late February Eleanor and Berengaria, accompanied by Count Philip of Flanders, had reached Naples and Richard sent some galleys to meet them there and convey them to Messina. But although Count Philip was allowed to embark, Eleanor and Berengaria were not. Tancred's officials said that their escort was too large to be accommodated in an already over-crowded city and sent them to Brindisi. This was obviously not the real reason, so Richard went to see Tancred to demand an explanation. The two Kings met at Catania on 3 March and spent five days together. According to Roger of Howden Tancred eventually confessed to Richard that he had been listening to Philip's insinuations. The French King apparently had warned Tancred that Richard's word was not to be relied upon;

that he had no intention of keeping the treaty they had made last October, and instead was planning to deprive Tancred of his kingdom. This is a curious story and however well-informed Roger of Howden was, he is unlikely to have overheard the private conversation of two Kings. None the less the fact that Eleanor and Berengaria were kept away from Messina suggests that Howden is doing more than simply repeating anti-French gossip. Tancred was understandably nervous about the crusaders but clearly he had nothing to fear from Philip's small force. His problem was Richard and the Angevin army. Although they were allies Richard's assault on Messina, and the circumstances in which the alliance had been forged, were hardly such as to dispel all Tancred's doubts. Yet it was vital that he read Richard's intentions correctly. The King of Sicily's insecurity was fertile ground for Philip's diplomatic skill – these were just the kind of fears he had played upon when separating Henry II from his sons. What Philip wanted is clear enough: he wanted to save his sister's honour. She had now been betrothed to Richard for more than twenty years. To be cast aside after so long would be an intolerable insult. As the news came that Eleanor and Berengaria had crossed the Alps and were travelling southwards through Italy so Philip's concern grew. But at the same time their journey may have raised his hopes of drawing Tancred over to his side. For Tancred too had news which gave him cause for grave concern. Henry VI had left Germany and was heading in the direction of Sicily. It is not hard to imagine Tancred's feelings when he learned that Eleanor and Henry VI had met at Lodi, not far from Milan, on 20 January 1191. Just what lay behind this meeting? Were Richard and his old mother planning to throw in their lot with Henry? These were the fears which Richard had to dispel when he met Tancred at Catania and, eventually, he succeeded. The two Kings exchanged gifts as a token of their renewal of friendship. Richard gave Tancred the sword Excalibur which had once belonged to King Arthur. Tancred's gift was more prosaic, but possibly more useful: four large transport ships and fifteen galleys.

The French King had been playing a dangerous game. Once Tancred was convinced that he had nothing to fear from Richard, then Philip became the victim of his own intrigue. He protested his innocence, claiming that the whole thing was a put-up job, a scheme devised by Richard to give him an excuse for breaking his promise to marry Alice. For two reasons, however, Philip's defence does not ring quite true. Firstly, because Tancred's agents had prevented Berengaria from leaving Naples – an unnecessary complication if it was just a charade. And, secondly, because the Count of Flanders, on his arrival in Sicily, took Richard's side against King Philip – which suggests that he did not believe the French King's story. At all events it is clear that Philip was now isolated and in a weak bargaining position. Richard drove home his advantage. He had no wish, he said, to discard Alice but he could never marry her since she had been his father's mistress and had borne him a son. It was a grim accusation, for Alice had been entrusted to the Old King's custody, but Richard claimed that he could summon many witnesses able to testify to its truth. In the face of this terrible threat to his sister's honour Philip gave up his struggle to save her marriage. In return for 10,000 marks he released Richard from his promise. Other clauses in the treaty between the two Kings drawn up at Messina in March 1191 regulated most of their outstanding differences, above all the question of Gisors and the Norman Vexin. This disputed territory was to belong to Richard and his male descendants, but would revert to Philip and his heirs if Richard were to die without a legitimate son. Elsewhere the treaty was based on the *status quo*. Richard confirmed Philip's rights over Issoudun, Graçay and Auvergne, while Philip confirmed Richard's rights over Cahors and the Quercy. There can be no doubt that Philip regarded this treaty as a humiliation. In a gesture which perfectly expressed his feelings he chose to set sail from Messina on 30 March, just a few hours before Berengaria arrived. In the opinion of Rigord, the chronicler of St Denis, the quarrel between the two Kings began at the moment when Richard rejected Alice.

Eleanor stayed about three days in Messina. Then this indomitable old lady, now about seventy years old, set off on the long journey back to Normandy. We know almost nothing about the girl whom she left behind in the care of Richard's sister Joan. Berengaria moves silently in the background of events. Contemporary writers found little in her either to praise or to blame. They dismiss her in a phrase: 'a lady of beauty and good sense', says one; 'sensible rather than attractive', says another. After they were married Berengaria and Richard did not spend much time together. There were times when force of circumstances gave them no choice in the matter, but there were times also when Richard preferred to do without her. The clearest evidence of this comes from the pen of Roger of Howden. He reported an incident, apparently in 1195, when a hermit came to the King and rebuked him for his sins. 'Remember the destruction of Sodom and abstain from illicit acts, for if you do not God will punish you in a fitting manner.' At first Richard ignored the warning but when, some time later, he was struck by an illness, he recalled the hermit's words. He did penance and, says Roger of Howden, tried to lead a better life. This meant regular attendance at morning church – and not leaving until the service was over; it meant distributing alms to the poor. It also meant avoiding illicit intercourse; instead he was to sleep with his wife, a marital duty which he had presumably been neglecting. Their marriage, however, remained childless.

Richard's inability to produce an heir and the hermit's warning are the two main planks on which the case for Richard's supposed homosexuality is based. In the last forty years it has apparently become impossible to read the word 'Sodom' without assuming that it refers to homosexuality. This tells us a good deal about the culture of our own generation: its unfamiliarity with the Old Testament, and its wider interest in sex. In fact, however, the magnificent maledictions of the Old Testament prophets are rarely complete without a reference to the destruction of Sodom and, more often than not, this phrase carries no homosexual implications. It refers not so much to the nature of the offences as to the terrible and awe-inspiring nature of the punishment. The picture which chiefly interested the prophets and the preachers who followed in their footsteps was the apocalyptic image of whole cities being overwhelmed by fire and brimstone. In the days when people read their Bible all the way through and when they appreciated the value of a good sermon no one understood the hermit's words to mean that Richard was a homosexual. So far as I have been able to discover the earliest reference to Richard's homosexuality dates from 1948. Thirteenth-century opinion was in no doubt that his interests were heterosexual. According to Walter of Guisborough Richard's need for women was such that even on his deathbed he had them brought to him in defiance of his doctor's advice. Although Walter of Guisborough was writing a hundred years later, his view of Richard's character was grounded in his reading of the contemporary chronicle of William of Newburgh. Then there is the legend, already referred to in the introduction, of Margery, the King of Almain's daughter. Yet another thirteenth-century legend links Richard with a nun of Fontevraud. As told by Stephen of Bourbon, a Dominican friar and a popular preacher, Richard wanted one of the nuns so badly that he threatened to burn down the abbey unless she was delivered to him. When the nun asked what it was that attracted him so much and was told that it was her eyes, she sent for a knife and cut them out, saying, 'Send the King what he so much desires.' The same story had been told by a contemporary of Richard, Peter the Chanter, a famous master in the schools of Paris, but in his writings he refers only to a king of the English, giving no name. Possibly he was just being cautious; we do know that Stephen of Bourbon claimed to have listened to Peter's sermons. But whomever Peter the Chanter may have had in mind it is clear that the thirteenth century did not suffer from the illusion that Richard preferred monks.

To all appearances the marriage of Richard and Berengaria turned out to be a failure, at least at the level of personal relationships. Certainly it proved to be childless and this, given the desire of most kings to have a son to succeed them, is generally taken as evidence for one kind of failure. But Richard acknowledged a child. Indeed his illegitimate son is a central figure in one of Shakespeare's plays. Not, of course, that Shakespeare's history can ever be relied on, and Philip Faulconbridge, the personification of sturdy English virtues, is doubtless a far cry from Philip, the boy from Aquitaine to whom Richard gave the lordship of Cognac as part of his campaign to hold the Counts of Angoulême in check. Even so, were *King John* as good a play as *King Lear* then Philip might have become as well known as Edmund, Gloucester's son. Unfortunately it is not. Inevitably we are in the realm of speculation but the probability is that

Berengaria was barren. An annulment might have been considered but in political terms the Navarre alliance had more than justified itself and was probably too important to be put at risk. Diplomatically, if not emotionally, the marriage was a success.

Berengaria's arrival in Sicily was described by the contemporary chronicler, William of Newburgh, in terms which show that he expected Richard to find pleasure in the marriage and, to judge from Ambroise, the opinion in the crusading army was that Richard loved her:

> most dear
> The King did love her and revere;
> Since he was Count of Poitiers
> His wish had wished for her alway.

The wedding, however, had to be postponed, not through any reluctance on Richard's part but because it was Lent. Still, though Richard could not marry in Lent, he could at least travel. Now that Berengaria had arrived, there was no reason why he should delay any longer in Sicily. He could marry in the Holy Land. So he prepared to go. The castle of Mategriffon was dismantled and stowed away, in sections, aboard ship. Then, on 10 April 1191, Richard's huge fleet, now numbering over 200 vessels, left Sicily behind.

On the third day out of Messina, Good Friday, a storm blew up. Richard was able to keep the greater part of the fleet together; at night-time a light was kept burning at the mast-head of the King's ship as a guide to the others.

> This fleet of mighty ships and men
> He guided, as the mother hen
> Doth guide toward the feed her brood,
> Such was his native knightlihood.

But when they reached their first rendezvous at Crete on 17 April it became clear that some twenty-five ships were missing, among them the great ship carrying both Joan and Berengaria. Richard sailed on to Rhodes and then waited there for ten days while his galleys scoured the seas in search of the lost ship. It was eventually found at anchor outside Limassol on the south coast of Cyprus. In company with some other ships it had raced ahead of the main fleet and had only just escaped being shipwrecked on the Cypriot shore on 24 April. Two other ships, less fortunate, were driven aground and some of the crew and passengers were drowned, including Roger Malcael, the King's vice-chancellor and seal-bearer. But when his body was washed ashore, the seal, which the vice-chancellor always wore on a chain round his neck, was recovered. Those who reached dry land were seized and informed that they would be held in custody until the ruler of Cyprus had decided what action to take.

Cyprus, an island famous for its cedars and vineyards, had long been part of the Byzantine Empire, but five years previously Isaac Ducas Comnenus, a member of the imperial family, had arrived there claiming, on the basis of forged documents, to be the island's new governor, just sent out from Constantinople. His deception was successful. The island's fortresses were placed in his hands. Then Isaac threw off the mask and governed Cyprus as an independent ruler calling himself Emperor. In order to maintain himself against the government of Constantinople, Isaac had made an alliance with Saladin and, in consequence, he had no intention of giving any help to crusaders. Ambroise, naturally, was shocked by the treaty between Christian and Muslim:

> And it was told of them as fact
> That they had sealed their friendship's pact
> By drinking one another's blood.
> 'Twas proved that this was no falsehood.

By the time that Isaac arrived at Limassol on 2 May some of the stranded crusaders had fought their way out of the fort in which they had been detained and, with the help of a well-timed landing party, had managed to join their fellows in the ships standing off shore. As soon as Isaac learned that Berengaria and Joan were aboard one of the ships he invited them to land. Fearing a trap, they declined the offer. They put him off from day to day but became increasingly alarmed as he mustered the forces with which he could, if he chose, launch an attack upon them.

Meanwhile it seems that something of what had been happening on Cyprus had been reported to Richard. On 1 May he left Rhodes and five days later, much to the relief of Berengaria and Joan, his fleet reached Limassol. When Isaac refused either to release the prisoners he still held or to restore the goods which he had seized, Richard gave the order to attack. Isaac had stripped Limassol bare of everything that could be moved and used it to fortify the beach: doors, benches, chests, planks, blocks of stone. The abandoned hulks of old ships were also pressed into service. Undaunted by the arrangements made to receive them, Richard and his men piled into small boats and rowed for the shore. As soon as they were in range, his archers opened fire on the defenders and then, with Richard at their head, they jumped out of the boats and charged up the beach. After a brief fight the Cypriots retreated and the victorious troops marched into Limassol, where they found a very satisfying amount of wine, meat and corn. That night Isaac pitched camp about five miles from the town, announcing that he would give battle the next day. But he had badly under-estimated his opponent. During the hours of darkness Richard disembarked his horses and had them exercised, while scouts were sent out to ascertain the enemy's position. When Isaac awoke next morning, he found his camp surrounded. The Cypriots, still rubbing the sleep from their eyes, were swiftly put to flight. Isaac himself just managed to escape but had no time to dress first. He left behind his treasure, his horses, his arms and his imperial standard, embroidered in cloth of gold, which Richard immediately decided to present to the abbey of Bury St Edmunds. Two crushing victories within twenty-four hours were quite enough to persuade many of the local landowners that it was better to submit at once; they came to Richard's camp and handed over hostages. By 11 May the ranks of those still loyal to him had thinned out to such extent that Isaac decided to sue for peace.

On that same day another group of visitors came to Limassol. At their head was the King of Jerusalem, Guy of Lusignan, and his brother Geoffrey, Richard's old enemy. But the Lusignans were no longer the troublesome vassals of Poitou. Guy and Geoffrey had come as suppliants, asking for Richard's support against the political manœuvres of King Philip – who had arrived in Acre on 20 April – manœuvres which were designed to push Guy off the throne. Richard agreed. There was already one Lusignan in his army, their nephew, Hugh, and in his role of Duke of Aquitaine he probably still considered himself their lord and protector. More important, by now it was only natural that he and Philip should take opposing sides. Guy of Lusignan and his party then did homage to Richard.

Next day, 12 May, Richard and Berengaria were married in the chapel of St George at Limassol and then Berengaria was crowned queen by John, Bishop of Evreux. So in a Cypriot town a Queen of England was crowned by a bishop of a Norman see. Richard was King of England, but he was also much more than that, and those whose lives became bound up with his found that they had to range widely through the whole of Christendom. In assigning to Berengaria a dower which comprised all his rights in the whole of Gascony south of the Garonne, Richard was doubtless fulfilling one of the terms of the marriage settlement negotiated with Sancho of Navarre.

Soon afterwards Isaac came to Richard's camp, ostensibly to confirm the peace terms which his envoys had offered and to swear allegiance to him. The terms, however, were so stiff that it is unlikely that Isaac ever had any intention of keeping them. Probably he hoped only to gain time and obtain some idea of Richard's plans. He did not stay long in the camp but slipped away after lunch, while his guards were having a siesta. Richard is said to have been well content when he learned that Isaac did not consider himself bound by the terms of the agreement. It gave him the justification he needed for his next great enterprise: the conquest of Cyprus. Part of his army he handed over to Guy of Lusignan with instructions to pursue and, if possible, capture Isaac. The rest were embarked in the galleys, half of which, under his command, sailed one way round the island, while the other half, commanded by Robert of Thornham, sailed round in the opposite direction. As they circumnavigated the island they captured coastal towns and castles as well as enemy ships. Having completed their circuit they returned to Limassol, where they were rejoined by Guy of Lusignan. He had not succeeded in tracking down Isaac; nevertheless, like the other commanders, he was able to report that Cypriots everywhere were prepared to recognize Richard as their lord. Typical of the stories about Isaac which were now being put into circulation and which were intended to show him up as a tyrannical usurper was the one which told how he cut the nose off a noble who was honest enough to advise him to submit.

Isaac, however, was confident that he and his followers could hold out in the great castles perched high in the mountains of northern Cyprus: Buffavento, Kantara and St Hilarion (or *Dieu d'Amour* as the Franks called it, claiming that it was the Castle of Love built for Cupid by Venus, Queen of Cyprus, a legend appropriate to the castle's romantic site). Isaac calculated that eventually Richard would have to move on to the Holy Land. When he was gone Isaac could come out of hiding and take over the island once again. It was not a badly laid plan but it came to nothing when the coastal fortress of Kyrenia fell into Richard's hands, together with Isaac's daughter. When Isaac heard the news of her capture he was beside himself with grief and agreed to surrender, making – or so it was said – only one condition: that he should not be put in irons. Richard accepted this, and then had silver chains made especially for him. By 1 June the whole of Cyprus was in Richard's hands. In area it was only about the size of East Anglia, but the mountainous terrain ought to have made conquest difficult. Richard, however, could plan a campaign as well as besiege a castle and at no time did he show his skill as a general to greater effect than in those few weeks in Cyprus. The operation was finely conceived and methodically carried out.

The conqueror reaped tremendous rewards. In addition to the spoils of war and the property confiscated from those who had fought against him, Richard imposed a fifty per cent capital levy on every Cypriot. In return he confirmed the traditional laws and customs of the island. But from now on these laws were to be enforced by Angevin officials backed by Angevin garrisons. As an outward sign of the new order Richard required all loyal Greeks to shave off their beards; they were obliged to look like Westerners. Two Englishmen, Robert of Thornham and Richard of Canvill, were put in charge of the government of the island. The capture of Cyprus was vitally important to the Christians in Outremer. In face of the overwhelming superiority of the Muslim land forces, Outremer owed its survival to sea power. The towns on the Palestinian and Syrian coast were kept going by the men and supplies ferried across the Mediterranean by the fleets of Venice, Pisa and Genoa. But the supply line was dangerously long. After the capture of Cyprus things were much better. The Christians now held an island base which could be used both as a supply depot and as a springboard for further crusades. In terms of military strategy the conquest of Cyprus turned out to be a master stroke. And one which had probably been in Richard's mind from the outset of his crusade. Centuries later, an observer of the occupation of Cyprus by British forces in 1878 commented: 'He who would become and remain a great power in the East must hold Cyprus in his hand.' Though reasonably safe from attack (not until 1571 did Cyprus fall to the Turks) it lay so close to the eastern shores of the Mediterranean that a man standing on the hills around Stavrovouni could see on the horizon the cedar-covered mountains of Lebanon. Richard was now very close to his destination.

9

ACRE AND ARSUF
1191

To understand the problems which were to face Richard on his arrival in the Holy Land we have to go back to September 1187. In that month Saladin, having already captured nearly all the cities and castles of the Kingdom of Jerusalem, chose to lay siege to Jerusalem itself. As a result his army was able to enter the Holy City on 2 October, the anniversary of Mahomet's ascent into heaven from Jerusalem. It was a brilliant stroke of propaganda skilfully utilized by Saladin's chancery in the jubilant letters which they circulated throughout the Muslim world. After Mecca and Medina Jerusalem was the most holy place in Islam and its recovery ensured that Saladin's name would never die. For his army it was the emotional climax of the campaign of 1187. But though the climax it was not the end. Saladin pushed his weary soldiers to lay siege to Tyre. Apart from a few isolated inland castles this great coastal fortress was now all that remained of the Kingdom of Jerusalem. But the defenders of Tyre, under the energetic command of Conrad of Montferrat, had made good use of the breathing space granted them. By November 1187 the city's fortifications were in first rate shape and Saladin's army had to face the tedious and uncomfortable prospect of a long-drawn-out blockade. If Tyre could survive the winter then it could serve as a beach-head for Christian reinforcements. In terms of military strategy it was a much more important city than Jerusalem, for once the Franks had lost the coast they could not hope to keep or recover the Holy Sepulchre. In later years there must have been moments when Saladin regretted that he had made a political rather than a military decision in September, but it is easy to be wise after the event and in the autumn of 1187 his momentum must have seemed irresistible.

Tyre survived. On 1 January 1188 Saladin called off the siege and Conrad of Montferrat became the hero of the hour. This ambitious, ruthless man, who had earlier had a narrow escape when his ship put in to Acre not knowing that it had already fallen, sensed that his star was in the ascendant and began to behave as though he were the real ruler of the kingdom. But in June 1188 Guy of Lusignan was released by Saladin on condition that he took no further part in the fighting. Guy, of course, had no difficulty in finding a clergyman who would release him from the oath he had sworn to Saladin. Good Christians were not expected to keep the promises they made to the infidels – 'the pagan cattle, the unbelieving, black-faced brood', as Ambroise called them. Unfortunately for Guy, Conrad refused to hand back Tyre so he found himself in the position of being a king without a kingdom and, in Conrad's eyes indeed, not even a king any more. As the months went by Guy's position became increasingly difficult. Then suddenly, in August 1189, he seized the initiative. He did what nobody, not Conrad, not Saladin, could possibly have imagined him doing. He marched south with a few followers and laid siege to Acre. Until its capture in 1187 Acre had been the chief port and the largest town in the Kingdom of Jerusalem. An army the size of Guy's had no hope of taking it. When Saladin arrived on the scene Guy would be trapped between the Acre garrison and the might of the main Muslim army. On the face of it, it was an act of incredible folly. His political opponents liked to write Guy off as a simple man but not even they had thought he could be as stupid as that. And yet it worked, as in Guy's apparently hopeless position nothing else could have worked. Guy set up camp on the hill of Turon, a mile east of Acre, and although he was unable to take the city, Saladin was equally incapable of dislodging him. It was a brave gesture which won him a good deal of sympathy and some political support; in April 1190 even Conrad had to recognize him as king. With each month that went by more reinforcements streamed into the Christian camp until eventually Guy was able to complete the landward blockade of Acre. The occasional Muslim supply ship got through, however, and this enabled the garrison to hold out. Thus a position of stalemate was reached. The Christians besieged Acre and Saladin besieged the besiegers. The stalemate was not broken until the arrival of the Kings in the spring and early summer of 1191.

But while the military stalemate continued, the balance of the political scales tipped again in favour of Conrad of Montferrat. Guy was King of Jerusalem by virtue of the fact that he had married Sibylla, the heiress to the kingdom. In the autumn of 1190, however, Guy lost both his wife and his two daughters, victims of one of the epidemics which were a normal part of life in the unhealthy atmosphere of an army camp. As in most wars disease did more damage than the weapons of the human enemy. With Sibylla dead, could Guy still claim to be king? Guy believed that as the anointed King he should retain the kingdom, but in legal terms the circumstances of his anointing and coronation in September 1186 were highly dubious. In that case perhaps Sibylla's younger sister, Isabella, should inherit her rights. It seemed to Conrad that Isabella ought to be queen and that he was just the sort of man to be her husband. True, it was rumoured that at least one of Conrad's two previous wives – one Italian, one Greek – was still alive, but then army gossip was notoriously unreliable. It was true also that Isabella had a husband already, Humphrey of Toron; he was unquestionably alive, indeed he was there in the camp. But then there were churchmen in the camp too and wherever there were churchmen, there marriages could be broken. If the Archbishop of Canterbury would not annul the marriage – and Baldwin, who arrived in October 1190, did in fact refuse to do so – then Conrad could try the Archbishop of Pisa. A Pisan after all would be attracted by the possibility of securing an extension of his home town's trading privileges in Outremer. So Isabella was abducted from her tent outside Acre and persuaded – by her mother – that her marriage to Humphrey was invalid. Despite Humphrey's protests, the marriage was annulled. On 24 November Isabella was wedded to Conrad. In canon law the marriage was both incestuous, because Isabella's sister had once been married to Conrad's brother, and bigamous, because her marriage to Humphrey was wrongly dissolved – as was later established by a papal commission. Legally a farce, the proceedings were none the less thought to make good political sense on the grounds that the kingdom needed a rough ruler with the skills and driving force which Humphrey of Toron clearly lacked. An open confrontation and the danger of an armed clash between Conrad and Guy was avoided because Guy remained at Acre while Conrad and Isabella went back to Tyre. But there were now two candidates for the throne. Thus Richard would have two problems to tackle on his arrival at Acre: first the beleaguered city would have to be taken and then the much more difficult question of the quarrel between Conrad and Guy would have to be faced.

On 5 June 1191 Richard set sail from Famagusta. He made his first landfall near the great castle of the Knights of St John at Margat. This castle was to be Isaac's prison. Then Richard sailed south, reaching Tyre on 6 June. The garrison of Tyre, however, acting on instructions from King Philip and Conrad of Montferrat, would not give him permission to enter the town. So Richard spent the night encamped outside the walls and next day continued on his voyage to Acre. Outside Acre his fleet intercepted a large supply ship flying the flag of the French King. On closer inspection it proved to be a blockade-runner, laden with supplies and reinforcements for the garrison of Acre. (In an earlier, successful attempt to run the blockade, not only had Saladin's sailors shaved off their beards and put on Frankish clothes, they had also ostentatiously kept pigs on the ship's upper deck, relying on the Christian patrols' knowing that the Muslims would never eat pork.) Richard's galleys closed with the supply ship and, after a fierce struggle, the blockade-runner was sunk. According to a Muslim account, when the ship's captain saw that defeat was inevitable, he scuttled his ship rather than see valuable supplies and siege equipment fall into enemy hands. A rumour prevalent among the Franks said that this equipment included a stock of two hundred snakes which the Muslims, with characteristically evil cunning, had planned to release in the camp of the Christian army. After this triumph Richard was given a joyous welcome when he joined the army besieging Acre on 8 June. The celebration lasted well into the night as the army danced and sang by the light of torches and bonfires. Observing the scene from the hills around Acre, Saladin's men gloomily noted the vast amount of siege equipment which Richard had brought with him.

For two years all eyes in the Muslim, as well as in the Christian, world had been focused on Acre. Baha al-Din Qaragush, one of Saladin's most experienced commanders and his outstanding military architect, had been placed in charge of the defence of the city. If it fell it would be a tremendous blow to the prestige of the victor of Hattin and liberator of Jerusalem. Richard's arrival stimulated the besiegers to greater efforts and put fear into the hearts of the enemy. His reputation had preceded him. The wooden castle of Mategriffon was raised again, this time outside the gate of Acre. By contrast Philip had made little impact on the state of the siege in the weeks since 20 April. According to Muslim sources he had brought with him six galleys to Richard's twenty-five. He had contented himself with setting up his siege-machines, chiefly stone-throwing mangonels, and bombarding the city walls, though according to Rigord of St Denis he did this so effectively that Acre would have fallen into Philip's hands like a ripe fruit had he not courteously chosen to delay the final assault until after Richard's arrival. The bombardment was intensified when Richard brought up his siege-machines to join those already erected by Philip, Hugh of Burgundy and the Templars and Hospitallers. Philip's best mangonel was given the traditional name of *Malvoisin*, 'Bad Neighbour' while another machine built with funds from the crusaders' common chest was called 'God's Own Catapult'.

The defenders of Acre directed their own artillery fire against the Frankish siege-machines. Being made of wood they were particularly vulnerable to the dreaded Greek fire. This was a naphtha-based mixture which was put into pottery containers and then hurled from catapults. The impression it made was vividly described by Joinville, the chronicler of St Louis's crusade in 1250: 'In appearance this Greek fire looked like a large tun of verjuice with a burning tail the length of a long sword. As it came towards you it made a thunderous noise – like a dragon flying through the air. At night it gave so great a light that you could see our camp as clearly as in broad daylight.' Then on impact the containers shattered and the mixture burst into flames. Since Greek fire could not be extinguished by water it was particularly devastating in sea-battles, but even in land warfare it was effective enough, and to counter it wooden structures had to be covered with hides or other materials soaked in vinegar or urine. Richard also had a belfry built, a moveable tower, with stations for crossbowmen and archers on each floor and with its top floor higher than the city walls to permit the lowering of a drawbridge on to the battlements across which a storming party could launch their attack. This was an extremely expensive item of siege equipment, but it is clear that even at the height of the struggle against Saladin the two Kings were also contending against each other and that in this contest Richard's greater wealth gave him the upper hand. Philip had offered pay of three besants (gold pieces) a month to any knight who would join his service, only to be outbid by Richard who offered four. Presumably for the same reason Richard's siege-machines seem to have been better guarded than Philip's and, as a result, to have suffered less from Muslim attack. In any event, under their joint bombardment, the walls of Acre were slowly but surely battered down.

Every now and then a section of wall collapsed as a result of being undermined. Undermining was the most efficient method of bringing down a wall. The miners tunnelled their way beneath the foundations, which they underpinned with timber props. The mine was then filled with brushwood, logs and other combustible material. When all was ready, this was set alight and the miners beat a hasty retreat. The props were burned through, the masonry above collapsed – and a party of assailants was ready and waiting to storm through the breach. Military architects tried to meet this threat by protecting exposed walls with a *glacis*. The broad base of this ponderous pyramid-like structure rested on the bottom of the moat and meant that any tunnel had to cope with heavy static pressure from above even before it reached the walls. But if the sappers did their job well enough then the only way to deal with a mine was by digging a counter-mine. That meant tunnelling into the mine from the defenders' side and then capturing it. The fate of a besieged town or castle would sometimes hinge upon the outcome of these desperate hand-to-hand struggles which took place in the darkness below ground. At one stage, having under-

mined and bombarded a tower until it was tottering on the point
of collapse, Richard was so anxious to finish the job that he offered
two besants to anyone who could bring him back a stone: at some
stage all of these techniques of siegecraft involved crossing the –
normally dry – moat and to do this the ditch had to be filled in,
with earth, rubble and all kinds of rubbish. One favourite story
among the besiegers of Acre was of a woman who was so enthusiastic
that, when mortally wounded, she begged that her body would be
thrown into the moat so that even dead she could continue to be
of some use.

Shortly after Richard's arrival both he and Philip fell ill. The
chroniclers called their illness *Arnaldia* or *Léonardie*, a fever which
caused their hair and nails to fall out. It was probably a form of
scurvy or trench mouth. At one point Richard's life was thought
to be in danger, but as soon as his condition began to improve he
insisted that he should be carried to the front line in a litter so that
he could continue to direct siege operations. At regular intervals,
when the Kings judged that the artillery and sappers had sufficiently
softened up the target, they gave the order for an assault against
some weak point in the city walls. When they saw the Franks
advancing, the defenders of Acre beat their drums as a signal to
Saladin. He immediately launched an attack on the camp of the
besiegers, who were thus forced to fight on two fronts. Time and
again the assault was beaten back. None the less the sustained
pressure was taking its toll. Inside Acre the beleagured garrison
was running short of food and war materials. The arrival of the
Angevin and French fleets meant that Muslim supply ships could
no longer hope to get through. The garrison kept in touch with Saladin by using carrier-pigeons and occasionally a messenger was able
to swim through the Frankish lines. But after nearly two years of
siege the defenders of Acre were exhausted and they needed something more than messages of support. Their courage was tremendous and compelled admiration even in the Christian camp: 'What
can we say of this race of infidels who thus defended their city?
Never were there braver soldiers than these, the honour of their
nation. If only they had been of the true faith it would not have
been possible, anywhere in the world, to find men to surpass them.'

But courage alone was no longer enough. On the night of 4 July Saladin made a last bid to take the besiegers' camp by storm. When this failed the capitulation of Acre became both inevitable and imminent. By now large sections of its walls were in poor shape and much of the moat had been filled in. On 12 July besiegers and besieged agreed on terms of surrender. The lives of the defenders were to be spared in return for a ransom of two hundred thousand dinars (gold coins), for the release of fifteen hundred prisoners now in Saladin's hands and for the restoration of the Holy Cross. When he heard of the conditions Saladin was horrified, but it was too late – Frankish banners were already waving over the city. Acre had fallen at last.

But, as the Christian army moved in to take possession of the city there occurred a fateful incident which was to have far-reaching consequences. Duke Leopold of Austria planted his banner by the side of the standards belonging to the Kings of France and England. For a brief while it stood there in triumph, but then some of Richard's soldiers tore it down and threw it into a ditch. Leopold was naturally offended. A few days later, having tried in vain to obtain satisfaction, he left Acre and returned to Austria. He held Richard responsible for the insult, undoubtedly correctly. The soldiers must have acted with, at the very least, their lord's tacit approval. Leopold had good cause to hate the King of England and two years later, when Richard fell into his hands, he took his revenge. What was it that lay behind the incident of the standard? Why did Richard humiliate Leopold? So far as the German chroniclers of the time are concerned Richard was simply an arrogant and overbearing man who wished to keep all the glory for himself. But to understand what it was all about we have to look more closely at Leopold of Austria's position in the crusader camp.

Leopold had reached Acre in the spring of 1191, somewhat earlier than the two Kings. From the moment of his arrival he found himself cast in the role of leader of the German contingent. This was because Frederick Barbarossa had never reached the Holy Land; in June 1190 he had been drowned in a river in Asia Minor. After his death the great German crusade broke up. Only a pitifully small remnant of Barbarossa's army managed to struggle on to Acre. They arrived in October 1190, carrying with them some bones from the body of the dead Emperor – bones which they hoped would one day find a fitting resting place in Jerusalem. In command of this contingent was Barbarossa's second surviving son, Duke Frederick of Swabia. In January 1191, however, Frederick's name was added to the long list of those who had succumbed to the diseases of the camp. Thus, when Leopold arrived, he found himself the most important German noble present. But despite his splendid family connections – he was related to both the Hohenstaufen and the Comneni – Leopold did not have the resources to make his presence felt in the Frankish camp. There were not many Germans at Acre; Leopold's own retinue was tiny; and he did not have the cash to attract other men to his banner as Richard had been doing ever since he reached Marseilles. Indeed, according to one English chronicler, Leopold could afford to stay in Outremer only because he was subsidized by the King of England. The Duke of Austria remained an unimportant outsider in a camp which had split into two factions. For him to raise his standard in Acre was totally unrealistic.

If the two Kings had allowed Leopold's standard to remain there they would, in effect, have publicly acknowledged that the Duke of Austria was entitled to share the plunder with them. Yet right from the start of the crusade, Richard and Philip had acted on the assumption that they would each take one half of their conquests. Only recently indeed, while they were both lying sick beneath the walls of Acre, the two Kings – who were never too sick to quarrel – had again quarrelled over booty. Philip had demanded a half of Cyprus and Richard had countered by arguing that either the arrangement applied only to Outremer itself or, if its scope was wider, then Philip should hand over half of Artois, for Count Philip of Flanders had died at Acre on 1 June and by the terms of a treaty he had made with Philip of France in 1180, his death meant that the French King could claim to be the new lord of Artois. Though neither King gave in to the other, the argument shows that they were still thinking in terms of a fifty-fifty division of the spoils. The two Kings were not simply being acquisitive. For some years now the barons of Outremer, faced by a succession of political and military crises, had made it plain that if a king from Western Europe came to their aid he could expect to be able to wield power within the Kingdom of Jerusalem – and to wield power he would have to be able to draw upon the Kingdom's financial resources. Since these resources now had to be reconquered, the agreement between Richard and Philip fitted perfectly naturally into the prevailing framework of political and legal custom. The problem arose partly owing to Leopold's awkward position in the crusader camp and partly owing to the fact that the two Kings were late-comers to the siege of Acre. The Duke of Austria was certainly not the only one to resent the way in which the newly-arrived Kings monopolized the rewards. There were many barons and knights who, having endured the rigours of the siege for months or even years, now found themselves out in the cold. Robbed of their just reward they were too poor to do anything but return home. Naturally they complained bitterly of the greed of the French and the English and, in a sense, Leopold had been acting as their spokesman. Undoubtedly, throughout the whole of this affair, Philip had taken the same line as Richard, but it was Richard who acted – and acted in a characteristically direct and high-handed fashion. Acre had fallen. It was a great triumph, but in the moment of victory the seeds of trouble had been sown.

With Acre once again a Christian city, the first task of the crusaders was to reconsecrate the churches. Their religious duty done, the crusaders turned to politics, to the thorny question of the crown of Jerusalem. Guy of Lusignan and Conrad of Montferrat formally submitted their claims to the judgement of Richard and Philip. On 28 July the two Kings delivered their verdict, which was a compromise. Richard's protégé, Guy, was to remain King until his death, but then the crown was to pass to Conrad and Isabella and their descendants. Meanwhile Guy and Conrad were to share the royal revenues; Conrad was to hold a large northern county consisting of Tyre and – if he could recover them – Sidon and Beirut. Guy's brother, Geoffrey of Lusignan, whose knightly skills had been much in evidence during the siege, was granted the lordship of Jaffa and Ascalon in the south. Now that his nephew Hugh IX *le Brun* was a grown man there was less scope for Geoffrey at home in Poitou, especially while Richard maintained his policy of excluding the Lusignans from La Marche. Jaffa and Ascalon,

however, would be more than sufficient to compensate Geoffrey –
if they could be reconquered. A few days later Richard announced
that he was going to lead the army to Ascalon.

King Philip had already made it plain that he wanted to go back
to France and on 29 July he finally made up his mind. He had never
wanted to be a crusader; he had been ill and an army camp in the
Middle East was a hypochondriac's nightmare. Moreover he had
a very good reason for wanting to be back in France as soon as
possible. His share of the inheritance of Count Philip of Flanders
meant more to him than the chance of entering Jerusalem in
triumph. If he wanted to be sure of Artois then to Artois he must
go. In vain Richard pressed Philip to join him in a declaration of
their intention to stay in the Holy Land for three years or until
Saladin had returned the Kingdom of Jerusalem in its entirety. In
vain the leading men in the French army, tears in their eyes, begged
their lord to stay. But on 31 July Philip left Acre. He was
accompanied as far as Tyre by Conrad of Montferrat, to whom he
had given his share of Acre, including half of the prisoners. Conrad
had no wish to remain in an army dominated by the lord of the
Lusignans. On 3 August the King of France embarked at Tyre and
sailed for home. Richard, of course, was well aware that once Philip
was in Paris he might try to occupy Gisors and the Norman Vexin
as well as Artois. To an unscrupulous and angry politician it was
a crusade-sent opportunity, a temptation not to be resisted. Before
he left Acre Philip once again promised to leave the Angevin lands
in peace; but he may well have reflected that Richard had many
times promised to marry Alice. In these circumstances it would have
been naïve of Richard to put any faith in Philip's promise and clearly
he did not. A group of Richard's men quickly caught up with
Philip's galleys and coasted back to Europe in their company. There
can be no doubt that they were going back to give warning of the
inevitable attack and ensure that preparations were made to receive it.

Among these men was Roger of Howden. Fortunately the historian can now call upon new sources to fill the gap created by the
departure of this excellent guide. From the moment of his arrival
in Acre, Richard's activities were observed and commented upon
by Middle Eastern writers, both Christian and Muslim. There is

the old French chronicle known as the *Estoire d'Eraclès*, which was begun by Ernoul, squire to Balian of Ibelin, one of the leading barons of Outremer. This was written to explain the disaster of 1187, a disaster in which the Ibelin family was deeply implicated. Since it throws the blame on Guy of Lusignan and therefore favours – as did Balian of Ibelin – Conrad of Montferrat's claim to the throne, the chronicle is frankly hostile to Richard. The latter's admirers returned the compliment. 'There was Balian of Ibelin,' Ambroise wrote, 'Falser than any friend of sin.' The *Estoire d'Eraclès* emphasizes Richard's cunning, ruthlessness and subtlety – but it also cannot help appreciating these qualities. After all, as the conqueror of Cyprus Richard was very much the saviour of the baronage of Outremer, for it was on the island that many of them found rich estates safe from the ever-present threat of Muslim invasion which was their lot on the mainland.

But above all, there are the accounts written by Arab historians, particularly Baha ad-Din and Imad ad-Din, both of whom were members of Saladin's household and very close to the master they loved and whose name they praised. The comparisons they made between the Kings of France and England make interesting reading. In Imad ad-Din's descriptions of the arrival of the Kings at Acre Philip cuts a very mediocre figure, while Richard is like a torrent sweeping all before him. For Baha ad-Din, Richard was 'a man of great courage and spirit. He had fought great battles and showed a burning passion for war. His kingdom and rank were inferior to those of the French King, but his wealth, reputation and valour were greater.' Richard's dignity seemed to be less than Philip's because they knew that he did homage to Philip, but it is clear that they feared the English King more. Elsewhere Baha ad-Din refers to his 'wisdom, experience, courage and energy' and to 'the cunning of this accursed man. To gain his ends he sometimes uses soft words, at other times violent deeds. God alone was able to save us from his malice. Never have we had to face a subtler or a bolder opponent.'

The Angevins, of course, looked upon Philip's departure as a traitorous desertion, a cowardly failure to fulfil his pilgrim's vow. And even in Capetian France, despite Philip's immense contribution to the extension of royal authority, his crusading record remained a permanent slur upon his reputation. In his life of Philip's grandson, St Louis, Jean de Joinville harked back to the contrast between the rival Kings: between Philip who 'returned to France, for which he was greatly blamed' and Richard who 'remained and performed great feats of arms' so that his example was held up to St Louis as that of 'the greatest king in Christendom'. Philip's early biographers, Rigord and William the Breton, did their best to defend their lord and explain his departure. According to Rigord Philip suspected Richard of treachery because he was exchanging gifts and envoys with Saladin, and this fact, together with his illness, made him decide, reluctantly, to leave. However, since he had the best interests of the crusade at heart, he took only three galleys with him, committing the rest of his army and treasure to Duke Hugh of Burgundy. William the Breton says that he left money to pay 500 knights and 1000 foot for three years. In fact what he really left behind was his share of the ransom of the prisoners of Acre and this had yet to be received. Thus in order to tide Hugh of Burgundy over until the ransom had been collected Richard had to lend him 5000 marks. Yet Richard must have felt that Philip's going was not all loss. In the vivid phrase of the Winchester chronicler, Richard of Devizes, Philip was to Richard like a hammer tied to the tail of a cat. Though his responsibilities and the demands made upon his treasure chest were now increased, at least there could be no doubt about who was in supreme command. It was, for example, now up to Richard to see that Saladin implemented the terms of the treaty made by his officers at Acre.

This was not going to be easy. The first step was to secure the return of the Muslim prisoners who had been moved to Tyre. Conrad was obstinate, however, and only when the Duke of Burgundy went to Tyre in person did he agree to hand them back. Apart from this Conrad would do nothing to help Richard, even though he was fighting to win a kingdom which Conrad could expect to inherit. To Ambroise, of course, Conrad was

> The false marquis who had sought
> By wealth and dealings underhand
> By wile and cheat to rule the land.

Saladin also had his problems. The terms of the Treaty of Acre
had shocked him. It is possible that after making so many financial
and military demands upon his emirs in the years since 1187 he
was simply incapable of bringing together so much money and so
many prisoners by the stipulated date, a month after the fall of Acre.
Some of the details of the treaty itself and of the subsequent negotiations between Richard and Saladin are obscure; not surprisingly
there are differences between the Christian and Muslim accounts
of what happened. It seems that because it took longer than expected
to recover the prisoners who had gone to Tyre, Richard had to agree
to interpret the treaty flexibly. Saladin was to be allowed to pay
the ransom in instalments: the first – and by far the largest in-
stalment – was due on 20 August. But neither side trusted the other.
It became clear that Saladin was still having difficulties in raising
the money and, in Richard's camp, men believed that he was spinning out the negotiations as a delaying tactic. The longer he could
pin Richard down in Acre, the harder the crusaders' task would
be. As the due date approached suspicions mounted and tempers
became increasingly frayed. Skirmishing between the armies continued and, on 19 August, a rumour – possibly deliberately manu-
factured – spread through the Frankish camp: Saladin, it was said,
had killed his prisoners. By noon on 20 August Saladin's envoys
had still not appeared. In the afternoon Richard marched his army
out of Acre. Then nearly 3000 prisoners were led out and, in full
view of Saladin's helpless troops, they were massacred. According
to Ambroise the Christian soldiers delighted in the work of but-
chery, seeing it as revenge for the deaths of their comrades who
had been killed during the siege. Only the commanders of the Acre
garrison were spared; they might fetch large ransoms or come
in useful later should an exchange of distinguished prisoners be
desired.

   Of all Richard's deeds this is the one most bitterly criticized. It
has been called both barbarous and stupid and has been cited to
show that there were no depths to which he could not sink in order
to relieve his frustrations. But it is not enough simply to condemn.
Of all wars those fought in a crusading spirit are the nastiest.
Even Saladin, by reputation the most courteous and civilized of

enemies, chose to massacre, two days after the battle of Hattin, all the Templars and Hospitallers who were in his hands – without giving them any chance of being ransomed. According to Imad ad-Din, he watched the slaughter with a joyful face, and looked upon it as an act of purification. Baha ad-Din indeed suggests that the Acre garrison may have been killed as a reprisal. In the eyes of the twelfth-century church the lives of unbelievers were of no account. They were, in any case, doomed to hell. There was even some virtue in accelerating the process. 'The Christian glories in the death of a pagan,' said St Bernard of Clairvaux, 'because thereby Christ himself is glorified.' In this world, if the lives of the Acre garrison had any value, it was as bargaining counters. So Richard deprived himself of a bargaining counter and, as a result, the money which had been collected for the ransom Saladin now distributed among his troops. But Richard had to move on; a bargaining counter which tied him to Acre was hardly an asset. Saladin was delaying things – even Baha ad-Din admits that – and to this extent he must share the responsibility. So too, though doubtless more willingly, must the Duke of Burgundy. All the leaders were, in some way, involved. According to Ambroise, when Richard realized that he was being tricked

> And how Saladin would do naught
> Nor give to those men further thought
> Who had guarded Acre in his stead,
> Richard a council summonèd
> Of nobles, and to them confided
> The case. They took thought and decided ...

If the crusaders were to leave Acre what else could they do? Baha ad-Din believed that the prisoners should have been led away into slavery. Although this seemed a natural solution to a Muslim, living in a society which kept slaves, it was perhaps less obvious to late twelfth-century Western Europeans who, through no particular virtue of their own, happened to live in a society which did not. Initially the prisoners taken at Acre had been offered freedom if they would accept baptism into the Christian faith. Many of them apparently took up this offer – but as soon as they were released, they crossed over to Saladin's lines. After this Philip and Richard said that there should be no more baptisms. Could the crusaders afford to march away from Acre leaving only a garrison to guard nearly 3000 Muslims? Merely to feed so many men would be difficult enough since, on Saladin's orders, the countryside around Acre had been thoroughly devastated. By mid-August, in fact, the prisoners had become an embarrassment rather than an asset and Richard and his fellow-soldiers had no compunction in ridding themselves of them in a fashion that was brutally efficient.

Two days later Richard led the army out of Acre. It had not been easy to persuade the soldiers to leave. After two years of grim struggle Acre had become a safe haven of pleasure. Saladin's secretary, Imad ad-Din, described in characteristically ornate language the activities of the prostitutes who had flocked to do business with the crusaders:

Tinted and painted, desirable and appetising, bold and ardent, with nasal voices and fleshy thighs ... they offered their wares for enjoyment, brought their silver anklets up to touch their golden ear-rings ... made themselves targets for men's darts, offered themselves to the lance's blows, made javelins rise towards shields ... They interwove leg with leg, caught lizard after lizard in their holes, guided pens to inkwells, torrents to the valley bottom, swords to scabbards, firewood to stoves ... and they maintained that this was an act of piety without equal, especially to those who were far from home and wives.

These ladies, however, had to stay behind in Acre. Washerwomen were still the only camp-followers whom Richard would allow to accompany the army on its march.

The goal of the march was Jerusalem, but it would have been foolhardy in the extreme to try to go there direct from Acre: the land was hilly and the supply line from the coast would have been impossibly long. So Richard decided to make for Jaffa. From there he would strike inland to Jerusalem. Whatever route he chose, he was now going to face the Turkish cavalry – the elite troops of Saladin's army – in open country. At Acre the besiegers had been safely entrenched behind their own line of fortifications and the renowned Turkish cavalry had never had a real opportunity to

demonstrate their skill. At Acre the Franks had faced military problems no different from those they would have faced in any siege
of a similar town in Europe. But now Richard would have to cope
with an unfamiliar style of warfare. He was to pass the test with
flying colours because he knew how to make the best use of local
advice and local experience.

The very different cavalry tactics employed by the Turks and the
Franks make a fascinating contrast. The Turks were essentially
mounted archers, though they each carried a small round shield and
a lance, sword or club as well as their bow. All their weapons, however, were lighter than those used by the Frankish knights and in
hand-to-hand fighting between equal numbers, the Franks held the
advantage. The Turks therefore used the speed and agility of their
horses to stay at a distance while sending in a rain of arrows upon
their enemies. They used the bow while riding at speed with such
dexterity that even in retreat they could turn in the saddle and shoot
at their pursuers. They used their mobility to encircle the enemy
and assail him from all sides at once. Only when their archery had
reduced the enemy to a state of near helplessnesss did the Turks
shoulder their bows and ride in for the kill.

The chief tactical weapon of the Franks was the charge of their
heavily armoured knights. Holding reins and shield in his left hand,
the knight held a lance rigid beneath his right arm, using the horse's
forward momentum to give power to the blow delivered by the
lance. If his lance shattered on impact the knight carried on the
fight with his sword. The weight of the charge was such that no
body of troops could stand up to it. It was said that a Frank on
horseback could make a hole through the walls of Babylon. If the
Franks succeeded in delivering a charge against the main body of
their more lightly-armed enemy, they won the battle. It was as
simple as that – or as difficult. If the timing of the charge were fractionally wrong, the elusive Turkish cavalry was able to scatter, leaving the Franks beating against thin air. And once the charge had
been delivered the Franks, having lost their tight formation, became
vulnerable to counter-attack. The Turkish horse-archers swarmed
all round their enemy like gnats round a man's head. To try to drive
them away with a charge was all too often like using one's hand

to beat off the gnats. The only observable result was a temporary agitation in the swarm:

> When to pursue them one essays
> Their steeds unrivalled like a swallow
> Seem to take flight, and none can follow.
> The Turks are so skilled to elude
> Their foemen when they are pursued
> That they are like a venomous
> And irksome gadfly unto us.

The Turks would turn repeatedly and harass the ponderous knights to their doom. Thus the charge had to be held back until exactly the right moment – and dashing knights did not always find it easy to be patient when under non-stop fire. Except at close range the light Turkish bow did not have the power to fire an arrow capable of piercing a coat of mail and wounding the body of the wearer, but it could penetrate far enough to stick in the mail, so that knights under Turkish attack were often thought to resemble hedgehogs or porcupines. More serious than his undignified appearance was the fact that the knight was liable to have his less well-armoured horse killed under him. It was in this situation that the foot-soldier came into his own. The knights and their horses had to be protected until the moment to charge came. The job of protecting them was given to the infantry, both spearmen and archers. They were drawn up in a defensive screen, surrounding the knights like a wall and forcing the Turks to stay out of effective archery range. This meant, of course, that when on the march the speed of the army's advance was dictated by the pace of the infantry. The Turkish horse-archers had the advantage of superior speed and mobility. If the Franks were to survive in this kind of warfare then the qualities they needed were steadiness and discipline – not the qualities popularly associated with the medieval knight, but qualities which he none the less possessed as much as any other well-trained soldier. In the judgement of a twelfth-century Syrian, Usamah, 'the Franks – may Allah's curse be upon them – are of all men the most cautious in warfare'.

Richard's march south to Jaffa was a classic demonstration of

Frankish military tactics at their best. He marched close to the sea-shore. Thus the army's right flank was protected by the sea and Richard's fleet. When Acre surrendered, a large part of the Egyptian fleet had been captured at anchor in the harbour so there was no-thing to fear from that quarter. The knights were organized in three divisions with their left flank protected by infantry. Since this meant that the foot-soldiers had to bear the brunt of the ceaseless Turkish attack, Richard divided them into two alternating halves: one half marched on the left, while the other took things easy, marching beside the baggage train between the knights and the sea.

Saladin, too, marched south, on a parallel course, keeping the main body of his troops at some distance from the Franks and send-ing in bands of skirmishers to harass them continually. Richard's men were under orders to ignore all provocations and to keep marching in close formation. No one was to break ranks. Saladin naturally concentrated on the rearguard, where the infantry was sometimes compelled to face about and fight off the Turkish attacks while marching backwards. On the very first day of the march the line became too extended, the rearguard under the Duke of Bur-gundy lagged behind and the Turks swooped in, breaking through the line and attacking the wagon train. Richard himself rushed back from the van and saved the situation. But it was a useful lesson. From then on Richard's orders were rigidly obeyed and rearguard duties were normally performed either by the Templars or the Hospitallers – the soldiers with most experience of this hard school of warfare. Baha ad-Din was particularly struck by the discipline of the infantry. 'I saw some of the Frankish foot-soldiers with from one to ten arrows sticking in them, and still advancing at their usual pace without leaving the ranks ... One cannot help admiring the wonderful patience displayed by these people, who bore the most wearing fatigue without having any share in the management of affairs or deriving any personal advantage.' One other happy result of that first day was the healing of an old enmity. The French knight William des Barres fought with such gallantry that Richard decided to forget the grudge he had borne for so long.

Day after day the army toiled on, past Haifa, over the ridge of Mount Carmel, and on past Caesarea. Everywhere they found that

Saladin's men had been there before them, razing fortresses to the ground and burning crops. But the presence of the fleet enabled Richard to keep his men supplied and give them occasional rests aboard ship. The heat was intense, and the Franks, heavily armoured, suffered badly. Sunstroke claimed many victims. And every day the arrows of the Turks claimed many more. Richard himself was wounded by a spear-thrust in the side, not very seriously. Yet still the army, in close formation, moved doggedly on. It was not to be harassed into defeat. By early September Saladin realized that his only hope of stopping it lay in committing a much larger proportion of his troops than he had risked up till now. He picked as his battleground the plain to the north of Arsuf. On 6 September the Franks were relieved to be unmolested as they marched through the forest of Arsuf; there had been a rumour that the forest would be set ablaze while they were in the midst of it. But as they emerged from the cover of the woods they saw why they had been left in peace. Saladin had spent the day drawing up a vast army – as it seemed to the crusaders – in battle array. The Franks, of course, had no choice but to advance. On 7 September, Richard took even more care than usual in organizing his line of march. In the van he placed the Templars; next came the Bretons and the men of Anjou; then King Guy with the Poitevins; in the fourth division marched the Normans and English guarding the dragon standard; after them came the French contingents, and bringing up the rear, in the position of greatest danger, the Hospitallers. They were drawn up into such a solid and tight formation that it was impossible to throw an apple into the ranks without its hitting a man or a horse. Richard and the Duke of Burgundy, with a retinue of picked knights, rode up and down the line of march observing Saladin's movements and checking and re-checking their own formation. As always the infantry had their vital defensive role to play. The only difference between the Battle of Arsuf and the fighting of the last two and a half weeks was that, by committing his main force to the attack, Saladin would be giving Richard a chance to deliver one of the famous Frankish charges, and if Richard could seize the moment, victory would be his.

In the middle of the morning Saladin made his move. The sight

and sound of the Turkish cavalry as it swept towards them was
something which Ambroise would never forget:

> With numberless rich pennons streaming
> And flags and banners of fair seeming
> Then thirty thousand Turkish troops
> And more, ranged in well-ordered groups,
> Garbed and accoutred splendidly,
> Dashed on the host impetuously.
> Like lightning sped their horses fleet,
> And dust rose thick before their feet.
> Moving ahead of the emirs
> There came a band of trumpeters
> And other men with drums and tabors
> There were, who had no other labours
> Except upon their drums to hammer
> And hoot, and shriek and make great clamour.
> So loud their tabors did discord
> They had drowned the thunder of the Lord.

Although the spears and arrows of the Frankish infantry took
heavy toll, the Turkish forces, supported by Bedouin and Nubian
auxiliaries, seemed to be everywhere, their horsemen charging in,
then wheeling round and charging again, pressing closer and closer.
The rain of arrows was so thick that even the bright sunlight was
dimmed. In the rearguard the Hospitallers came under terrible
pressure. Several times during the day, the Master of the Hospital
begged for permission to charge. Each time Richard said no; they
must wait until he gave the signal for a general assault – six clear
trumpet blasts, two in the van, two in the centre, two in the rear
– and that would not be until the Turkish army was closely engaged
and their horses had begun to tire. The Hospitallers held on grimly.
As the day wore on, the heat became more and more oppressive;
so did the dust and the deafening noise of drums and cymbals. The
Hospitallers began to feel that the signal would never come and that
they would be branded as cowards for submitting so patiently to
the unending onslaught. Moreover they were losing horses at an
alarming rate. Goaded beyond endurance, two of the knights, the

Marshal of the Order and Baldwin Carew, lost their nerve and charged. At once the rest of the Hospitallers and the French knights galloped after them, scattering the infantry screen, which was unprepared for the rearguard's sudden move. This was the critical moment. The Hospitallers' counter-attack, premature though it was, had to be supported at once otherwise the rearguard, having lost contact with the main army, would be gradually smothered by the superior numbers of the Turks. Without hesitation Richard and his own knights charged too, ordering the Bretons, Angevins and Poitevins to join them. The massed Frankish cavalry drove all before it.

> Their soldiers stood aghast
> For we descended on the foes
> Like thunder, and great dust arose.
> They suffered a most fearsome rout
> So that for two leagues all about
> Fugitives filled the countryside,
> Who once were boastful in their pride.

But under an experienced captain like Saladin it was at precisely this moment that the Turks were most dangerous. If in their excitement the Franks pressed the charge too far, the knights, having lost their close order, could find that they had galloped headlong into a trap. Richard was well aware of the danger. The Normans and English had been held in reserve; the royal standard was to act as a rallying point. Thus when the Turks counter-attacked in their turn there was a basis upon which the Franks could re-form their lines. Then in a fierce struggle which marked the climax of the battle, with both sides having thrown in their reserves, the day was won by a series of charges led by Richard and William des Barres. Saladin withdrew and the army continued on its southward march, though that night many returned quietly to the battlefield to plunder the bodies of the slain.

Saladin's prestige had suffered a second great blow. First Acre, now Arsuf. The legend of his invincibility had been destroyed. His troops were demoralized and though the skirmishing continued unabated they were unwilling to face the Franks again in pitched battle. 'We were all wounded,' wrote Baha ad-Din, 'either in our bodies or in our hearts.' By contrast Richard now stood at the height of his fame. Although the Hospitallers had anticipated his signal, Richard's swift reaction and masterful handling of the next few minutes had conjured victory out of imminent confusion. Naturally his soldiers praised – and doubtless magnified – Richard's own part in the hand-to-hand combat. 'There the king, the fierce, the extraordinary king, cut down the Turks in every direction, and none could escape the force of his arm, for wherever he turned, brandishing his sword, he carved a wide path for himself, cutting them down like a reaper with his sickle.' Richard's bravery and prowess inspired the loyalty and admiration of his followers, but it was his superb generalship which really counted.

Three days later, on 10 September, the Frankish army reached Jaffa. In destroying its walls, Saladin had done so much damage that the army could find no lodging within the town; so they camped in an olive grove outside. Richard now held the port nearest Jerusalem. The obvious course was to march inland and head directly for the Holy City. But did Richard have enough troops to lay siege to Jerusalem and protect his supply line? If Saladin succeeded in cutting his communications, Richard would be in serious trouble. In his march from Acre to Jaffa, Richard had had one flank protected by the sea and for supplies had relied heavily on his fleet; inland the Turkish harassing tactics might be far more effective. The main Turkish army, moreover, although it had been defeated, was still intact. It lurked at Ramlah, while Saladin himself took a contingent to Ascalon further down the coast. The great harbour fortress of Ascalon was the key to the vital road which linked Egypt and Syria. Saladin wanted to defend both Jerusalem and Ascalon but in the opinion of his emirs he did not have enough troops and they forced him to choose between them. Saladin opted to hold Jerusalem. This meant that he had to dismantle Ascalon to prevent a useful base from falling, intact, into Christian hands. On the day on which Richard entered Jaffa, Saladin began to evacuate the population of Ascalon.

What would Richard do now? Sensing the strategic importance of Ascalon, he had no wish to let Saladin demolish the town unhindered. He sent the lord-designate of Ascalon, Geoffrey of Lusignan, in a galley to reconnoitre the situation from the sea. On his return, a meeting of the army council was held. Despite Richard's wishes, the majority argued in favour of staying where they were and re-fortifying Jaffa, on the grounds that it was the most convenient port for Jerusalem. As always there was a divergence of views between those who saw the need to think in terms of military strategy, of holding terrain as well as winning it, and those who were pilgrims and who wanted, above all, to enter the Holy City and fulfil their vow. Reluctantly Richard gave way to the majority view. At least to stay at Jaffa for a while would give the soldiers the rest they badly needed after the exertions on the road to Arsuf. The decisions made in September 1191 are a useful reminder that neither Saladin nor Richard was an autocratic ruler; both were forced to take account of the feelings of the men on whose co-operation they relied if they were to achieve anything.

But Richard was still confident of success. A letter written on 1 October reveals his optimistic frame of mind: 'With God's grace we hope to recover the city of Jerusalem and the Holy Sepulchre within twenty days after Christmas and then return to our own dominions.'

JERUSALEM AND JAFFA
1191-1192

DURING September and October 1191 the Franks settled down to rebuild Jaffa and enjoy the comforts of the town and its surrounding orchards.

> There was great wealth of pasture ground
> And there did grapes and figs abound,
> Almonds, and pomegranates too
> Which in such great profusion grew
> And which so copiously did fill
> The trees that all might eat at will.

Ambroise was less happy about the women who travelled down from Acre to entertain them:

> Back to the host the women came
> And plied the trade of lust and shame.

Jaffa, however, was a small town and, after a while, some of the soldiers hankered after the more hectic excitements of Acre. Richard himself was forced to go to Acre and haul them back to their duty. When he returned, he brought with him Berengaria and Joan. Despite the relaxed atmosphere at Jaffa, the enemy were never far away and on one occasion Richard was very nearly captured. He had ridden out with a handful of knights on a reconnaissance and hawking patrol but was then lured into a Turkish ambush. Several members of his escort were killed and Richard himself only escaped because one knight, William de Préaux, had the presence of mind

and courage to pretend that he was the King. Thinking they had
captured Richard, the Turks broke off the fight and made off into
the hills. Arab writers were impressed by the loyalty of a man who
was willing to sacrifice himself for his lord. On the Frankish side
people were alarmed by the narrow escape and did their best to dis-
suade the King from taking part in skirmishes, but apparently in
vain. The patrols continued, and if Richard saw a fight nothing
could stop him from rushing into it.

But if this kind of behaviour was rash and short-sighted Richard
was at the same time thinking ahead and on a much grander scale.
Floating through his mind was not just the recovery of Jerusalem
but also the conquest of Egypt. Throughout the twelfth century
this had been a favourite scheme of the Kings of Jerusalem – and
possibly a mistaken one, since the end result of their attacks on
Egypt was the unification of Egypt and Syria under one ruler, Saladin. But once this unification had been achieved there could be no
doubt that the project made good sense: Saladin's hold on Jerusalem
was made possible by the wealth of the Nile Valley. In the thirteenth
century the maxim that 'the keys of Jerusalem are to be found in
Cairo' became the principle on which crusade strategy was based.
Richard mentioned his plan for an Egyptian campaign the following
summer in a letter he sent to the Genoese in October 1191. His
policy up until then had been one of alliance with the Pisans, since
this had been the line taken by Guy of Lusignan, while Conrad of
Montferrat and Philip of France looked to the Genoese. But difficult
though it was to persuade those old and bitter rivals, Pisa and
Genoa, to co-operate, it was also obvious that any significant military advance such as an attack on Egypt would require maximum
maritime support. So, in October 1191, we find Richard both confirming and offering privileges to the Pisans and Genoese on his
own behalf and persuading his protégé, Guy of Lusignan, to do the
same.

In the meantime he had once again opened negotiations with
Saladin. Baha ad-Din's account of an exchange of views between
Richard and Saladin gives a useful insight into the attitudes of the
two sides. Richard began by pointing out that 'the Muslims and
the Franks are bleeding to death, the country is utterly ruined and

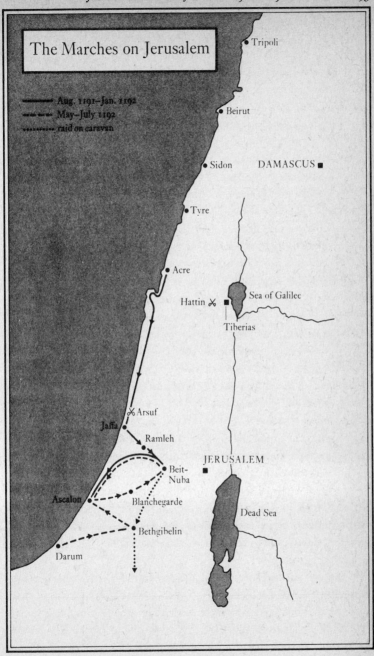

The Marches on Jerusalem

——— Aug. 1191–Jan. 1192
- - - May–July 1192
.... raid on caravan

Tripoli

Beirut

Sidon

DAMASCUS

Tyre

Acre

Hattin ⚔

Sea of Galilee

Tiberias

⚔ Arsuf

Jaffa

Ramleh

JERUSALEM

Beit-Nuba

Ascalon

Blanchegarde

Dead Sea

Bethgibelin

Darum

goods and lives have been sacrificed on both sides. The time has come to stop this. The points at issue are Jerusalem, the Cross, and the land. Jerusalem is for us an object of worship that we could not give up even if there were only one of us left. The land from here to beyond the Jordan [*Oultrejourdain*] must be consigned to us. The Cross, which for you is simply a piece of wood with no value, is for us of enormous importance. If you will return it to us, we shall be able to make peace and rest from this endless labour.' In reply Saladin explained that 'Jerusalem is as much ours as yours. Indeed it is even more sacred to us than it is to you, for it is the place from which our Prophet made his ascent into heaven and the place where our community will gather on the day of Judgement. Do not imagine that we can renounce it. The land also was originally ours whereas you are recent arrivals and were able to take it over only as a result of the weakness of the Muslims living there at the time [i.e. of the First Crusade]. As for the Cross, its possession is a good card in our hand and could not be surrendered except in exchange for something of outstanding benefit to Islam.' On another occasion Saladin claimed that even if he wanted to cede Jerusalem, popular indignation would make it impossible. (And it is true that when Jerusalem was restored to the Christians in 1229, it was immediately – if only temporarily – recaptured by a host of poorly armed Muslim peasants.)

In most of the negotiations of October and November 1191 Saladin was represented by his brother al-Adil Saif ed-Din, whom the Franks called Safadin. He was a diplomat of consummate skill and, after Saladin's death, it fell to him to hold the empire together. Like the rest of the crusaders, Richard liked and admired al-Adil, and in mid-October he put forward some apparently startling peace proposals. If Saladin would grant Palestine to his brother, then he, Richard, would arrange for al-Adil to marry his sister Joan. As a dowry he would give her the coastal cities from Acre to Ascalon. The happy couple could live at Jerusalem, to which the Christians should be given free access. Al-Adil was intrigued – or amused – by the idea and passed it on to Saladin, who accepted it at once, somewhat to the surprise of his advisers. But Saladin believed that the whole thing was just a joke of Richard's and he did not want to spoil it. Sure enough, when al-Adil's envoy next saw Richard, the King told him that Joan had flown into a towering rage when she heard of her brother's plan, swearing that she would never consent to being an infidel's wife. Perhaps, Richard continued in the same vein, the best way of solving the problem would be for al-Adil to turn Christian. Later on, Richard had the idea of substituting one of his nieces in place of the reluctant Joan. Unquestionably these negotiations were not to be taken at face value. Richard was not the man to be caught in a fog of romantic optimism. He was mustering an army ready to move out of Jaffa and in the meantime was becoming acquainted with the enemy, whether by skirmishing with him and exchanging blows or by meeting him and exchanging compliments and gifts. All contacts, however light-hearted, were ways of assessing the mood in Saladin's camp. And Saladin's camp, of course, was by no means united. The setbacks of the last few months had brought tensions and rivalries to the surface. It is possible that the death of Saladin's nephew, Taqi al-Din Umar, on 9 October 1191 had already precipitated a quarrel over the succession to his lands between al-Adil and Saladin's eldest son, al-Afdal – a quarrel which prefigured the succession dispute which followed the death of Saladin in 1193. Certainly, if the *Estoire d'Eraclès* is anything to go by, there was a school of thought among the Frankish baronage of Outremer which believed that Saladin was at odds with al-Adil and feared that his brother might actually marry Joan and set himself up as an independent ruler. Conceivably then Richard's proposals may have been intended as probes to investigate and widen splits at Saladin's court.

But if this was the game which Richard was playing, then it is clear that he was on a poor wicket. For al-Adil and Saladin were playing the same game – and to greater effect. By ostentatiously negotiating separately with both Richard and Conrad of Montferrat, they gave the Franks good cause to fear that the split in the Frankish camp might soon become irreparable. Ever since the end of July Conrad of Montferrat, dissatisfied with a compromise which left the crown in his younger rival's hands, had held aloof from the crusade. Despite repeated requests he had refused to give Richard any help. Indeed he had told Saladin that he would break with the crusaders if he were given Beirut and Sidon. But since he had, in effect, already broken with them, Saladin saw no reason to give away two valuable towns for nothing. To have any hope of obtaining Beirut and Sidon, Conrad would have to take up arms against Richard, and even Conrad did not dare to go quite as far as that. In these circumstances Saladin was perfectly happy to talk peace, but he had no intention of making peace. There were no peace terms, he believed, which would prevent the crusaders from treacherously launching an attack as soon as he was dead; it was better for him to carry on the Holy War until he had expelled them from Palestine or dropped dead in the attempt.

On 31 October 1191 Richard left Jaffa and began the last stage of his journey to Jerusalem. The advance was extremely slow. Throughout November – while continuing to negotiate – and December he concentrated on rebuilding the castles on the pilgrims' road from Jaffa to Jerusalem – castles which Saladin had dismantled. Saladin withdrew to Jerusalem, contenting himself with sending out patrols to raid Richard's lines of communication and to attack any foraging parties which were not properly guarded. In one such attack a foraging party was heavily outnumbered and even when Richard sent the Earl of Leicester and the Count of St Pol to reinforce it, the Franks were in great difficulties when the King himself arrived on the scene. Quickly weighing up the situation, his companions advised him not to intervene: 'You will not succeed in rescuing them. It is better that they die alone than that you risk death in this attack, and so endanger the whole crusade.' But, although Richard was familiar with the argument and doubtless appreciated it, he was also moved by another code of values: 'I sent those men there. If they die without me, may I never again be called a king.' Once again Richard charged into a skirmish, and emerged unscathed. Indeed, since the elaborate courtesies of his negotiations with al-Adil were giving rise to rumours that he was going to betray the army, Richard liked to ride back from adventures of this kind carrying the heads of Turks as a public demonstration of his devotion to the cause of the crusade. By 22 November the main army had reached Ramlah and there they stayed for six weeks while the winter rain beat steadily down. The difficulties of campaigning in this kind of weather meant that winter was traditionally the season when armies were disbanded and soldiers went home. Saladin kept his army together until 12 December, but he was at last compelled to give way before the pressure of his emirs and their troops and the threat of deteriorating morale. When he learned that the bulk of Saladin's army had dispersed, Richard moved his headquarters up to Latroun. Here he spent Christmas and then ordered the main crusading army to advance up to Beit Nuba, only twelve miles from the Holy City.

The weather was appalling; heavy rain and violent hailstorms; mud everywhere. Their food was soggy and rotten, their clothes wet through, and their arms and armour rusty. Yet the soldiers were in jubilant mood, and they gave thanks to the God who had brought them so far:

> God may we now our voices raise
> In thanks, in worship and in praise!
> Now we shall see Thy Holy Tomb!
> No man felt any grief or gloom,
> Or any sadness or distress,
> For all was joy and happiness.

But not everyone was so optimistic. Those who knew the country, and who were sufficiently far-sighted to see what would happen if Jerusalem were captured, took a wiser and sadder view. Foremost among these men were the Templars and Hospitallers. They pointed out that if Richard laid siege to Jerusalem, he would almost certainly be caught between the garrison and a relieving army. What hope was there of escaping from that trap when they were so far from the sea? (In fact, the morale of the troops who still remained with Saladin in Jerusalem was so low that the city might have fallen fairly soon.) But if they did take Jerusalem, what then? The enthusiastic crusaders, pilgrims to the Holy Sepulchre, would all go home, their pilgrimage completed, their vows fulfilled. How many could be persuaded to live in Jerusalem and defend it? As they could see, it was not exactly a land flowing with milk and honey. The answers to these questions were obvious. Despite the mounting difficulties they had never quite abandoned their dream of saving Jerusalem, but now that they had at last arrived at their destination there could be no escape from the realities of the situation. They could no longer decide to press on and hope; there were no more corners to be turned. At a meeting of the army council held in January 1192 the inevitable decision was taken: Richard gave the order to retreat. To most of the ordinary soldiers, the pilgrims, it was a bitter blow. The weather conditions, which had been bearable while they were marching forward to the Holy City, were now intolerable. Even the elements seemed to be mocking them:

> When they were burdened with a load
> Of goods and through the thick mud strode,
> They stumbled to their knees and fell.
> Then to the devil down in hell
> Men cursing gave themselves. My lords,
> Think not that these are idle words:
> Never was goodly company
> So deeply sunk in misery.

And to these men Richard, the conqueror of Cyprus and of Acre, the victor of Arsuf, was now the general who turned back from the gates of Jerusalem.

The council which had voted to retreat had also decided that the most sensible course was to take Ascalon and rebuild it. This was sound military strategy but it was not for this that many soldiers had crossed the sea. Most of the French contingents, who were said to have been in favour of laying siege to Jerusalem, retired to Jaffa – some even to Acre. It was with a much diminished army that Richard reached Ascalon on 20 January 1192. For the next four months Richard's forces remained there, making it the strongest fortress on the coast of Palestine. They received no help from Conrad of Montferrat and precious little from anyone else. The Duke of Burgundy rejoined them for a while in early February but then went back to Acre as soon as Richard announced that he could not afford to lend him any more money.

Acre was in chaos. The Genoese and the French tried to seize control of the city and were joined by a flotilla of galleys under the command of Conrad of Montferrat. But in a three days' battle the Pisans defended the city against this coalition. Richard was on his way north when he received their appeal for help. He reached Acre on 20 February to find that the news of his approach had forced Conrad and Hugh to beat a hasty retreat to Tyre. Richard managed to bring about a temporary reconciliation between the Pisans and the Genoese; then he went north to see Conrad. The two men met at Casal Imbert on the road to Tyre. Conrad again refused to join the army at Ascalon and, on both sides, angry words were spoken. Richard then presided over a council meeting at which Conrad was formally deprived of his share of the revenues of the Kingdom of Jerusalem. However, since the Marquis of Montferrat had the support of most of the local baronage and the French, it was extremely difficult to put this judgement into effect, even though Richard himself remained at Acre for six weeks in an effort to keep control of the situation. The rebuilding of Ascalon, meanwhile, went on under the watchful eye of its new Count, Geoffrey of Lusignan. Most of the building costs were met out of Richard's pocket, but some profitable raids on caravans travelling between Egypt and Syria suggested that the fortress would soon be self-sufficient.

On 31 March 1192 Richard returned to spend Easter with his army at Ascalon. While he reconnoitred Gaza and Darum and planned a further advance down the coast, the French, according to Ambroise, were enjoying themselves at Tyre:

> Those who were present there assured
> Us that they danced through the late hours
> Of night, their heads bedecked with flowers
> Entwined in garland and in crown;
> Beside wine casks they sat them down
> And drank until matins had rung;
> Then homeward made their way among
> The harlots ...

Throughout the spring both Richard and Conrad continued their separate negotiations with Saladin. From Richard's point of view, the need for a settlement became urgent as a result of news which reached him on 15 April. His brother John was making trouble in England and King Philip, unmindful of the oath he had sworn, was

threatening the borders of Normandy. Richard would have to return
to his ancestral lands. But what would happen in Outremer when
he was gone? Conrad was not prepared to co-operate with Guy of
Lusignan; if the feud continued, Saladin would almost certainly be
able to recover the ground he had lost in the last twelve months.
The kingdom desperately needed a king who could rule effectively
– which meant a king whose authority was undisputed. Compared
with this harsh fact the question as to who had the better legal right
was a matter of secondary importance.

 With this in mind, on 16 April Richard called a meeting of the
army council at Ascalon – within twenty-four hours of the arrival
of the messenger sent by the chancellor of England, William Longchamp. He gave the assembly a choice of kings: Conrad or Guy.
Unanimously the council opted for Conrad. Richard's biographers
and historians of the crusades have always said that this decision
came as a shocking surprise to the King, but this is hardly likely.
It is true that up till then he had consistently taken Guy's side. In
practice, however, this had simply meant that Richard had been
King of Jerusalem, not Guy. If Richard had wanted Guy to take
over the direction of affairs, there would have been no need to call
a meeting of the army council and offer it a choice of kings. Richard's
army already recognized a king, Guy, and this meeting only made
sense if a policy change was being considered. In all probability
Guy's formidable brother, Geoffrey of Lusignan, had already decided to renounce the lordships of Ascalon and Jaffa and return
home to Poitou. Once Richard left, Guy's position would become
even more vulnerable. Naturally he could not be dropped without
a word of regret and so, very properly, Richard expressed his sorrow
at what had happened before announcing that he would abide by
the decision of the council. While Richard was king in reality, Guy
could perfectly well be king in theory. But not even Richard had
been able either to defeat Conrad of Montferrat or to secure his
co-operation, and left to his own resources Guy had little or no
chance against this clever and totally unscrupulous opponent.
If Guy had succeeded in recapturing Acre it might have been
different but, as it was, in the eyes of the barons of Outremer
he was still the man who had lost the Battle of Hattin. All this

must have become crystal clear to Richard during the six weeks
he spent at Acre – if not earlier. Fortunately Richard was in
a position to compensate Guy in magnificent style. He had earlier
sold Cyprus to the Templars for 100,000 besants. So far they had
paid only forty per cent of the purchase price and their attempt to
raise the money by imposing a tax on the Greek Cypriot population
had provoked a rebellion. It looked as though Cyprus was going
to be more trouble than it was worth. Thus they were easily persuaded to sell out to Guy in return for 40,000 besants. Richard did
not press Guy for payment of the balance of 60,000 besants and
it was, in fact, never paid. The Lusignans were to rule Cyprus for
the next three hundred years, until 1489.

Meanwhile, Conrad of Montferrat had to be told of his good fortune, so Richard sent Count Henry of Champagne to take the news
to Tyre. Count Henry was a distinguished crusader who had already
been in the Holy Land for nearly two years. As the nephew of
both King Richard and King Philip, he was in a good position to
heal the divisions between the Angevin and French forces.
For this reason indeed he had acted as commander of the army
besieging Acre from the time of his arrival in the summer of
1190 until the coming of the two Kings in 1191. In the last few
months he had become clearly aligned with Richard's party, preferring to remain at Ascalon rather than withdraw to Tyre with the
Duke of Burgundy. (It is possibly this which accounts for the description of Duke Hugh in Joinville's *Life of St Louis* as 'bold but
sinful, enterprising but unwise', since Joinville was the hereditary
seneschal of Champagne.) When Count Henry reached Tyre and
told his news, Conrad fell on his knees and thanked God, praying
– or so Ambroise heard – that he should not be permitted to be
crowned if he were not worthy to be king. There was great urgency,
so it was agreed that he should be crowned at Acre within the next
few days. Count Henry left, in order to make preparations for the
coronation. But no one had reckoned with the assassin's knife.

On 28 April Conrad had expected to dine at home with his wife
Isabella. She, however, took so long over her bath that he eventually
gave up and went round to the house of his friend, the Bishop of
Beauvais, in the hope of dining there. Unfortunately the Bishop had

just finished his dinner so – doubtless reflecting that it was not his lucky day – Conrad headed home again. Turning a corner, he was met by two monks, one of whom seemed to have a letter for him. As Conrad went to take the letter, they stabbed him and he died soon afterwards.

Who were the killers? And why had they chosen to kill Conrad? Before he was executed, one of them confessed that they had disguised themselves as monks in order to worm their way into Conrad's confidence. In reality they were both followers of Rashid ed-Din Sinan, a legendary figure in the Near East and popularly known as 'The Old Man of the Mountain'. From 1169 until his death in 1193 Rashid was the leader of the Syrian branch of a revolutionary religious movement which had been founded in Persia at the end of the eleventh century. The orthodox Muslims who ruled Persia looked upon the followers of the new teaching as heretics and tried to suppress them. But these heretics did not submit meekly to persecution. They created a secure base for themselves in the great mountain fortress of Alamut, and they struck back at those who attacked them. Their chosen weapon was the assassin's dagger. In the early twelfth century the new teaching, together with its terrorist techniques, was carried into Syria and it was here that its devotees were given the name by which they are remembered: assassins. The word 'assassin' comes from the Arabic *hashish*. Their enemies accused them of taking hashish; to outsiders it seemed the easiest way of explaining why they acted the way they did. There is no good evidence to prove that they really did take hashish, but there is no doubt at all about the fact that they used murder as a political weapon. Thus, in the course of the twelfth and thirteenth centuries, a new word entered the languages of Europe: assassin, a dedicated killer.

The description of the Assassins given by the late twelfth-century German chronicler Arnold of Lübeck, illustrates very well the impact which the Old Man of the Mountain made on the European imagination:

This Old Man has by his witchcraft so bemused the men of his country that they neither worship nor believe in any God but him. He entices them with promises of an afterlife in which they will enjoy eternal pleasure and so he makes them prefer death to life. He only has to give the nod and they will jump off a high wall, breaking their skulls and dying miserably. The truly blessed, so he tells them, are those who kill others and are themselves then killed. Whenever any of his followers choose to die in this way, he presents them with knives which are, so to speak, consecrated to murder. He then gives them a potion which intoxicates them, plunging them into ecstasy and oblivion. Thus he uses his magic to make them see fantastic dreams, full of pleasures and delights. He promises them that they will live in such dreams for ever if they die when killing at his command.

Because many of their deeds were done by stealth, the power of the Assassins was easily magnified. There was no way of knowing where they would strike next. A story involving Saladin tells us much about the nature of the power attributed to Rashid ed-Din. According to this tale the Old Man of the Mountain sent a messenger to Saladin with instructions to deliver the message only in private. Naturally Saladin had the messenger searched, but no weapon was found. Then Saladin dismissed everyone but a few trusted advisers. The messenger refused, however, to deliver his message. So Saladin sent everyone away except his two personal bodyguards. Still the messenger was reluctant, but Saladin said: 'These two never leave my side. I look upon them as my sons. Deliver your message or not, as you choose.' Then the messenger turned to the two bodyguards and said: 'If I ordered you in the name of my master to kill Saladin, would you do so?' They said they would, and drew their swords saying, 'Command us as you wish.' The messenger ordered them to sheathe their swords and then all three left the Sultan's camp. Saladin was dumb-founded. Rashid ed-Din Sinan's message had been delivered. We have to remember that Saladin was the champion of Muslim orthodoxy and was prepared to order the crucifixion of heretics. He was therefore in much greater danger of assassination than were most Christians, though in 1176 he seems to have reached an accommodation with the Syrian Assassins. But before that date there were at least two attempts on his life. At one stage he is said to have been able to sleep only in a specially constructed wooden tower.

But why should the Assassins have wanted to murder Conrad of Montferrat? Nobody really knew the answer to this and all kinds of rumours spread rapidly. Some said that Saladin had bribed Rashid to kill both Richard and Conrad, but the Old Man killed only one of them because he knew that, with both out of the way, the Sultan would have a free hand to deal with the Assassins. Others blamed Richard. The Assassins' own confession was said to have implicated the King of England, but even if such a confession was made, it would not be very reliable evidence. It was a normal part of the Assassins' technique to provide the murderer with a 'cover story' of this kind in order to spread mistrust and suspicion in the opposing camp. Richard was the obvious man for the Assassins to implicate: he and Conrad had always been political enemies, and an observer, even if he had heard the news of their recent reconciliation, might well have thought that there was something suspicious about so complete a reversal of Richard's attitude. Only someone who understood the situation in England and Normandy could make sense of Richard's sudden switch. There were many French crusaders who were prepared to believe anything that was said against Richard, particularly when it became clear that the man who had most obviously gained from Conrad's death was Richard's nephew and political associate, Henry of Champagne. Fortunately for Richard, however, he was explicitly cleared of the charge in a letter written by the Old Man of the Mountain himself and sent to Leopold of Austria. At least the letter was intended to look as though it had been written by Rashid. In fact it was a forgery. Someone was trying to dispel the rumours. But useful rumours never die and to accuse your enemies of hiring Assassins to murder you became a standard tactic in European propaganda warfare in the 1190s. A hundred years later a piece of Capetian propaganda masquerading as a historical poem actually turned Richard into another Old Man of the Mountain, describing how he trained young English boys to be assassins, indoctrinating them with the belief that they would go to heaven whenever a successful mission ended with their own death.

At this distance in time it is no easier than it was then to know what really lay behind the murder of Conrad. Everything we know about Richard and Saladin (at least after the 1171 *coup d'état* by which he seized power in Egypt) suggests that they would not have stooped to assassination. The most straightforward explanation is that offered by the chronicles of Outremer – which reflect neither a Capetian nor an Angevin nor a Muslim point of view. They say that Conrad had offended Rashid by an act of piracy and this was the Old Man's revenge. It was not the kind of explanation to appeal to amateur politicians. It was far too simple for that. They preferred to look for deeper causes and for plots of Machiavellian subtlety. None the less on the evidence available it seems that this is probably what happened.

Conrad's death threw the political situation into a state of total chaos. The Duke of Burgundy tried to seize the town but Isabella, claiming to be following her dead husband's instructions, shut herself up in the castle and said she would hand over the keys to no one except Richard or the duly elected King of Jerusalem. But who might that be? Was Guy of Lusignan now King again? There were some who feared that, with Pisan support, he might renew his bid for the throne. Where did Isabella's first husband, Humphrey of Toron, stand now? If the marriage to Conrad had been invalid, was she still married to Humphrey? (There was yet another version of Conrad's death which made out that it had been plotted by Humphrey.) Or could Isabella, the twenty-one-year-old, twice-married heiress to the kingdom, find a third husband? Henry now became Richard's candidate for the throne and they both realized that in this confused state of affairs, when almost anything might happen, speed was essential. The best way of ending the political uncertainty was for Henry to marry the lady before anyone else did – and then let the lawyers argue the question of the legal validity of the wedding at their leisure. So although there are signs that both Richard and Henry shared the lawyers' doubts, this is what happened. On 5 May, after a week's widowhood, Isabella married Henry. Ambroise took a rather more romantic view of the Count's motives:

> The French delayed not in the least
> But sent straightway to fetch the priest
> And caused the Count to wed the dame.

My soul, I should have done the same,
For she was fair and beautiful
And so, may God be merciful
To me, the Count, unless I err,
Was well disposed to marry her.

After the wedding Henry and Isabella were installed in the royal palace at Acre:

The Count is richly lodged. Ah, would
That I had anything so good.

In the last twenty days events had moved with bewildering speed. On 15 April Guy had still been King of Jerusalem. By 5 May he was lord of Cyprus, while the Kingdom of Jerusalem was welcoming its third ruler in as many weeks. Henry, however, never assumed the title of king – either because he could not be crowned in Jerusalem or because of worries about the validity of his marriage. After Richard's departure he became the effective ruler of the Kingdom until 1197, when he accidentally stepped backwards through the open window of an upper room and was killed. Isabella then married, as her fourth husband, Guy of Lusignan's brother, Aimery, who died of a surfeit of fish in 1205. Thus by the time she was thirty-three, Isabella had been divorced once and widowed three times. When she herself died soon afterwards, the world must have seemed a safer place for husbands.

From Richard's point of view, the accession of Henry of Champagne meant that, for the first time, he had all the forces of the kingdom at his disposal. He decided to seize the opportunity to add to the length of the coastline in Christian hands, and increase the pressure on Saladin's line of communication between Egypt and Syria. Summoning Henry and the French army to join him he ordered an attack on the fortress of Darum, twenty miles south of Ascalon. In fact, after five days of fierce fighting, Darum fell on 22 May 1192, one day before Henry and the Duke of Burgundy arrived. But, in a fine gesture, Richard at once handed the captured town to the new lord of Jerusalem. Now that there was a new spirit of co-operation among the Christians they would surely succeed. This time, moreover, they would not be hampered by the winter mud and rain. But on 29 May Richard received another messenger from England, the vice-chancellor, John of Alençon, with yet more disquieting news about a conspiracy between John and Philip Augustus. Richard was now caught in a terrible dilemma: which mattered most – Jerusalem or the Angevin Empire? It would have taken John of Alençon about eight weeks to travel from London to Jaffa. What had happened in those weeks – and, if he left now, what would happen in the next two or three months? Jerusalem at least was near at hand. Should he try again to take it? It was a forlorn hope, if ever there was one, but did he want to be known as the King who did not even try? If by some miracle he took Jerusalem there would be no one in Europe who could stand against him, the conqueror who had restored the Holy City to Christendom. But suppose he failed, and then came home too late?

The army council met and decided that, whatever Richard did, they would attack Jerusalem. When this news was leaked to the soldiers their joy was so great

> That they went not to bed, but danced
> Till after midnight, still entranced.

Only Richard was unable to join in the general celebration. He withdrew to his tent and stayed there for several days, troubled and despondent. Finally one of his chaplains, William of Poitiers, managed to talk to him and revive his spirits. He reminded the King of all the past triumphs which God had allowed him to enjoy, of all the dangers which he had, by God's grace, escaped. Now that he had been brought to the verge of the ultimate victory, it would be a shameful thing to retreat.

> Now it is said by great and small
> Who wish you honour, one and all,
> How unto Christendom have you
> A father been, and brother, too,
> And if you leave it without aid
> 'Twill surely perish, thus betrayed.

Richard listened in silence and even after the chaplain had finished, he still said nothing, but next day he announced that he would stay in Palestine till the following Easter and that all should at once prepare for the siege of Jerusalem.

On 6 June the army, in cheerful mood, marched out of Ascalon. Five days later they reached Beit Nuba without encountering any opposition. Their only losses were two soldiers who died of snakebites. Henry of Champagne had gone to Acre to fetch reinforcements and Richard ordered his men to wait for their arrival. Saladin had withdrawn to Jerusalem. Apart from the usual skirmishing between foraging and reconnaissance patrols the main army was left in peace. Ambroise reports that in the course of one skirmish the King rode to the top of a hill from where he had a clear view of Jerusalem: this may well have been the hill known as Montjoie, the spot from which the men of the First Crusade first saw the Holy City. It was the nearest Richard ever came to Jerusalem. In thirteenth-century legend this moment was given a more dramatic turn: when the King realized that he was within sight of Jerusalem he flung up his shield to cover his eyes and, weeping, begged God that he might not have to look upon the city if he could not deliver it.

To the soldiers kicking their heels at Beit Nuba, Count Henry seemed an interminable time coming. As so often in the history of the crusades the convenient discovery of a relic helped to keep up morale. Apparently a fragment of the Holy Cross was in the neighbourhood, buried in order to keep it out of infidel hands. Richard and his knights were led to the spot by the man who had hidden it:

> Abbot of Saint Elias, who fed
> On nothing more than roots and bread.
> With his great beard that grew untrimmed
> A very holy man he seemed.

Finding this piece of the Cross was a comfort. Comfort of another kind was provided by a resoundingly successful raid on a rich caravan, with the result that an immense quantity of booty ranging from chessboards to camels was distributed among the soldiers. But exciting though these episodes were, they were no substitute for a siege of Jerusalem. Eventually Count Henry arrived and by 29 June the entire force was encamped at Beit Nuba. Baha ad-Din gives a graphic picture of the alarm at Saladin's headquarters – the emirs blustering bravely but in reality ready to abandon the city at a moment's notice, Saladin himself perplexed and unable to sleep. Yet as far as the leaders of the crusade were concerned nothing had changed. They were back where they had been six months earlier, except that this time Saladin had a larger army and would be able to cut off the supply line to the coast if they committed their forces to an attack on Jerusalem. Moreover Saladin had blocked up or polluted all the springs around Jerusalem, so the army would be in a waterless region in midsummer. Richard, however, had put forward an alternative plan: an attack on Egypt. A combined fleet of Pisan and Genoese ships had already played an important part in the capture of Darum – an ideal starting-point for the march across the Sinai Desert – and, so Richard assured his fellow-commanders, it was now lying moored at Acre, ready to transport all their supplies to the Nile Delta. He himself was ready to lead an army of 700 knights and 2000 men-at-arms, paid out of his own resources, along the coast road into Egypt. It was agreed that the two alternatives – the siege of Jerusalem or the attack on Egypt – would be put before a committee of twenty (five Templars, five Hospitallers, five barons of Outremer and five nobles of France) and that the whole army would abide by whatever the committee decided.

The committee opted in favour of an Egyptian campaign – as Richard undoubtedly knew it would, since fifteen of its twenty members were local experts and Richard was always careful to work in close consultation with them. Here, it seemed, was the fruition of the idea which had been in the back of Richard's mind since he opened negotiations with the Genoese in the previous October. The Duke of Burgundy and the French contingent, however, refused to co-operate. For them it was Jerusalem or nothing. Richard was prepared to go to Jerusalem, he said, if the army insisted, but he would not lead them there. He would go as their comrade, their fellow-pilgrim, but not as their commander. He would not lead them into a trap. But the army did not insist, could not. It was hopelessly split into two camps and therefore condemned to ineffectiveness. Hugh of Burgundy composed an insulting song about Richard, and his troops relieved their feelings by singing it loudly; Richard replied in a similar vein. However, apart from this minor contribution to the troubadours' art the army achieved nothing. On 4 July the withdrawal began. For Richard it must have been a day of misery. In agreeing to stay on in the Holy Land he had risked far more than the rest. He knew now that he had failed to liberate Jerusalem or to conquer Egypt; and for all he knew he might already have succeeded in losing the Angevin Empire.

By various routes the army returned to the coast. Richard reopened negotiations with Saladin and they were quickly able to come close to a settlement. Saladin agreed to allow pilgrims into Jerusalem and to cede the coast to the Christians, provided that they demolished Ascalon. Richard, however, refused to consider the demolition of a fortress on which he had spent so much time and money. Indeed he chose to strengthen it by reinforcing its garrison with troops drawn from Darum. Darum, no longer required as a base for an attack on Egypt, was dismantled to prevent its falling into Saladin's hands and being used as the supply depot in a siege of Ascalon. While the argument about Ascalon continued Richard moved to Acre, arriving there on 26 July. He had for a while been contemplating a strike to the north, against Beirut.

But Saladin moved first. On 27 July his army appeared outside the walls of Jaffa. After resisting bravely for five days, the town surrendered and was sacked. The garrison withdrew into the citadel, but their position was hopeless and they could do no more than buy a little time. They came to terms with Saladin. They would capitulate if they were not relieved by three o'clock next day, 1 August; naturally they had sent a message to Acre as soon as they saw Saladin's army, so they hoped that by now Richard was well on the way. He had in fact received the news at Acre on the evening of 28 July and had at once set off to the rescue. Henry of Champagne with a force of Templars and Hospitallers took the land route, but was halted at Caesarea by a report that the road was blocked by a second Muslim army. Richard's company, together with the Pisans and Genoese, went by galley but were held up by contrary winds off Mount Carmel. As a result it was not until late on the night of 31 July that his fleet reached Jaffa. When dawn came, it looked as though Richard had arrived too late. The whole town and the shoreline were swarming with Muslim soldiers. The beleaguered garrison must have signalled their presence to the fleet, but Richard did nothing; presumably he feared a trap, knowing that Frankish banners could be waved by Muslim hands. As the hours went by and still nothing happened the garrison began to give up hope; some of them laid down their arms and left the citadel.

At this point, just when Jaffa seemed well and truly lost, a priest jumped from the citadel into the harbour below, his landing cushioned by shallow water and sand. He swam out to the galleys. As soon as Richard realized that a remnant of the garrison was still holding out, he hesitated no longer. The red-painted royal galley under its red flag shot forward. Leaving off his leg armour, Richard jumped into the water and waded ashore, followed by his men. This charge, preceded by crossbow fire, cleared the shore. Once they had established a beachhead, some of the troops were detailed to seize all the timber they could lay their hands on and put up a barricade. The others, led by Richard, pressed forward and entered the town. The Turks were in a state of complete confusion: some still had their minds bent on plunder rather than war, while others believed that the garrison had already surrendered and were taken by surprise when it sallied out in support of Richard. In no time at all they were either dead or in flight. On that day, says Ambroise, the King's prowess exceeded Roland's at Roncesvaux.

Saladin's attack on Jaffa had been a brilliant and unexpected thrust. If it had succeeded it would have effectively cut the coastal strip of the re-born Kingdom of Jerusalem into two separate parts, and it had come within inches of success. It had failed because Richard had arrived in the nick of time; and against him, his knights and his crossbowmen there were no Muslim troops who fought in expectation of victory. Had he arrived eighteen hours later, however, he would have found Saladin securely in control of Jaffa. More important still, having seized the initiative in this dramatic fashion, Saladin would have been well on the way to winning back his reputation of 1187 and to re-asserting his authority over his emirs.

Ironically it may be that Saladin had moved too fast. Throughout it had been a war in which both sides knew a great deal about their opponents' plans. Fought in a country where the overwhelming bulk of the population either was Muslim or spoke Arabic and dressed in Arab fashion it was, at the 'civilian' level, impossible to tell friend from foe. Scouts and spies moved freely from one side to the other. Thus Saladin had learned of Richard's intention of besieging Beirut as early as 23 July; and he had moved at once. If he had not been so well-informed his attack on Jaffa might have come when Richard was at Beirut rather than at Acre, and Richard then might have arrived too late – unless, of course, his voyage had been helped by a following wind. It is possible to speculate endlessly, but it is clear that it had been a close-run thing and that the Frankish gains of the last twelve months had been placed in great jeopardy.

From Jaffa Saladin withdrew about five miles inland and at once resumed peace negotiations – or rather truce negotiations since for an orthodox Muslim there could be no peace to end the Holy War, only a truce. As before, Ascalon proved to be a stumbling-block. Saladin therefore decided to try a surprise attack on Richard before his land army had had time to link up with his amphibious force and while he was still desperately short of horses. By pitching his camp outside the battered town walls Richard had challenged Saladin to battle and Saladin decided to take up the challenge. During the night of 4 August the Turkish cavalry moved quietly forward. Luckily the King received just enough warning of their approach to be able to get his troops into battle array, though some of his soldiers were only half-dressed. The front rank knelt down, each man protected by his shield and pointing a lance at the enemy. Behind them were the crossbowmen, working in pairs; while one discharged his bolt, the other wound a second crossbow. The Turks charged but stopped and veered away as soon as they saw that this formidable defensive hedgehog would not break and run. In the end it was Richard and his ten mounted knights who went over to the attack against an enemy that was reluctant to fight now that it had lost the element of surprise. In the eyes of some of his followers the day was won by the King's personal courage and prowess:

The King was a giant in the battle and was everywhere in the field, now here, now there, wherever the attacks of the Turks raged most fiercely. On that day his sword shone like lightning and many of the Turks felt its edge. Some were cloven in two from their helmet to their teeth; others lost their heads, arms and other limbs, lopped off at a single blow. He mowed down men as reapers mow down corn with their sickles. Whoever felt one of his blows had no need of a second. He was an Achilles, an Alexander, a Roland.

These were the qualities which made him a legend. In reality the day was won by the professional competence with which he arrayed his troops and by the poor morale of the Turks, still suffering from the effects of their ejection from Jaffa and critical of Saladin's leadership.

This marked the end of Saladin's counter-attack. Both sides were now completely worn out, and Richard himself fell seriously ill. (It was said that he began to recover from the moment when he heard that Hugh of Burgundy had died at Acre.) For him it was time to make peace and go home. Aware of Richard's anxieties, Saladin was still attracted by the idea of prolonging the struggle and driving the Franks out before he died, but his emirs had had enough:

Look at the state of the country, ruined and trampled underfoot, at your subjects, beaten down and confused, at your armies, exhausted and sick, at your horses, neglected and ruined. There is little forage, food is short, supply bases are far away, the necessities of life are dear. All supplies have to come from Egypt, confronting the murderous perils of the desert.

(This last sentence shows why Saladin cared so much about Ascalon and the threat it posed to the road from Syria to Egypt.) According to Imad ad-Din, the emirs also argued that if a truce were agreed, the Franks would go back to Europe. Thus when, after a period of recovery, Saladin decided to renew the war, there would be almost no one in Palestine to stand against him. Faced by his troops' reluctance to fight, Saladin could not help but see the force of these arguments. But in his negotiations with Richard he remained adamant on the subject of Ascalon.

Eventually Richard gave way, worn down by an illness which

made him feel a physical as well as a political need to return. He insisted only that the newly-built fortifications should be razed to the ground before Ascalon was handed over. On these terms, on 2 September, Richard's and Saladin's representatives agreed to a three-year truce. From Tyre to Jaffa the coast was to remain in Christian hands. Jerusalem, of course, was kept by the Muslims, but pilgrims were free to visit the city. Many of his followers took advantage of this opportunity, but Richard did not. He would enter Jerusalem as a conqueror, but not on conditions laid down by unbelievers. Instead he travelled to Acre to recover his health and make arrangements to leave. He freed William de Préaux in exchange for ten Muslim prisoners. Finally on 9 October 1192 he set sail. The Third Crusade – his crusade – was over. In that it had not taken Jerusalem it was a failure, but given the political and military problems with which Richard and his fellow-commanders had to cope, it is amazing that they achieved as much as they did. Certainly Saladin feared that the coastal towns might be used as bases from which the rest of Palestine would be conquered. While Saladin was alive there was not much chance of that, but after the great Muslim leader was gone, who could tell? Saladin himself had grave misgivings. It was already obvious that his death would be followed by a struggle for power within his family. Had Richard stayed in the Holy Land until the next Easter – as he had once said he would, and as he nearly did since 9 October was just about the latest date in the year at which it was safe to sail – he might have achieved his ambition. By one of the ironies of history, Saladin died on 4 March 1193, more than three weeks before Easter. But by that time Richard was a prisoner in Germany.

PRISONER
IN GERMANY
1193-1194

HOMEWARD bound from Acre Richard made good time. On average the return journey from the Holy Land to Venice took ninety days, twice as long as the outward passage, and winter voyages were normally slower than average. But by the end of the first week of December, sixty days after leaving Acre on 9 October 1192, Richard was already approaching Venice. For most of the journey he had been aboard the *Franche-Nef*, a big ship which was able to sail on in weather conditions which sent galleys scurrying to port. If he had kept up this kind of pace on the overland route from Venice to Normandy he would have been back in his own dominions in January 1193. If he had returned at that date it would have been obvious to all, both contemporary writers and historians, that the arrangement he had made for the government of his lands in his absence had worked extremely well. He would have returned to an undiminished Angevin Empire.

There had been some difficulties – as was inevitable when Richard had a brother as ambitious and as crooked as John; and Richard had certainly not helped matters when he named Arthur as his heir in the treaty he made with Tancred in October 1190. None the less, for almost a year after the sealing of that treaty, Richard's chief official in England, William Longchamp, Bishop of Ely, papal legate, justiciar and chancellor of England, remained in control of the situation. Not surprisingly, his relations with John had been tense, and Richard had heard something of this in February 1191 while he was still in Messina. He had provided Walter of Coutances, Archbishop of Rouen, with letters authorizing him, if need be, to take charge of affairs. But there was clearly no crisis, no sense of urgency. Walter of Coutances waited at Messina until Eleanor and Berengaria had arrived there on 30 March, and then he returned with Eleanor at a leisurely pace, not reaching England until the end of June. Longchamp meanwhile had achieved an uneasy compromise with John, chiefly by agreeing to do all he could to help him to the throne in the event of Richard dying on the crusade. (This was, in any case, what any sensible politician would have done; there would be nothing to be gained from supporting the claims of a small child.) Throughout the summer of 1191 Longchamp continued to rule England and John was accepted as the heir apparent. But in September the chancellor made a fatal mistake, giving the unscrupulous John the chance he had been waiting for. Richard's and John's half-brother, Geoffrey, now consecrated Archbishop of York, decided to return to England in defiance of his oath to remain out of the country for three years. He landed at Dover, where Longchamp's brother-in-law was the constable of the castle. Discovering that the constable's men intended to arrest him, he took refuge in St Martin's Priory. Here he was besieged for four days and then, on 18 September 1191, Longchamp's men went in after him and dragged him outside by his arms and legs, his head banging on the pavement as they pulled him away from the altar of the priory church.

This act of violence reminded men of the death of Thomas Becket, with Longchamp in the part of Henry II. Almost to a man the English clergy turned against him; from that day there was no act of tyranny, no offence, whether political, sexual or financial, of which they did not think him capable. John and his partisans had no difficulty in stirring up such strong feeling against him that he was forced to flee the country in ignominy. Some idea of the propaganda techniques used by John's friends can be obtained from the widely circulated account of the scene on Dover beach one day in October as Longchamp, described by his enemies as being small, ape-like and excessively fond of boys, looked about for a boat in which he could cross the Channel. It is best left in the immortal, if unreliable, words of Hugh Nonant, John's chief propagandist and, in his spare time, Bishop of Coventry – a man of whom it was said (again by his enemies) that when he confessed a lifelong catalogue of sins on his deathbed, no confessor could be found who was willing to absolve him.

Pretending to be a woman – a sex which he always hated – he changed his priest's robe into a harlot's dress. The shame of it! The man became a woman, the bishop a buffoon. Dressed in a green gown of enormous length, he hurriedly limped – for the poor little fellow was lame – from the castle heights to the sea-shore, and then sat down to rest on a rock. There he attracted the attention of a half-naked fisherman who was wet and cold from the sea and who thought that the Bishop was the sort of woman who might warm him up. He put his left arm round Longchamp's neck while his right hand roamed lower down. Suddenly pulling up the gown he plunged unblushingly in – only to be confronted with the irrefutable evidence that the woman was a man. The fisherman then called his mates over to have a look at this truly remarkable creature.

According to Hugh of Nonant, Longchamp's servants eventually managed to rescue him from the fisherman but after further adventures of this kind the chancellor ended up in Dover gaol, where he was left to cool his heels for a week before being released and finding his way to Flanders. But although John's friends could assassinate a man's character, they could not secure for their patron the power which he coveted. The chancellor's place at the head of the administration was taken by Walter of Coutances and John's subsequent behaviour clearly indicates that he was disappointed with the results of his victory over Longchamp.

In January 1192, within a month of his return to France, Philip Augustus asked the seneschal of Normandy, William FitzRalph, to meet him at a conference between Gisors and Trie. There he produced a forged version of the Treaty of Messina of March 1191. According to this document the Norman Vexin was Alice's dowry and since Richard had now married someone else, Philip claimed that it should now be handed back to him, together with his sister. William FitzRalph and the barons of Normandy refused to comply with this demand. Philip left the conference in anger, swearing he would take the Vexin by force. His first step was to invite John to Paris. It was believed that he would offer to make John lord of all the Angevin lands in France if he would step into Richard's shoes and marry Alice (the fact that John was married already was clearly not a problem). At this point Eleanor of Aquitaine intervened. Hitherto she had stayed in Normandy but now she crossed hastily to England to confront her youngest son. Under pressure from his mother and Walter of Coutances – above all swayed by the threat that if he went to see Philip they would confiscate all his estates – John did as he was told. King Philip tried to organize an invasion of Normandy, but his nobles refused to join in an attack upon the lands of an absent crusader, so this plan too came to nothing.

Inevitably Philip's return meant that throughout the Angevin Empire Richard's castles were put into a state of readiness. These preparations achieved the desired effect. Only in Aquitaine did Philip succeed in shaking the loyalty of any of Richard's vassals. Taking advantage of the fact that Élie de la Celle, the seneschal of Gascony, was incapacitated by illness, a number of lords rose in rebellion. Chief among them were Count Élie of Périgord and the Viscount of Brosse. But once he had recovered his health, the seneschal lost little time in regaining the initiative. He captured the castles of the chief nobles and either destroyed them or kept them in his own hands. Behind the revolt lay not only the intrigues of Philip Augustus but also the natural desire of the Count of Toulouse to recover the lands of which he had been deprived in 1188. It was here that the Navarre alliance, cemented by Richard's marriage to Berengaria, proved its worth. Berengaria's brother, Sancho of Navarre, brought a large force of knights to the seneschal's aid and together they took the war into Count Raymond's lands, advancing right up to the walls of Toulouse itself. Thus, at the end of 1192, it was apparent that the Angevin Empire, despite Philip's best endeavours, had held firm. The only real trouble was not in England but in Aquitaine, and even here Richard's arrangements – his choice of officials, his diplomatic marriage – had proved more than adequate to cope with the situation.

All this time Richard kept in touch with what was happening. Reports and messengers went to and fro in either direction. It was not an ideal way of keeping his finger on the pulse of political activity in Western Europe, but the practical difficulties involved were not so very different from those faced every day by the papacy in its government of the churches of Christendom – and as a crusader king, Richard could command a quasi-religious authority of his own. Nonetheless, the great gulf in time and space fixed between him and his subjects tended to mean that, like even the most masterful popes, he reacted to events rather than controlled them. By January 1192, for example, he had heard both sides of Longchamp's fall and he sent Andrew de Chauveny – a fine knight but one who had broken his arm and was now out of action – to Rome, where he was able to discuss the case with clerks representing both Walter of Coutances and William Longchamp. According to Roger of Howden, Andrew de Chauveny let it be known that although Richard was prepared to accept the fact that this minister could no longer be saved, he was not prepared to countenance any further increase in John's power. While Richard was in Outremer, Rome seems to have functioned as a clearing-house for the exchange of information. Andrew de Chauveny, there in March 1192, would certainly have heard of Philip's attempts to seize the Vexin and win over John – a subject on which Richard was to receive confused and conflicting reports throughout May. Most important of all were the reports which dealt with Aquitaine, since it was in response to them that Richard planned the route that he would take on his journey back home.

The capture and imprisonment of Richard was one of the most important political incidents in late twelfth-century Europe; its consequences included not only a severe weakening of the defences of Normandy, but also the complete overthrow of the Kingdom of Sicily. Yet to this day the circumstances which led to Richard's being arrested in Vienna by agents of Duke Leopold of Austria remain a mystery. All we can do is guess. Our starting-point must be the late date of Richard's departure from Acre. This meant that it was already mid-November by the time the *Franche-Nef* reached Corfu. Up to this point he had probably followed the route which Philip had taken in the summer of 1191. From Corfu he could – as Philip had done – make contact with the officials of King Tancred of Sicily at Otranto or Brindisi, and they would have supplied him with the latest news. It may have been at this time that he learned of the invasion of Toulouse undertaken by Élie de la Celle and Sancho of Navarre. In the face of Count Raymond's enmity any plan of disembarking at a north Italian or south French port and returning to Aquitaine through Provence would now have to be shelved. To travel by a road further east through France or the Rhineland would be to run the risk of capture by Philip or Henry VI. Tancred, who watched all of the Emperor's movements with great care, undoubtedly knew of the meeting at Milan in December 1191 between Philip and Henry VI, and of the renewal of their friendship. After the failure of his 1191 campaign, when his wife Constance fell into Tancred's hands, the Emperor was planning a new invasion of Sicily and his diplomatic and naval preparations included treaties with both Pisa and Genoa. For Richard to coast westwards towards Barcelona in the hope of returning home through Aragon and Navarre was to run the risk of being sighted and intercepted by forces sent out by Pisa, Genoa or Toulouse. Moreover, the Mediterranean winter was closing in, and the longer he stayed at sea, the greater the risk of shipwreck; for this reason sea-borne commerce normally came to a halt during the winter months. (The twelfth-century customs of Pisa went so far as to forbid all maritime activity after 30 November.) Quite apart from the difficulties involved in navigating the Straits of Gibraltar – where both sides were held by Muslim powers – the weather alone is sufficient to explain why Richard could not afford to return home via the Atlantic coast. According to the great twelfth-century Arab geographer Edrisi the Atlantic was a forbidding sea of darkness, its sombre-hued waters torn by gales in which the waves rose to frightening heights; the English, he wrote, were the chief of the audacious sailors who ventured upon it, but even they sailed only in the summer.

Richard was clearly in a very awkward position. All routes home appeared to be blocked. He resolved that if his enemies would not grant him safe conduct through their territories, he would try to get back without informing them. He decided to travel through Germany, where he would be least expected and least looked for. He left the *Franche-Nef* at Corfu (she was later seen at Brindisi) and hired two or three galleys to take him northwards along the Dalmatian coast. The weather had the last word. They were shipwrecked on the Istrian coast somewhere between Aquileia and

Venice. Fortunately Richard and his few companions escaped un-harmed. Since he planned to travel incognito he had embarked on the galleys with only a handful of men: loyal knights like Baldwin of Béthune and William of L'Étang, his most trusted clerk, Master Philip of Poitiers, and some Templars.

At least one of their squires could understand German and Richard himself knew a great deal about German politics, partly through his own family connections and perhaps also as a result of more recent conversations with the man who had carried his stan-dard throughout the fighting at Jaffa: a man known to the crusaders as Henry the German. Thus Richard rejected the idea of taking the direct route from Venice: through Verona, the Brenner Pass, Tirol, Swabia and then down the River Rhine. This north-westerly road would have taken him right into the centre of Henry VI's power. Instead, by travelling north-east towards Bohemia he hoped to reach lands ruled by a group of German princes who were hostile to Henry VI. The key figures in this group were the Welf (or Guelf) family and the greatest of the Welfs was Richard's brother-in-law Henry the Lion, formerly Duke of both Bavaria and Saxony. Henry VI's efforts to raise money to finance his forthcoming invasion of Sicily were driving more princes to join the Welfs: among them the new Duke of Bohemia, Ottokar, his brother Wladislaw of Moravia, Hermann of Thuringia, and Albert of Meissen. Once Richard had reached Bohemia or Moravia he would be able to travel on roads controlled by his kinsmen and their friends until he reached a Baltic or a North Sea port. Moreover, in midwinter, the passes in the central Alps would be very difficult, while the road to Bohemia went via the Pontebba Pass over a fairly low range. The disadvan-tage of this route was that it would take him through Styria and Austria, lands belonging to the Duke whose standard had been cast down at Acre. But where every route, whether by land or by sea, bristled with problems this was probably the best chance.

Richard hoped that, disguised as pilgrims returning from the Holy Land, he and his party would escape detection. Almost at once, however, they succeeded in arousing the suspicions of the local prince, Count Meinhard of Görz, a kinsman of Conrad of Montfer-rat. Anyone who was interested in Richard's whereabouts was bound to investigate reports of a group of Norman and English pilgrims being seen in the vicinity. And if it is true that these pilgrims spent money on a lavish scale it was unlikely that anyone would be deceived by their disguise. A German chronicler says that when Richard was captured he was found in a kitchen, roasting meat on a spit, hoping that by doing this servile work he would escape recognition. Unfortunately the kitchen hand was wearing a magnificent ring, worth many years' wages. The details of this story are probably false but in common with the accounts in other chronicles it suggests that the travellers – despite their elaborate pilgrim's attire, long hair and flowing beards – did not take enough trouble to conceal their wealth. Meinhard of Görz captured eight of Richard's knights. At Friesach, in Carinthia, six more of his household were arrested while Richard himself, riding through the night with just three companions, managed to escape. Although the roads were now watched, they struggled on for three more days along the valleys of the Mur and Mürz. In an effort to avoid their earlier mistakes they no longer stopped to buy food, but eventually, near Vienna, hunger caught up with them. So, shortly before Christmas 1192, less than fifty miles from the safety of the Moravian border, Richard fell into the hands of Leopold of Austria. After this time no one in England had a kind word for the Austrians: 'they are savages who live more like wild beasts than men,' wrote Ralph of Diss.

Leopold sent Richard to a strong castle built high on a rocky slope overlooking the Danube: the castle of Dürnstein. The castle is in ruins today, but a legend still clings to its broken walls, the legend of Blondel, the faithful minstrel who travelled the length and breadth of Germany in search of his missing lord. He visited castle after castle and outside each one sang the first lines of a song which he and Richard had composed together. At last, at Dürnstein, he heard the refrain. In its earliest known form, the legend was told by a Rheims minstrel in the second half of the thirteenth century. There is not a shred of evidence to indicate that there is any truth in the story – but it was good publicity for minstrels. There was, in fact, very little mystery about Richard's captivity. Both Leopold of Austria and his lord, the Emperor Henry VI, were keen to take full advantage of their victim and this was best done by trumpeting and proving to the world that they held the King of England prisoner. By 28 December Leopold had informed the Emperor. He at once summoned the Duke to bring Richard to his court at Regensburg. The bargaining was about to begin.

To Henry VI the news came as a godsend. He was in deep political trouble. His Sicilian plans had, so far, proved to be both expensive and disastrous. Within Germany itself almost every move he made provoked fresh opposition. Germany was a kingdom ruled by princes. Although the Hohenstaufen King was by far the greatest of the princes, for him to try to impose his own will in every corner of his vast kingdom was to invite rebellion. But making concessions and compromises did not come easily to Henry VI. He was inclined to insist upon his rights as king, come what might. In 1191 the election of a new Bishop of Liège had led to quarrels between two local princes: the Duke of Brabant and the Count of Hainault. In this north-western part of his kingdom the Emperor had little real power and yet Henry's response to the dispute was to try to impose a third candidate of his own. In November 1192, one of the rival candidates, Albert of Brabant, was murdered by a group of knights who were widely believed to have been carrying out Henry VI's orders. The result of the storm of protest which followed was that the Emperor found himself faced with two major theatres of rebellion: the Welfs and their allies in the north and east; the princes of the Lower Rhineland, led by two formidable churchmen, the Archbishops of Cologne and Mainz, in the north-west. With something like half the princes of Germany in open revolt there was a very real threat that Henry would be deposed. It was at this critical juncture that fortune delivered Richard into his hands.

For more than a year kings and princes haggled over Richard's body, the body of a man who was a crusader and supposedly, therefore, under the protection of the church. But in the eyes of politicians the most valuable piece on the chessboard of Europe had come on to the market and the bidding for him was correspondingly fierce. Events in the Byzantine Empire as well as in England, France and Germany depended upon the outcome of the auction. The first deal to be negotiated was the sale of Richard to Henry VI – a complicated matter since both Emperor and Duke were pursuing designs of their own and neither trusted the other an inch. On 6 January 1193 Leopold of Austria and Meinhard of Görz arrived at Regensburg, bringing their prisoners with them. The first meeting between Henry VI and Richard I, the two rulers who dominated Europe in the 1190s, was a brief one. Fearing that the Emperor intended to kidnap Richard, Leopold sent him back to Austria for safe-keeping. It then took six weeks of bargaining before Henry VI and Leopold finally agreed terms on 14 February. Out of the total of 100,000 marks which was, in effect, the reserve price placed on Richard's head, it was agreed that the Duke should have 75,000 marks. 50,000 marks of this was disguised as a dowry for Eleanor of Brittany, Richard's niece, who was to marry one of Leopold's sons at Michaelmas. In addition Richard was to release, without ransom, the prisoners he had taken in Cyprus, Isaac Comnenus and his daughter. On his mother's side Leopold was related to the Comneni and by insisting that the wrong done to them be righted he could cover a good piece of business with the veneer of a good deed. (Isaac was, in fact, released. No sooner was he out of prison than he made a bid to seize the throne of Constantinople. But sudden death – he may have been poisoned – put an end to his hopes of a new empire.) Leopold and Henry VI also agreed that Richard in person should come with fifty galleys and two hundred knights to assist the German King on his next invasion of Sicily. On these conditions Leopold was willing to hand Richard over to the Emperor, but in exchange he demanded two hundred hostages from Henry VI as a guarantee that he would keep his side of the bargain. All this had been a matter for Henry and Leopold to settle; Richard himself had no say in any of it.

By this time, of course, all Christendom knew what had happened. The Pope excommunicated Leopold – and one of the terms of the treaty of 14 February laid down that Richard should obtain his captor's absolution! Philip of France had been told the news by Henry VI himself: 'Inasmuch as he is now in our power and has always done his utmost to annoy and disturb you, we have thought it right to notify Your Highness, for we know that these tidings will bring you most abundant joy.' Philip wrote at once to Leopold begging him not to release Richard without consulting him and then passed the information on to the man he believed could make the best use of it. By mid-January 1193 Count John was already on his way to France. At Paris he did homage to Philip for Normandy and all of Richard's other lands including – or so it was said in England – England. He promised to marry Alice and to hand over Gisors and the Norman Vexin to Philip. He then returned to England to stir up rebellion. He asked for help from William, King of the Scots, but William would have nothing to do with such treacherous schemes. In 1189, in return for 10,000 marks, Richard had released William from the humiliating terms which Henry II had imposed on the King of the Scots while he held him prisoner in 1174; William had no intention of turning against Richard now that he was a prisoner. John also sought help from Philip's father-in-law, Baldwin, Duke of Hainault and, since the death of Count Philip at Acre, Count of Flanders. Here, at least, he found willing allies. A fleet was assembled at Wissant, ready to invade England in the spring. But Eleanor and the justiciars mustered levies to defend the southeast coast and, apart from a few rash troops who were promptly captured, the invasion never materialized. The best that John could do was to levy some Welsh and Flemish mercenaries and use them to garrison the castles of Windsor and Wallingford. He then claimed to be King, asserting that his brother Richard was dead. A few believed him, but Eleanor, the justiciars and the barons did not. They knew John and they knew that Richard was alive; indeed they knew that the Bishop of Bath, Savaric de Bohun, probably on his way back from Rome, had seen the Emperor – to whom he was distantly related – and had opened the question of Richard's release in January, while Henry was still negotiating with Leopold.

A copy of Henry VI's letter to Philip had come into the hands of Walter of Coutances. He summoned the great council of the realm to a meeting at Oxford on 28 February 1193. The council sent two Cistercian abbots to Germany to seek further information. On 19 March they found Richard at Ochsenfurt, a small town on the river Main not far from Würzburg. Duke Leopold was taking him to Speyer to hand him over to the Emperor. Richard greeted the two abbots warmly. They were the first visitors able to give him reliable information on recent events in England and Normandy, so he questioned them closely. Although he grieved over his brother's treachery, a poor return for the estates and titles which he had showered upon him, he consoled himself with the thought that John was not the man to take a country if there was anyone to resist him. The abbots accompanied Richard on the last three days of his journey to Speyer. According to Howden, during this difficult time the King's conduct won the admiration of all who met him: courteous, dignified even in captivity, self-possessed and able to rise above the vicissitudes of fortune, a man born to command. At the imperial court at Speyer Richard had to undergo the ordeal of being, in effect, put on trial. He was accused of betraying the Holy Land (presumably by making peace with Saladin), of plotting the death of Conrad of Montferrat (one of Henry VI's most loyal supporters was Conrad's brother, Boniface of Montferrat) and of breaking agreements he had made with the Emperor. Roger of Howden does not specify what these agreements were, but Henry VI was presumably referring to Richard's alliance with Tancred of Sicily and his support for Henry the Lion. To these charges, however, the King replied so forcefully and persuasively that he won the court round to his side. Envoys from Philip Augustus were present and, in their master's name, they formally defied Richard, that is they declared that all ties of friendship and mutual aid between the King of France and his vassal were now at an end. But Philip's envoys took back to Paris with them the memory of Richard's bearing and it is clear that even William the Breton, Philip's court poet, was impressed. 'When Richard replied he spoke so eloquently and regally, in so lionhearted a manner, that it was as though he had forgotten where he was and the undignified circumstances in which he had been captured and imagined himself to be seated on the throne of his ancestors at Lincoln or at Caen.' Sensing the mood of the meeting Henry VI dropped his accusations and instead praised Richard, giving him the kiss of peace and promising to bring about a reconciliation between him and King Philip. This scene moved the onlookers to weep with joy. Richard had, for the moment, succeeded in dispelling the threat of a Capetian-Hohenstaufen alliance against him. But kiss or no kiss, he still had to pay the Emperor for his freedom. On 25 March he agreed to pay 100,000 marks and supply Henry with the services of fifty galleys and two hundred knights for a year. There is evidence to show that Hubert Walter, Bishop of Salisbury, was at Speyer on 30 March and almost certainly he had also been there during the crucial discussions of 21-25 March. There is no doubt that by this time Richard had recognized in Hubert his most capable and trustworthy political adviser and minister. In the autumn of 1190 Hubert had gone to Acre in the company of Baldwin of Canterbury. After the Archbishop's death on 19 November 1190 he took charge of the English contingent at the siege until the arrival of Richard himself. From then on he had been one of the King's inseparable companions in Outremer and won a great reputation – among the Muslims as well as with the Franks – as a soldier, diplomat and administrator. He had probably been one of those whom Richard left behind in the *Franche-Nef* when he began his bid to return home in disguise. At any rate he was still in the Kingdom of Sicily when he heard the news of Richard's capture. He at once went to Rome, presumably to make sure that Celestine III excommunicated Leopold of Austria and did everything possible to obtain the King's release, and then hurried on to Germany. It had been, said Richard in a letter written to his mother on 30 March 1193, 'an exhausting and dangerous journey'. The King showed his gratitude and good judgement by asking Eleanor to see that Hubert was elected to the archbishopric of Canterbury, which had remained vacant ever since Baldwin's death. Hubert and the two abbots then took their leave and headed for England.

It seems likely that Richard expected a speedy release as soon as he had supplied the hostages which the Emperor required. But Henry VI had no intention of letting this trump card slip out of his hand as quickly as that. Despite the theatrical gesture he had made at the Easter court at Speyer he saw no reason why he should not listen to further approaches from Philip and play one king off against the other. He sent Richard, under close guard, to the castle of Trifels, in the mountains west of Speyer. This was to remove him from the German political arena where, as the proceedings at Speyer had shown, he had many sympathizers and, in effect, to place him in solitary confinement. It was not at all to Richard's liking – though it was reported in England that he kept his spirits up by playing practical jokes on his guards and making them drunk. He was rescued from Trifels by the diplomacy of another old friend, William Longchamp, who despite being driven out of England had forfeited neither Richard's trust nor his office as chancellor. Longchamp persuaded Henry VI to allow Richard to return to the imperial court, which by now had moved on to the palace at Hagenau, and he also negotiated a date for the King's release: as soon as 70,000 marks had been paid and hostages for the rest handed over. This had been arranged by 19 April 1193, at which date Longchamp was sent back to England with letters from both Richard and Henry VI exhorting the prisoner's subjects to find the money as quickly as possible. Richard – or Longchamp – suggested various ways of raising money and added that he would like to know how much each noble contributed 'so that we may know how far we are bound to return thanks to each'. As soon as Eleanor and the justiciars in England received this letter they issued orders levying a twenty-five per cent tax on income and on the value of moveable property, and appropriating the year's wool crop from the Cistercian monasteries as well as gold and silver plate from churches throughout the country. Similar letters were sent to the other parts of Richard's dominions and similar measures taken – though possibly not with that high degree of bureaucratic thoroughness which characterized English government.

Inevitably, while all this was going on, Philip and John had not been idle. War had broken out in three different parts of the Angevin Empire. In England John was able to benefit from the continuing uncertainty about Richard's future but even so he gained very little ground. The justiciars repaired and garrisoned the royal castles, raised armies and succeeded in driving John's forces back into the castles of Windsor and Tickhill, where they were besieged. They were believed to be on the point of capitulation when Hubert Walter arrived from Germany – he landed on 20 April – and suggested that a six months' truce be made. If a great deal of money was to be raised quickly – and John's estates in England and Normandy were to contribute to this – then domestic peace was essential. The justiciars, naturally hesitant about taking extreme measures against

a man who might soon be king, agreed at once. By the terms of
the truce John was allowed to retain the castles at Nottingham and
Tickhill but had to hand over Windsor, Wallingford and the Peak
to his mother for the duration of the truce. In Aquitaine Ademar
of Angoulême, claiming to hold his county as a fief of France – i.e.
not subject to the Duke of Aquitaine – began to raid the Duke's
estates in Poitou. But here too Richard's officials stood firm.
Ademar's troops were beaten back and he was captured. In the third
theatre of war, however, there was a different story to tell. Here
Philip himself took charge of operations and he succeeded in
delivering a shattering blow to the defences of Normandy. On 12
April the great frontier castle of Gisors and its near neighbour
Neaufles were surrendered to the King of France.

The decisive weakness here was political, not military. Henry II
and Richard had spent huge sums on the fortifications of Gisors
and the other castles of the Norman Vexin, but Philip did not have
to try his strength against this massive bulwark. Gisors was not
blockaded or battered into submission. Its castellan, Gilbert de
Vascœuil, yielded without a blow being struck. English and Norman
writers were unanimous in condemning him as a traitor. Unquestionably he did betray his lord's trust, but equally clearly he was
in a very awkward position and must have found it hard to weigh
present against future loyalties. Gilbert had been in Sicily during
the winter of 1190–1 and he was well aware that neither Henry VI
nor Philip Augustus had any cause to love Richard. If Richard were
not released, what would happen to Gisors? There could be no
doubt that on the day that John, with Philip's help, became Duke
of Normandy, Gisors would become a Capetian possession. No one
else in the whole Angevin Empire was as exposed as the castellan
of Gisors. Many other frontier lords succumbed to the pressure
which Philip exerted in the spring of 1193: the lords of Aumâle
and Eu, Hugh of Gournay, William of Caïeux, Count Robert of
Meulan and Count Geoffrey of Perche. At least three of these men
had been on crusade with Richard: William of Caïeux, Hugh of
Gournay and Geoffrey of Perche; to one of them, indeed, Count
Geoffrey, Richard had given a niece in marriage. Yet these associations did not prevent them from making their castles available

to Philip's troops. Their problem was that as marcher lords they
held estates on both sides of the border and could rarely afford to
be unambiguously loyal to one lord only. They were always walking
a political tightrope between the King of France on the one hand
and the Duke of Normandy on the other. It had been these same
lords who had joined the revolt of 1173–4 against Henry. If they
did not leap on to the bandwagon in time they were always likely
to be run down. Following Philip's acquisition of Artois after the
death of Philip of Flanders the lords of north-eastern Normandy
were in a particularly vulnerable position. It was hardly surprising
that some of them won an unenviable reputation as turncoats in
those difficult times when Richard was in prison or John was on
the throne. But morally and militarily there were differences as well
as similarities between their case and that of Gilbert de Vascœuil.
They could claim that they had a duty to protect their ancestral
estates whereas Gilbert had no lands around Gisors and Neaufles;
he was there purely as Richard's castellan, his only duty was to his
lord. In military terms, moreover, the fall of Gisors and the other
castles of the Vexin might have been crushing, for it opened the
road to the heart of Normandy, to Rouen itself.

Without hesitation Philip advanced to lay siege to the ducal capital. He had with him a large army, including a Flemish contingent
under Count Baldwin, and – according to Roger of Howden's information – no less than twenty-three siege-machines. At first there
was confusion and uncertainty in Rouen, but the arrival of another
of Richard's crusading companions, Robert, Earl of Leicester, stiffened the resolve of the defenders. When Philip called upon the
city to surrender he was told that the gates were open and he could
enter any time he liked. The King of France was not the man to
walk into an obvious trap. He settled down to a siege but seems
to have been disconcerted by this obvious display of confidence on
the part of the defenders. After only a fortnight he set fire to his
siege-machines and moved off in search of easier game. Verneuil
held out against him but he soon captured two more border castles,
Pacy and Ivry – and since Pacy belonged to Robert of Leicester
its fall was particularly satisfying. Despite the setback before the
walls of Rouen, April and May 1193 were good months for Philip.

From now on the castle of Gisors was to be a thorn in Richard's flesh. In a very real sense the events of these months were to cast a shadow over the rest of Richard's reign.

The defences of Normandy were strong but its outer walls had been undermined by the possibility that Richard would never be freed. Normans may well have remembered another twelfth-century Duke of Normandy, Robert, captured by Henry I in 1106, and still in prison when he died nearly thirty years later. Both John and, to greater effect, Philip played upon this theme for all they were worth. Philip, of course, did his best to turn possibility into reality. He arranged to meet Henry VI at a conference on 25 June. Ostensibly Henry was going in order to reconcile the two Kings, but Richard was convinced that if this meeting took place he would soon find himself in a French prison from which there would be no escape. Philip could offer the Emperor either cash or political help, or a combination of the two. With Philip's assistance, for example, Henry VI might be able to attack the rebels of the Lower Rhineland from two sides at once. At all costs Richard had to prevent this alliance. The prisoner became diplomat. Throughout the early summer of 1193 he was busy and eventually he succeeded in reconciling Henry with some of the rebels. Owing to their vital commercial links with England and Normandy the princes of the Lower Rhineland were inclined to listen carefully to what Richard said, while Henry was prepared to make peace if the settlement included the money he needed to finance his Sicilian campaign. The June meeting between Philip and the Emperor did not take place. Instead Henry VI swore that he was innocent of complicity in the murder of Albert of Brabant and allowed a new episcopal election to take place at Liège. With Richard as mediator, he came to terms with the Rhineland rebels and with Hermann of Thuringia and Albert of Meissen. As part of this same political process the terms of the King's ransom were re-negotiated and finally settled at Worms on 29 June. Richard would be freed when the Emperor had received 100,000 marks and hostages for an additional payment of 50,000 marks, which would have to be made within seven months of Richard's release. Within the same period Eleanor of Brittany would have to be sent to Austria to marry Duke Leopold's son. The additional sum of 50,000 could, however, be remitted if Richard succeeded in persuading the most important rebel, Henry the Lion, to make peace with the Emperor. In other words, Richard had managed to thwart Philip's plans but only at considerable financial cost to his own subjects.

When Philip heard of this latest treaty between Henry and Richard he sent John a message: 'Look to yourself; the devil is loose.' Acting on this belief the King of France made peace with Richard's agents in Normandy in order to consolidate the gains he had already made. The first clause of the treaty made at Mantes on 9 July 1193 simply stated that Philip could keep all the lands he had taken. After his release, Richard was to pay Philip 20,000 marks. As security for this payment four key Angevin castles were handed over; Loches, Châtillon-sur-Indre, Drincourt and Arques. The Count of Angoulême was to be freed and neither he nor his vassals were to be in any way penalized for their war against the Duke of Aquitaine. From Richard's point of view these were harsh terms but probably he knew better than Philip did that it would be many months yet before he was free. In these circumstances it was worth agreeing to almost anything so long as a halt was called to Philip's advance. But the campaign in Normandy was only one aspect of Philip's war against Richard. On the diplomatic front the struggle continued. Philip still harboured hopes of launching an invasion of England and to this end had entered into negotiations for a marriage alliance with Denmark. On 15 August 1193 he married Ingeborg, the daughter of King Cnut VI. As a successor of the famous Cnut, the eleventh-century conqueror and King of England, Cnut VI possessed both a tenuous claim to the throne of England and a fleet. Philip was interested in both of these assets but, unfortunately for Ingeborg, he had lost interest by the morning after the consummation of the marriage. He repudiated his new wife and tried to return her to the custody of the Danish envoys who had escorted her to France, but they refused to take her back and departed in haste, leaving Ingeborg to her fate. For years Philip was to endure the condemnation of the church rather than have Ingeborg as his queen. His dream of a new Danish invasion of England had became a domestic nightmare.

In his pursuit of Richard, however, Philip was not a man to be put off by minor disappointments. It did not take long to have his marriage dissolved on grounds of consanguinity by some pliant Capetian bishops – among them, of course, his cousin the Bishop of Beauvais, who had performed a similar service on behalf of Conrad of Montferrat during the siege of Acre. The Pope disapproved, but Philip felt himself free to look around for a new wife. Hoping to create some kind of counterweight to Richard's influence among the princes of Germany he proposed himself as a husband for Agnes, heiress of Henry VI's uncle, Conrad of Hohenstaufen, Count Palatine of the Rhine. But here too Philip was disappointed. Agnes's mother, believing that the King of France's record as a husband left something to be desired, connived at her secret marriage to Henry of Brunswick, Henry the Lion's son and Richard's nephew. Since this marriage was a step in the direction of a reconciliation between the Welf and Hohenstaufen families it also brought Richard a little nearer to freedom. But the people who contributed most to the King's release were his subjects the tax-payers in England, Normandy, Anjou and Aquitaine. By Christmas 1193 Henry VI had received so much of the ransom money that he fixed 17 January 1194 as the day of Richard's release. The Emperor also announced that he planned to make Richard King of Provence and had set 24 January as coronation day. This plan, if it had been carried out, would have made Richard ruler of a kingdom stretching from the Alps to the River Rhône, and including the port of Marseilles. Although this territory was in theory a part of the empire, in practice Henry VI did not have the power to impose a king over the heads of the local magnates. Richard would have been king in title only. Yet since one of his vassals in this new 'kingdom' would have been the Marquis of Provence, known – under another hat – as Count Raymond V of Toulouse, even this would have given Richard a legal lever which might have come in useful in his relations with this neighbour whose county he claimed. So far as Henry VI was concerned it would certainly have added to the dignity of his empire and might conceivably have been a diplomatic asset if the King of England, in his role as King of Provence, had owed him homage.

But in mid-January 1194 all of these schemes were shelved when

Philip and John put in a new bid for Richard. By pooling their resources they decided that they could afford 150,000 marks for possession of the prisoner; alternatively they offered Henry either 100,000 marks if he would detain Richard until the autumn (i.e. until after the end of the next campaigning season), or £1,000 a month for as long as he cared to keep him captive. Henry was tempted. He postponed the date of Richard's release and summoned another meeting of the princes of the empire to Mainz on 2 February. Once again, however, Richard's contracts with the German princes, particularly those of the Lower Rhineland, paid handsome dividends. They compelled the Emperor to stand by the agreements he had made. And so, on 4 February, on completing the payment of 100,000 marks and giving hostages – including two sons of Henry the Lion and a son of the King of Navarre – for the 50,000 marks still outstanding, Richard was freed. Henry VI did succeed, though, in persuading Richard to become his vassal. On his mother's advice, Richard resigned the Kingdom of England to Henry VI in order to receive it back as a fief of the empire. He was to pay his overlord £5000 a year. Richard was now a vassal of Philip for his continental lands and a vassal of Henry VI for his island kingdom. But it was worth it. At long last he was a free man.

According to Howden's calculations he had been in prison for one year, six weeks and three days. There had been times when he had almost given up hope, and the better known of Richard's two surviving songs dates from one such period – probably the early summer of 1193, when he knew of the plan for a conference between Philip and Henry and while the desertion of some of those barons who had been on crusade with him was still fresh in his mind.

> Feeble the words, and faltering the tongue
> Wherewith a prisoner moans his doleful plight;
> Yet for his comfort he may make a song.
> Friends have I many, but their gifts are slight;
> Shame to them if unransomed I, poor wight,
> Two winters languish here!
>
> English and Normans, men of Aquitaine,
> Well know they all who homage owe to me

That not my lowliest comrade in campaign
Should pine thus, had I gold to set him free;
To none of them would I reproachful be –
Yet – I am prisoner here!

This have I learned, here thus unransomed left,
That he whom death or prison hides from sight,
Of kinsmen and of friends is clean bereft;
Woe's me! but greater woe on these will light,
Yea, sad and full of shame will be their plight
If long I languish here.

No marvel is it that my heart is sore
While my lord tramples down my land, I trow;
Were he but mindful of the oath we swore
Each to the other, surely do I know
That thus in duress I should long ago
Have ceased to languish here.

My comrades whom I loved and still do love –
The lords of Perche and of Caïeux –
Strange tales have reached me that are hard to prove;
I ne'er was false to them; for evermore
Vile would men count them, if their arms they bore
'Gainst me, a prisoner here!

And they, my knights of Anjou and Touraine –
Well know they, who now sit at home at ease,
That I, their lord, in far-off Allemaine
Am captive. They should help to my release;
But now their swords are sheathed, and rust in peace,
While I am prisoner here.

Richard was set free at Mainz, still a long way from his threatened
lands. His enemies, realizing that their last opportunity had come,
launched a new attack. Philip set his armies in motion in order to
take possession of the territories which John had surrendered to
him in a treaty made in January 1194. These included the whole of
Normandy east of the Seine except for the city of Rouen and its en-
virons; John also conceded Vaudreuil and the lands east of the

River Itun. Further west he granted Moulins and Bonsmoulins to the Count of Perche, whose ancestors had held these castles until 1168. Vendôme was granted to Louis of Blois. He recognized the validity of Count Ademar's claim that Angoulême was independent of the duchy of Aquitaine. Perhaps most serious of all, he surrendered the key fortresses of the Touraine: Tours, Azay-le-Rideau, Amboise, Montbason, Montrichard, Loches and Châtillon-sur-Indre. John was clearly a desperate man. In order to oust Richard he was prepared to undo all his father's and his brother's work and be content with an Angevin Empire which was not only much truncated but also critically weakened by the loss of vitally important frontier regions. As yet, of course, John's grants existed only on paper. It was up to the beneficiaries to turn them into reality. Philip began in Normandy. In February he captured Evreux, Neubourg and Vaudreuil, thus gaining control of both banks of the Seine to within easy striking distance of Rouen. He may have threatened the ducal city for a second time before withdrawing to Paris, and then going south to Sens, where he received the homage of two more of Richard's Aquitainian vassals, Geoffrey de Rancon and Bernard, Viscount of Brosse.

While these further inroads were being made into his dominions Richard was on his way back to England. His progress was leisurely but during the weeks of his journey down the Rhine he was knitting together a system of alliances which was to be a prominent feature of the European political scene for the next twenty years. In return for pensions from his seemingly inexhaustible treasure chest he received the homage of the Archbishops of Mainz and Cologne, the Bishop of Liège, the Duke of Brabant, the Count of Holland and several other lords from the Lower Rhineland. Since he obtained no direct military aid from these alliances they have sometimes been judged to be expensive luxuries, but they were to become part of a coalition which was to hem in Philip Augustus and deprive him of his own most valuable ally, the Count of Flanders. Finally, on 13 March, Richard landed at Sandwich. At the shrines of Canterbury and Bury St Edmunds he gave thanks for his safe return.

The long captivity in Germany had cost him and his subjects dearly. On the other hand, the provisions he had made for defending and governing his dominions during his absence on crusade had worked well. For more than two and a half years, from July 1190 to March 1193, the Angevin institutions of government functioned remarkably well, in Aquitaine, in Anjou, in Normandy and – despite the bit of trouble between John and Longchamp – in England. Some of the credit for this must go to the seneschals, bailiffs and provosts, the justiciars and sheriffs who were left in charge of affairs while Richard was away, and some also to the King who had chosen and appointed them. While Richard was on crusade, even though there were some observers who feared that he might not return, it was possible – and simplest – to go on behaving as though he would. But his imprisonment provoked a totally unforeseeable crisis. The exploitation of this crisis by his most ruthless enemy, Philip of France, twisting John's ineffectual and treacherous ambition to his own purposes, forced men to face up to the possibility that Richard might never return. With Philip on the move they could no longer just wait and see; they were compelled to weigh up the probabilities, consider their loyalties and choose sides. Since the leader of one side was in prison while the other rode with his knights it is hardly surprising that many of those who lived in exposed frontier positions chose as they did. Compared with the loss of support which King Stephen suffered in Normandy while he was in captivity – from February to November 1141 – Richard's continental possessions survived quite well. None the less Philip had encouraged some of the more restless lords of Aquitaine to rise in revolt and he had himself made strategically important gains in the Loire and Seine valleys. On his return Richard was faced with a daunting task – and one which would inevitably involve heavy expenditure on war, to add still further to the already unprecedented financial burdens placed upon his subjects. 100,000 marks was a vast sum, a king's ransom, perhaps twice his total annual income from England. Most of it had clearly gone into the coffers of Henry VI. In 1193 and 1194 there seemed no end to the Emperor's good fortune. On 20 February 1194 King Tancred of Sicily died, and the heir to the throne was a small child. In May Henry marched across the Alps, his war chest full of Angevin silver. On 22 November 1194 he was crowned King at Palermo.

Of Richard's enemies there were two who had little cause to celebrate. The first of these was John. Once Richard had been released
it was evident that John's gamble had failed miserably. His castles
in England were besieged and were certain to fall. It was said that
the castellan of St Michael's Mount in Cornwall died of fright when
he heard the news that Richard had landed. In Normandy Philip
had granted him custody of Arques, Drincourt and Evreux but even
if he managed to hold them against his brother they could in no
way compensate him for the loss of the estates which Richard had
given him in 1189. The best John could do was to throw himself on
his brother's mercy. He had achieved nothing except to cause some
damage to the empire which he still had a chance of inheriting and
to give the world further evidence of his ineptitude and treachery.

The second was Richard's captor, Leopold of Austria. For daring
to imprison a crusader he was excommunicated and ordered to pay
back the ransom money. He refused. He had, in any case, received
very little of it. His chief hope lay in the dowry which Eleanor of
Brittany was to bring with her when she married his son. But seven
months passed from the day of Richard's release and there was still
no sign of the promised bride. He threatened to execute his hostages
unless Richard sent his niece to Austria, and one of the hostages,
Baldwin of Béthune, was given the task of carrying this news
to the King. The threat worked. In December 1194 Baldwin of
Béthune set off again for Austria, escorting both Eleanor and the
daughter of Isaac Comnenus. But on 26 December, while Leopold
was out riding, his horse fell and crushed his foot. By the next day
the foot had gone black. The surgeons advised amputation but Leopold could find no one who had either the strength of mind or the
heart to perform the painful operation. Despite the Duke's pleadings
not even his son and heir could steel himself to the task. Eventually
Leopold himself had to hold an axe close to the bone of his leg and
order a servant to drive the axe through with a mallet. After three
blows the gangrenous foot was removed. But it was too late. On
the last day of the year Leopold died, after having made his peace
with the church and promised to make full restitution to Richard.
The hostages returned home. In the eyes of the Angevins, God's
justice had been done.

12

RECOVERY
1194-1199

THERE was no need for Richard to stay long in England. Most of the castles held in John's name had already capitulated. The only two still holding out against the siege operations mounted in mid-February by Hubert Walter, now Archbishop of Canterbury and chief justiciar, were Tickhill and Nottingham. The garrison of Tickhill sent two knights to see if Richard was indeed in the country and when they confirmed the truth of the stories, the castle was surrendered. The garrison of Nottingham was made of sterner stuff. Richard arrived there on 25 March 1194 to the accompaniment of 'a great blowing of horns and trumpets'. But the defenders were convinced that the fanfare was just a trick and fought on. Some men who were standing close to Richard were hit by archery fire from the battlements, so the King gave the order for an immediate assault on the castle. Richard himself took part in the attack, wearing only a light coat of mail and an iron headpiece but protected by large, strong shields which were carried in front of him. They took the outer bailey and then the barbican. The coming of darkness put an end to the fighting. During the night the garrison burned down the castle's outer works, calculating that since they could no longer hold them it was better to deprive the besiegers of as much cover as possible. Next day Richard pressed the attack by other means. He brought up his siege-artillery and had gallows erected in full view of the garrison. Some of the soldiers captured on the previous day were hanged. The message was clear. If they continued to hold out they would all suffer the same fate. On 27 March two of the defenders were given safe-conduct to visit the camp of the besiegers.

'Well,' said Richard, 'what can you see? Am I here?' When the
two knights reported back, fourteen members of the garrison left
the castle at once and all the rest surrendered on the next day. Their
lives were spared, but they had to pay stiff ransoms. Richard wanted
to free the hostages now in Germany and raise an army to recover
his lost lands; every penny would count.

After an enjoyable day's hunting in Sherwood Forest – the nearest
he ever came to the purely legendary figure of Robin Hood –
Richard returned to Nottingham and to an important council meeting. There was a great deal of business to be done: legal proceedings
to be taken against John and his partisans; and, above all, ways of
raising men and money to be devised. Men who may have thought
they had bought their offices in 1189 were informed that, in reality,
they had only leased them for a term of years, and that the term
was now expired. If they wished to remain in such lucrative positions they would have to make new financial arrangements. Danegeld was revived in the form of a new land tax, called a carucage,
but, as in 1189, the greatest yield came from innumerable deals
made with individuals seeking office or favour or with communities
like the Jews or the citizens of Lincoln, who wanted protection or
privilege. Richard was anxious to go to Normandy and it was rather
against his will that he was persuaded of the need for some kind
of public demonstration of the fact that not only had the King
returned to his kingdom but he had returned with his full
sovereignty unimpaired either by the long imprisonment or by the
homage done to the Emperor. So on 17 April, in full regalia and
wearing a crown, he walked in procession in Winchester cathedral,
accompanied by his mother, Queen Eleanor, and by most of the
prelates and barons of England. (This was not a coronation, but a
crown-wearing. Although it was similar to that undergone by King
Stephen after his release from captivity in 1141, it was also a rather
more unusual event than that had been, since until the 1150s kings
had been accustomed to wearing their crown two or three times a
year.)

The crown-wearing took place on the Sunday after Easter. For
Richard the coming of spring meant the coming of the campaigning
season. His thoughts would have echoed the words of Bertrand de

Born, the writer of war songs, who believed that the poetry was in the pleasure:

I love the gay Eastertide, which brings forth leaves and flowers; and I love the joyous song of the birds, re-echoing through the copse. But I also love to see, amidst the meadows, tents and pavilions spread; it gives me great joy to see, drawn up on the field, knights and horses in battle array.

And it delights me when the skirmishers scatter people and herds in their path; and I love to see them followed by a great body of men-at-arms; and my heart is filled with gladness when I see strong castles besieged, and the stockades broken and overrun, and the defenders on the mound enclosed by ditches all round and protected by strong palisades.

And I like to see the lord who is foremost in the attack, mounted, armed and fearless, for thus he inspires his men to serve him boldly. And then when battle's joined everyone will follow him with a good courage, for no man wins respect until he has given and taken many a blow.

Maces and swords, helms of different hues, shields that will be riven and shattered as soon as the fight begins; many vassals clashing together until the steeds of the dead and wounded run aimlessly about the field. And once he has entered the fray let each man of high birth think of nothing but the breaking of heads and arms; for it is better to die than to be vanquished and live.

I tell you, I find no such pleasure in food, or wine, or sleep as in hearing the shout of 'At them!' on both sides, and the neigh of horses that have lost their riders, and the cries of 'Help! Help!'; in seeing men great and small go down on the grass by the ditches; and in seeing the dead, with the pennoned stumps of lances in their ribs.

> Take this song to my Lord Yea and Nay
> And tell him that he delays too long in peace.

Richard, whom Bertrand called 'Yea and Nay' not because he was of a fickle, changeable disposition, but because his words were few and to the point, needed little encouragement. He waited impatiently while an army, including Welsh and Brabançon mercenaries, mustered at Portsmouth. On 2 May, he ordered men and horses to embark, and then – against the advice of his sailors – put out to sea in the teeth of a gale. But there was no way his fleet of one hundred big ships could cross the Channel in this weather and next day he put back into Portsmouth to wait until the storm had blown itself out. Not until 12 May was the sea calm enough. Then he left England, never to return. There was no need to. He had left his kingdom in the care of one of the most outstanding government ministers in English history, Hubert Walter. As a nephew of Henry II's justiciar Ranulf Glanville, Hubert gained his early administrative experience under the Old King, but it was on crusade with Richard that he had really come to the fore. In the first flush of enthusiasm after the fall of Jerusalem several bishops had taken crusader's vows, but only two of them, Baldwin of Canterbury and Hubert of Salisbury, had fulfilled them. When Hubert returned from the Holy Land he was a famous and much-respected man. There were plenty of influential candidates for the archbishopric, left vacant since Baldwin's death at Acre in November 1190, but Hubert was unquestionably the King's man and, as such, he was elected archbishop in May 1193. At Christmas he was appointed chief justiciar in succession to Walter of Coutances and eventually, in March 1195, he was also made papal legate.

This cluster of the great offices of church and state in the hands of one man, combined with the King's steady support for his minister, gave Hubert Walter an unassailable position. There were, of course, critics – whether disappointed and bitter men like Gerald of Wales or austere saints like Hugh of Lincoln, who, on his deathbed, asked for God's and Hubert Walter's forgiveness for sometimes failing to rebuke the Archbishop when rebuke was called for. Both critics in their different ways expressed the strict official line of the church: churchmen should not become involved in worldly affairs. Since the church was unwilling to renounce its worldly wealth and privileges a degree of involvement was unavoidable, but the sight of a clerk as deeply immersed in secular business, financial, judicial, even military, as Hubert Walter was, always made ecclesiastics uncomfortable, whether they attacked him for it – or whether they went out of their way to justify him, as Ralph of Diss did. It seems to have made the Archbishop himself uncomfortable too: in 1198 he resigned his justiciarship, and his place was taken by a layman. Yet despite this resignation he continued to work at Richard's side and under a new king took office again as chancellor. Without government business to occupy his mind he felt – or so

Gerald of Wales said – 'like a fish out of water'. From the King's point of view, however, it was a very comfortable arrangement. Since the sheer size of his dominions inevitably meant that for most of the time he was an absentee ruler it was convenient and reassuring to know that all important business, whether of church or state, went through one pair of trustworthy hands. This is what Henry II had hoped to achieve when he appointed his chancellor Thomas Becket as Archbishop of Canterbury; and what Richard had hoped from Longchamp. Becket was a disaster; Longchamp failed but might not have done in less unfavourable circumstances; Hubert Walter was a resounding success. No king had a better servant than him. He controlled the machinery of government in an age of administrative reform and expansion, in an age of experiment, when the government took over direct management of some of the country's most important economic resources – the tin mines, the ports – in an age which witnessed the emergence of an influential group of specialized and professional civil servants – in short, in a crucial period in the awful history of bureaucracy. The motive which lay behind this rapid development was war and the financial needs of a king who was waging a relentless war for the recovery of his lost inheritance. In 1196 Hubert calculated that he had sent Richard eleven hundred thousand marks in the last two years; this fantastic total is either a chronicler's error or a minister's pardonable exaggeration – the point remains that Hubert did everything the King required. Richard could safely leave England in his hands.

On landing at Barfleur the King received a tumultuous welcome. Everywhere he went he found himself in the midst of a jubilant crowd. Old and young joined in the dancing and singing: 'God has come again in His strength. It's time for the French King to go.' The French King, indeed, had launched a fresh attack on Normandy, planning again to take possession of lands which John had granted him in the treaty of January 1194. On 10 May Philip laid siege to the important castle of Verneuil. The garrison had already withstood one siege in 1193 and were confident of repeating that success. They mocked Philip by opening the gate and inviting him to enter; then by drawing a caricature of him on it for him to look at when it was shut. But presumably they owed much of their confidence

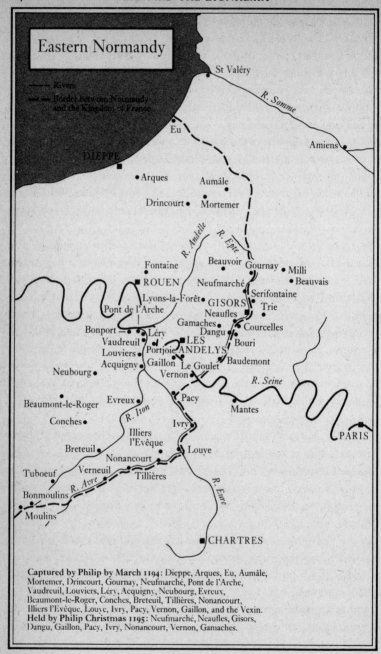

Eastern Normandy

— Rivers
— — Border between Normandy
and the Kingdom of France

St Valéry

R. Somme

Eu

Amiens

DIEPPE

• Arques   Aumâle

Drincourt •   • Mortemer

R. Andelle

R. Epte

Fontaine   • Beauvoir   Gournay   • Milli

■ ROUEN   Neufmarché   • Beauvais

Lyons-la-Forêt   GISORS   Serifontaine

Pont de l'Arche   Neaufles   • Trie

Bonport —   Gamaches •   • Courcelles
         • Léry   Dangu •
Vaudreuil   LES   • Bouri
Louviers   Portjoie ANDELYS
Acquigny   Gaillon Le Goulet   Baudemont

Neubourg •   Vernon •

                    R. Seine

Beaumont-le-Roger   Evreux •   • Pacy

Conches •   R. Iton   Mantes •

                    Ivry •

Illiers
l'Evêque

Breteuil •   Louye •   PARIS

Nonancourt •

Tuboeuf •   Verneuil
      R. Avre   Tillières

Bonmoulins •

R. Eure

Moulins •

■ CHARTRES

Captured by Philip by March 1194: Dieppe, Arques, Eu, Aumâle,
Mortemer, Drincourt, Gournay, Neufmarché, Pont de l'Arche,
Vaudreuil, Louviers, Léry, Acquigny, Neubourg, Evreux,
Beaumont-le-Roger, Conches, Breteuil, Tillières, Nonancourt,
Illiers l'Evêque, Louye, Ivry, Pacy, Vernon, Gaillon, and the Vexin.
Held by Philip Christmas 1195: Neufmarché, Neaufles, Gisors,
Dangu, Gaillon, Pacy, Ivry, Nonancourt, Vernon, Gamaches.

to the belief that Richard was already on the way to relieve them. In reality he was still at Portsmouth on 10 May, held up by storms in the Channel. As a result Philip had one last chance to gain more terrain before Richard's arrival. But one of Philip's allies did not wait to see the outcome of the siege before changing sides. John went to Lisieux, where Richard, worried about Verneuil, was spending a restless night in the house of John of Alençon. There John came to him and fell at his feet, begging forgiveness. It was given at once; generously, said Richard's admirers, but also casually and contemptuously. 'Don't be afraid, John, you are a child. You have got into bad company and it is those who have led you astray who will be punished.' It was some time before he received some of his estates back, and even then the castles were withheld from him, but the 'child' (now twenty-seven years old) had been treated better than he deserved – and, as John of Alençon told him to his face, very much better than he would have treated Richard. Whereas Richard's fault was over-confidence – he feared no one – his brother was ill at ease with anyone who possessed either power or intelligence, and he was afraid to trust them. Just then John had a scheme to show his brother that he could be of use to him. In February Philip had put him in charge of the town of Evreux. In May John returned there, killed the French in the town and took possession of it in Richard's name. It is no wonder that Capetian as well as Angevin writers looked upon him with distaste.

From Lisieux Richard hurried on to reach Tubœuf, some twenty kilometres west of Verneuil, on the morning of 21 May. Here he was met by a knight from the Verneuil garrison who had managed to ride through the French lines, presumably in search of aid. According to Rigord of St Denis, Philip's siege-machines had already brought down a section of the castle wall, so help was urgently needed. It seems clear that in his haste Richard had gone on well ahead of the large army he had brought across from England. Instead of advancing to challenge Philip to battle – a tactic which always alarmed the French King – he dispatched one force of knights, men-at-arms and crossbowmen to break through the French lines and reinforce the garrison (which they did) while ordering other troops to ride round to the east of Verneuil to cut Philip's supply lines. After being on the brink of success Philip's position began to deteriorate. On 28 May he received the news that John had now betrayed him as well and had seized Evreux. At once he rode off in the direction of Evreux and although he left sufficient forces at Verneuil to maintain the siege, they decided to withdraw next day, leaving their siege-artillery to be captured by Richard. Philip's sudden departure had been the last straw for his troops, already demoralized by the threat to their supplies and by the knowledge that Richard's main armies were now well on their way from Normandy and Anjou. After harassing the retreating French, Richard entered Verneuil on 30 May, in triumph and in joy. To show his appreciation of the garrison's courage and loyalty he kissed each man in turn and promised them rich rewards. The tide of war had turned.

Nevertheless Philip was far from being a beaten man. He drove John out of Evreux and sacked it. It was both an act of revenge for the killing of his troops there and an acknowledgement of the fact he could no longer hope to hold on to the town. He was, however, still in a position to threaten Rouen and he made this plain for all to see by crossing the Seine and attacking the castle of Fontaine, a bare four or five miles from the ducal capital. John and the Earl of Leicester were at Rouen but had nothing like enough strength to challenge the French royal army, which was able to press the siege uninterrupted. Even so it took Philip four days, from 10 to 14 June, to capture what was a very small castle. Having made his gesture he demolished Fontaine and withdrew. In order to hold back the tide before it gathered momentum he began to make overtures for a three years' truce.

Richard meanwhile had been hunting bigger game. By 14 June his forces had captured three castles, all of them more important than Fontaine and one of them, Loches, a major fortress. The massive army which had mustered at Verneuil had been divided in half. An Anglo-Norman contingent went north and took Beaumont-le-Roger, a castle belonging to Robert of Meulan, one of the marcher lords who had declared for Philip in 1193. The levies from Anjou and Maine stormed and demolished the castle of Montmirail on the Maine–Perche border. Richard may have been at Beaumont-le-

Roger but his chief concern now was for his lands futher south. His marriage alliance with Navarre was still paying dividends. Berengaria's brother Sancho had marched into Aquitaine with a large force, including 150 crossbowmen, and had been busy laying waste the lands of Ademar of Angouléme and Geoffrey de Rancon. Sancho was then called back to Navarre by the news that his father, King Sancho VI, was dying, but his army moved into Touraine to besiege Loches, where it had been arranged that Richard would join them.

Loches was one of those castles which had first of all been ceded to Philip in July 1193 as a security for the payment of 20,000 marks and then permanently surrendered by John in January 1194. The loss of this key fortress seems to have been associated with a general collapse of the Angevin position in Touraine since, when Richard reached Tours on 11 June, he confiscated the houses and goods of the canons of St Martin's and was offered 2000 marks by the townspeople – which suggests that they felt that they too had done something to incur his wrath. By the time of Richard's arrival at Loches on the next day the Navarrese troops had been there for a while without making any perceptible progress; probably they had not brought the equipment needed to crack a nut of this size and could do no more than blockade the castle. But on 13 June, in one fierce and prolonged assault, Richard took the castle by storm and captured a large garrison.

After reasserting his authority in Touraine, Richard's next task was to subdue the rebels in Aquitaine. He had given his chief officials in Normandy, the seneschal, the constable and the Archbishop of Rouen, authority to make a local truce for a year, but Philip wanted a general truce including all participants everywhere, so the talks broke down. The French King then marched south in an attempt to curtail Richard's freedom of movement in what had now become the main theatre of the war. It was not easy, however, for Philip to do this without giving his opponent the chance to bring him to battle, and this was precisely the opportunity which Richard was waiting for. Early in July he moved up to Vendôme (another town surrendered by John in January) and pitched camp there, barring the road which Philip would have to take if he wanted to make his presence felt in the Loire valley. As soon as Philip's scouts reported

that Richard's army lay just in front of them, the French King sent
word that he would attack in the morning and then promptly made
off in the opposite direction. Near Fréteval on 4 July Richard caught
up with the French rearguard and soon the whole of Philip's army
was in flight. Richard led a determined pursuit in the hope of catch-
ing Philip himself. According to Howden, when one horse tired,
Mercadier was at hand to provide Richard with another. Although
Philip managed to elude his pursuers, the French wagon train did
not. The rich booty included horses, tents, siege-engines and much
of Philip's treasure. In addition, by capturing the French King's
chapel, Richard had captured the royal archives, including documents with the names of those of his subjects who had been prepared
to join the enemy. Despite his eagerness to hunt down the man
whom he had learned to hate, Richard was still a cautious tactician.
One of his most experienced captains, William Marshal, had joined
neither the pursuit nor the plundering of the wagon train, but had,
on Richard's orders, held his troops together ready to deal with any
attempt by the French to rally and counter-attack. That evening,
as Richard's men celebrated, boasting of their great deeds, the
knights they had captured and the booty they had won, the King
praised William, and, by implication, praised himself: 'The marshal
did better than any of you. If there had been any trouble he would
have helped us. When one has a good reserve, one does not fear
one's enemies.' To lose his artillery was a humiliation for any commander and within the space of forty days Philip had retreated twice,
once at Verneuil where he lost his artillery and once at Fréteval
where he lost his whole wagon-train. Philip had been driven from
the field and Richard now had a free hand in Aquitaine.

From Vendôme Richard moved south. We know nothing about
the campaign except what Richard himself wrote in one brief letter
to Hubert Walter: 'Know that, by the grace of God, who in all things
upholds the right, we have captured Taillebourg and Marcillac and
the whole land of Geoffrey de Rancon; also the city of Angoulême,
Châteauneuf-sur-Charente, Montignac, Lachaise and all the other
castles and the whole land of the Count of Angoulême in its entirety;
we captured the city and citadel of Angoulême in a single evening;
in all we took full 300 knights and 40,000 soldiers.' Since this note

was sent from Angoulême on 22 July it looks as though Richard had had a busy fortnight. The old and formidable alliance of Geoffrey de Rancon and the Count of Angoulême had apparently been overwhelmed in a campaign of shattering power and decisiveness, thanks in part to the fact that the groundwork had already been laid by Sancho of Navarre. The capture of Angoulême was the culminating point of two months of remarkable military success; the relief of Verneuil, the taking of Loches, the pursuit at Fréteval and the capture of Taillebourg. As Ralph of Diss observed, 'from the castle of Verneuil to Charles's Cross [in the Pyrenees] there was no one to stand out against him.' Once again lack of evidence means that we know almost nothing about the administrative measures which were taken to secure this restoration of Richard's authority after the uncertainty of the last eighteen months. A few scattered clues, however, suggest that the relatively well-documented methods used in England were also employed south of Normandy. Moreover, the men whom Richard had learned to trust were those who had been on crusade with him and whose political and administrative competence had been tested in arduous and unfamiliar circumstances. Just as Hubert Walter came back from the crusade to be justiciar of England, so Robert of Thornham and Geoffrey de la Celle came back to be seneschals of Anjou and Aquitaine.

Normandy remained the problem and the exception to this rule. It was Normandy which had felt the weight of King Philip's main thrust in 1193 and 1194 and it was here that Richard continued to rely upon an old servant: William FitzRalph. As seneschal throughout the last twenty years of the twelfth century he is a figure of great importance in the history of Norman law and administrative custom, but in political terms he counted for less than the justiciar and the other seneschals because in the last years of his reign Richard concentrated his attention on Normandy, so the seneschal was inevitably overshadowed by the Duke himself. In the truce talks of June 1194 and in the events of the next two weeks Philip had tried to maintain his threat to Richard's position in the Loire Valley and beyond, but when he turned and ran at Fréteval it became clear that his priorities were elsewhere. Although he was prepared to make gestures of support for rebels in Richard's southern lands

– as he had been doing since 1182–3 – he would not put up a determined fight on their behalf. In Normandy it was different. Economically and strategically the Seine valley was vitally important to the King of Paris. Philip would fight tooth and nail to hold on to the gains he had made here; when he did his best to stir up trouble in Aquitaine it was only in an attempt to distract Richard's attention. In the end, by accident, Philip's tactic worked and Richard was killed in Aquitaine. This, however, does not alter the basic pattern of the last four years of Richard's rule – a struggle for dominance in the region between Paris and Rouen, a struggle which revolves around castles and bridges across the Seine, a struggle which concerns control of territory and the flexible deployment of resources within that territory.

After Fréteval, while Richard went south to the Saintonge and Angoumois, Philip sped back north. In his absence a Norman army commanded by Count John and the Earl of Arundel had laid siege to Vaudreuil. After the loss of the Norman Vexin in 1193, the castle of Vaudreuil had become the key fortress on this border, controlling access to the Seine bridge at Pont de l'Arche, only ten miles south of Rouen. Vaudreuil's importance in the eyes of the Norman Dukes is indicated by the fact that, together with Rouen, Caen and Falaise, it was one of those castles where they stored their treasure. Its fall in February 1194 had been a bitter blow – and to Philip, of course, a great triumph. He did not intend to let it slip out of his grasp. It throws a sharp light on John's career if we remember that the prince who besieged it in July 1194 was the same man who had granted it to Philip just six months earlier. From Châteaudun to Vaudreuil was a journey which Philip accomplished in three days – a marvellous feat, according to his biographers, since it normally took a week for an armed force to cover the hundred miles. Certainly it was quick enough to take John and the Earl of Arundel by surprise. Philip's forced march to Vaudreuil shows that Angevins were not the only ones to possess what W. L. Warren has called 'the ability of Henry II and Richard I to pop up as through a trap-door, with the suddenness of a Demon King'. The French King then attacked John's camp at dawn and won a thoroughly convincing victory. While the Norman cavalry rode to safety most of the infantry, together with John's siege-artillery, were captured. Philip's success at Vaudreuil in mid-July showed that the spectacular gains which Richard was still registering elsewhere could not be repeated on the Norman–French frontier. Here it was going to be a hard slogging match, with each forward push requiring methodical preparation. In these circumstances both sides were glad of a truce.

The truce of Tillières, sealed by Philip's representatives on 23 July, was due to last until 1 November 1195 and, like all truces, was based on the principle of *status quo*. Both sides were to keep what they held on the day of the truce. This meant that Philip kept Vaudreuil with the dependent fortifications at Louviers, Acquigny and Léry, as well as Gisors and the Norman Vexin, Vernon, Gaillon, Pacy, Illiers-l'Evêque, Marcilly-sur-Eure, Louye, Tillières-sur-Avre and Nonancourt. Other lands, mostly in the north-east of Normandy, which Richard acknowledged to be held by Philip's partisans included the lordships of Eu, Arques, Aumâle, Mortemer, Beauvoir and Neufmarché. Among these partisans of Philip's were Norman marcher lords like William of Caïeux, Hugh of Gournay and Count Robert of Meulan. The terms of the truce make plain the size of the task confronting Richard. Not only had he lost control of a large part of eastern Normandy but there was also a band of countryside further west where Philip's troops had devastated the land and demolished the fortifications. According to the terms of the truce Richard was only allowed to rebuild four such castles: Drincourt in the north-east, and Le Neubourg, Conches and Breteuil to the west of Evreux. Two of the rebels in Aquitaine were also included in the truce: the Viscount of Brosse and the Count of Angoulême. Since the truce was agreed on 23 July 1194 it seems probable that it was negotiated by Richard's Norman representatives in ignorance of the most recent developments in Aquitaine and this may account for the story, reported by Roger of Howden, that the terms displeased Richard. None the less, since he had completed his conquest of the lands of Geoffrey de Rancon and Ademar of Angoulême by 22 July, he may have been content with the *status quo* of 23 July. Even in Normandy it is clear that there had been some recovery since the nadir of February 1194. Philip may well have tried to hold on to some places which he finally chose to destroy. Evreux and Drincourt certainly came into this category; Conches, Breteuil and Le Neubourg probably did.

There was no chance, however, that the truce would be observed for long. In part this was because the complicated criss-cross of allegiances in the marches was bound to lead to argument, and thus to an outbreak of skirmishing. The truce had not tried to resolve any of the problems in this region, as a peace – if it hoped to achieve any sort of permanence – would have had to do. It had simply left the situation as it happened to be on one day. The position within the lordship of Drincourt, for example, was clearly unstable. Philip counted the tenants of Drincourt among his followers since he insisted that they should be included in the truce, but Richard's Norman supporters presumably held Drincourt itself since this was one of the four fortresses which Richard was expressly permitted to rebuild. But the position was not only unstable, it was also basically intolerable. Truce or no truce, the Duke of Normandy was bound to seize any opportunity of lessening the dishonour of knowing that Capetian banners were waving over his castles. That he did so to good effect seems clear from the peace negotiations of the summer of 1195, since Philip was then prepared to hand back all of his conquests except the Norman Vexin, Gaillon, Vernon, Ivry and Pacy. It is hard to imagine why Philip would be so generous unless his other conquests were either already lost or on the point of being lost. Roger of Howden confirms the fact that the truce was frequently broken and that finally by the summer of of 1195 Philip preferred to demolish many Norman castles on the grounds that he could no longer hold them. But unfortunately except in one case – that of Vaudreuil – the details of this process are entirely lost to us, and even at Vaudreuil the evidence is scrappy and by no means straightforward.

It is clear that there was one memorable incident, a conference of the two Kings near Vaudreuil in July 1195. Philip had already decided to destroy the great castle and was using the conference simply as a device to gain time to enable his engineers to complete the job of undermining the walls. Only when Richard heard the crash of the walls did he understand what Philip was up to. Swearing that by God's legs he would see to it that saddles were emptied that day he at once gave the order to attack. Philip beat a hasty retreat across the River Seine and then had the bridge at Portjoie broken down after him. Baulked of his prey Richard returned to Vaudreuil and took possession of it and of those of the French King's army who had been left behind. Although this was a dramatic story, told in vivid terms by at least four contemporary writers, it cannot be precisely dated. Wherever he possibly can Roger of Howden takes the trouble to give a precise date, but in this case he says that it happened 'on a certain day'. This imprecision, taken together with his vague phrases about 'frequent breaches of the truce' and 'many castles demolished', makes it regrettably clear that after the summer of 1194 our hitherto most reliable informant knows very little about events in Normandy. Thus although Roger of Howden tells us nothing about any military activity on Richard's part in the twelve months leading up to the capture of Vaudreuil, this does not entitle us to assume that Richard had in fact remained at peace, collecting money, overhauling the military system and giving instructions for tournaments to be organized in England. If the incident on the day of the Vaudreuil conference had been isolated as well as memorable it would make Philip's decision to undermine the castle an inexplicable act of folly.

On the other hand, to turn from the chronicles to the evidence of charters only seems to create more problems, since these suggest that on at least two occasions *before* July 1195 Richard's chancery was issuing charters from Vaudreuil, in January 1195 and in June. What really happened in and around this key fortress during the first six months of 1195 will probably always remain a mystery, but it is possible that on more than one occasion Richard had been able to hold court right at the gates of the castle, that he had in other words reduced the Vaudreuil garrison to impotence. A garrison which can no longer dominate the territory around its castle is an expensive luxury, which Philip might well have chosen to do without. The records of the Norman exchequer for the financial year ending in September 1195 show that Richard spent large sums on the castle at Pont de l'Arche only three or four miles north of Vaudreuil, close to the Cistercian monastery which Richard founded at Bonport, and controlling the bridge across the Seine which

carried the road to Rouen. As long as the bridge at Pont de l'Arche
was in Richard's hands he could at will bring across forces, mustered
at Rouen and supplied from that city's ample resources, which were
large enough to ensure that the Vaudreuil garrison stayed behind
their castle walls. Pressure of this kind, exerted over a long period,
though it might lead to skirmishing, would not necessarily culmi-
nate in a stirring military action of the type to attract the attention
of chroniclers. It could, none the less, be an extremely effective
means of waging war, and the generally held notion that there was
a period of peace between July 1194 and July 1195 should probably
be rejected. In its place we should envisage a period of sustained
military pressure against some of Philip's Norman castles, gradually
robbing them of their function, depriving them of the revenues and
resources which they would normally expect to draw from the
countryside around them.

Richard, of course, would not have been the only commander
to wage this war of attrition. By the summer of 1195 Philip was
ready to cut his losses on Normandy's north-eastern frontier as well
as at Vaudreuil. Events there are even more obscure than in the
Seine valley. But if Richard's problem in the marches of Normandy
had been caused by the uncertain allegiance of the marcher lords
then one obvious course was to install men of proven loyalty in these
lordships. One family which was committed to Richard's cause
throughout the 1190s was the Lusignan family: in Outremer, in
Cyprus and in Poitou. The head of the family, Hugh IX *le Brun*,
had a younger brother, Ralph of Exoudun, and to him Richard
granted the hand of the heiress to the county of Eu. Ralph first
appears as Count of Eu in August 1194. Another rich lady whose
estates lay in the same region, the widowed Countess of Aumâle,
was given in marriage to Baldwin of Béthune, recently returned
from Austria. The date of the wedding is uncertain; we know only
that Richard paid all or part of the expenses and that it happened
between January and September 1195. There is, of course, a very
big difference between being given a countess and being given the
countess's estates. The terms of the truce of Tillières imply that
Philip had granted the lordship of Aumâle to Hugh of Gournay and
when, in August 1195, Philip gave his sister Alice – now at last

returned to him – in marriage to Count William of Ponthieu he bestowed upon them the county of Eu and the town of Arques. There were, in other words, two claimants for both Eu and Aumâle, one recognized at Richard's court and one at Philip's. Obviously it would not be surprising if Ralph of Exoudun and Baldwin of Béthune were keen protagonists of the war in north-eastern Normandy; they had much to win. And the evidence of the peace negotiations of 1195 suggests that they had, in fact, been winning.

That Richard held the military initiative throughout the quasi-truce of 1195 is made clear by the existence of a few fragments of evidence for another campaign – a campaign about which Roger of Howden knew nothing. At his accession to the throne in 1189 Richard had surrendered all his rights over Auvergne and the lordships of Issoudun and Graçay. But since Philip, in Richard's eyes, had stolen parts of Normandy he felt justified in looking for compensation on another front. According to the northern chronicler, William of Newburgh, the only writer to give any account of this campaign, Richard's Brabançons first captured Issoudun and some other fortresses in Berry and then advanced into Auvergne, capturing the Count and his castles. William of Newburgh looks upon this as a splendid extension of Angevin power, but apart from implying that it took place during the summer when Vaudreuil fell, he gives no date for this campaign. Modern writers, if they mention the capture of Issoudun at all, tend to assume that it happened while Richard had his hands full at Vaudreuil and that the victorious Angevin army was a purely mercenary force under Mercadier's command. But the records of the Norman exchequer include a payment for barons and knights going to the King at Issoudun in wartime, and a charter in Richard's name was issued at Issoudun on 3 July 1195. The King may well have left Mercadier in charge when he returned to Vaudreuil but it looks as though Richard himself supervised the early stages of the successful campaign in Berry.

Peace talks were resumed off and on throughout this period. War and diplomacy went hand in hand and chroniclers often found the schemes put forward at peace conferences more interesting than the routine of warfare. Ralph of Diss, for example, reports a Capetian suggestion that the dispute should be settled by a duel between five champions on each side and says that Richard was delighted with the idea – on condition that he and Philip should each be one of his five; the scheme was dropped. Plans of this nature were simply propaganda exercises – public statements to show that both sides believed that they were in the right and were prepared to prove it by due process of law. Equally, both sides were anxious to show that they were genuinely concerned about the outcome of the struggle between Christian and Muslim and so, when bad news came from Spain at the end of July 1195, it was obviously appropriate to talk again about patching up their quarrel. At a peace conference in August Richard returned Alice to her brother and Philip seemed to be willing to renounce a large part of his conquests in Normandy, but in reality both sides still had hopes of improving their bargaining position and the terms were never ratified; nor did either King send any aid to the Christians in Spain. It could well be that Alice's husband, the Count of Ponthieu, was too eager to gain possession of his newly acquired rights in Eu and Arques for a peace along the lines mooted in August 1195 to be feasible. Early in November, while Richard was at Verneuil, expecting to meet the French King for more peace talks, some of Philip's men launched a raid in the far north-eastern corner of Normandy. The raid was extremely successful. Dieppe was sacked again and some ships in the harbour were attacked with Greek fire and went down in flames. The Count of Ponthieu would be an obvious leader of a raid against the chief local rival to his own port of St Valéry. At this point the desultory war of raid and counter-raid boiled up to a new climax. Philip, counting on Richard's attention being distracted by events in Normandy, made a bid to recover the ground lost in Berry. He may well have hoped that the levies of Aquitaine would have their hands full with a war against the new Count of Toulouse, Raymond VI, and possibly also with a rebellion in the Périgord. The coast seemed to be clear in Berry when Philip laid siege to Issoudun and succeeded in capturing the town. The castle, however, held out and the defenders managed to get a message through to Richard. When the news came he was at Vaudreuil. Immediately he sent orders for his armies to converge on Issoudun while he himself, travelling at breakneck speed – covering three days' journey each day, says Howden – went on ahead. On reaching Issoudun he broke through Philip's lines and entered the beleaguered castle. Since Richard only had a small force with him the French King pressed on with the siege but in the next few days more and more Angevin troops appeared on the scene and it soon became apparent that it was not Richard but Philip who was caught in the trap. He was now outnumbered and in no position even to flee as he had at Fréteval. There was no alternative but to accept Richard's conditions and this he did on 5 December 1195. The two Kings then separated, agreeing to meet again after Christmas to ratify the peace terms. In the meantime a short truce was to be observed.

The peace conference took place, as arranged, near Louviers in the Seine valley between Vaudreuil and Gaillon. By comparing the terms of peace of January 1196 with the truce of July 1194 we can see that Richard had made tremendous gains. In Normandy he had recovered everything except the Norman Vexin and the castles of Neufmarché, Vernon, Gaillon, Pacy, Ivry and Nonancourt. In Berry he had regained Châtillon-sur-Indre (one of the castles surrendered in July 1193), La Châtre, Saint-Chartier, Châteaumeillant, Issoudun and Graçay. In Aquitaine Philip formally recognized that the Count of Angoulême, the Viscount of Brosse and the Count of Périgueux were vassals owing homage and service to the Duke of Aquitaine. Philip also agreed to abandon his ally, the Count of Toulouse, if the latter did not want to be included in the peace. All in all the Peace of Louviers marked a very considerable step forward on Richard's part. Moreover, the peace terms contained the seeds for further advances. Richard had been able to insist that one of the castles of the Vexin, Baudemont, should be held by a partisan of his, Stephen of Longchamps. It was also agreed that the Norman estates of Hugh of Gournay would revert to the Duke after Hugh's death – or earlier if Hugh chose to return to Richard's allegiance. Hugh of Gournay's position had clearly been undermined, since the Peace of Louviers reveals that some of his knights had been fighting on Richard's side. In these circumstances it is not surprising to find him back in the Angevin camp by the following year. The Peace of Louviers could only be an interim settlement;

while Philip held a foot of the land which Richard considered to be rightly his, a permanent settlement was impossible.

Although the peace with Philip could be no more than a breathing-space, Richard now felt strong enough to risk stirring up war on a new front. In the spring of 1196 he summoned Constance of Brittany to attend his court. After the death of her first husband, Richard's brother Geoffrey, she had been given in marriage to Ranulf, Earl of Chester. She, however, stayed in Brittany while he preferred to live in England or Normandy and in general it seems that the duchy had gone very much its own way after Henry II's death. Although Richard held Constance's daughter, Eleanor, in his custody and had, more than once, arranged marriages for her, he needed more than this if he were to reassert the traditional Norman ascendancy over the Bretons: he needed custody of the heir to the duchy. Arthur was now nine years old and it was time he left his mother's care. Unfortunately the situation very quickly became hopelessly confused. No sooner had the Duchess Constance set foot on Norman soil than she was kidnapped by her husband and carried off to his castle at St James-de-Beuvron. Alarmed and, rightly or wrongly, holding Richard responsible for this, Constance's Breton advisers, who had Arthur in their charge, appealed for help to Philip and threw off all allegiance to the Duke of Normandy. Richard's response was to invade Brittany. The rebels were inevitably forced to bow before his superior military resources and – according to William the Breton – before the ruthlessness with which he waged war, not stopping even for Good Friday. But although Richard won his war, he lost the dispute. Arthur's guardians took him first into hiding and then to the safety of the court of King Philip. From Brittany, on 15 April, Richard wrote to Hubert Walter, asking him to send knights who were prepared to serve in a long campaign: he expected war with the King of France. They were to be in Normandy by 2 June.

In granting Arthur asylum at his court Philip made a public declaration of hostile intent against Richard, but if he were to put his threats into practice he needed allies who could offer him help, not allies like the Bretons who were in desperate need of his help. To play the part of protector to a young prince driven into exile was all very fine, but Philip needed good soldiers as well as a good cause. So in the spring and early summer of 1196 the French King was at work winning allies in the north-east, in the Low Countries where lords were richer both in money and in men than were the barons of Brittany. The surrender of Eu and Arques in the Treaty of Louviers meant that Philip had to find compensation for the Count of Ponthieu if Alice's new husband was to remain content with a wife who had been scandalously used then discarded by the Angevins. Count Reynold of Boulogne also had interests in north-eastern Normandy and Philip presumably had to persuade him that the Treaty of Louviers did not mean that the Capetians had no further ambitions in that area. But Philip's greatest success was in persuading the new Count of Flanders and Hainault, Baldwin VI, to join the alliance, since Baldwin, at that time still only the heir to his parents' counties, had been among the princes who did homage to Richard on his way back from Germany in 1194. By June 1196 Baldwin was ready to follow in his father's footsteps and fight at Philip's side. During that month all three of these princes were to be found at the French court. The ground had been well prepared for the attack Philip launched against Aumâle in July.

Philip had a large army, including a contingent led by Count Baldwin, and plenty of siege-machines. But Aumâle was stoutly defended and Richard was able to profit from Philip's presence in the north. He captured Nonancourt; according to the French chroniclers, its castellan surrendered without a fight and then, repenting of his treason, went to the Holy Land and became a Templar. From Nonancourt Richard marched to the relief of Aumâle; and there, in an attack on the French camp, he was defeated. Only the French chroniclers give any details; the English either say nothing or hint that Richard, anxious to avoid a bloody battle, turned away and sent his troops to devastate Capetian terri-tory instead. Either way it is clear that Richard tried to relieve Aumâle and failed. To some extent, the story that he was reluctant to fight is supported by William the Breton's account of Richard giving the order to attack only after some hesitation, after having weighed the likelihood of defeat against the certain dishonour if he were to withdraw without even attempting to help the defenders.

Richard was not in the habit of publicizing his defeats, so the evidence is unsatisfactory, but in all probability he had been forced to attack a well-entrenched French camp and had been driven off with some losses. A week or so later, on about 20 August, Aumâle surrendered. Richard had to pay 3000 marks in order to ransom the garrison he had been unable to save. The French artillery had given the castle such a severe battering that Philip decided to complete the job of demolition rather than repair and try to hold it.

The rest of the summer went badly for Richard. He laid siege to Gaillon and was wounded in the knee by a crossbow bolt. Philip re-took Nonancourt. The one bright spot was the capture of Gamaches, one of the castles of the Norman Vexin, by John. But though in the field Richard suffered several setbacks during the summer of 1196, it was precisely in this period that he set in motion the strategy which was to bring victory. The aim, of course, was to reconquer the Vexin and to achieve this Richard set himself two tasks. The first was to build a secure base-camp from which he could strike at the Vexin. The second was to deprive Philip of his two most valuable allies, the Count of Toulouse and the Count of Flanders.

It was probably late in the summer of 1196 that Richard began to build his base-camp: Château-Gaillard, or rather that whole complex of fortifications on the Seine at Andeli, crowned by the castle on the Rock of Andeli which is his most famous monument. It is evident that the desirability of fortifying this site had occurred to both Kings, since it was expressly forbidden in the Peace of Louviers. But in March 1196 Richard visited the Isle of Andeli, one of several small islands in the river at this point and one on which the Archbishop of Rouen had built a toll-house for the collection of dues from ships passing up and down the Seine. The landed estates of the church of Rouen, many of which lay in the Vexin, had suffered very badly in the war – which had only strengthened the Archbishop's resolve to hang on to one of his most lucrative assets, the manor of Andeli. Richard returned to Andeli again in April, May and June. He was clearly attracted to the site and may have begun negotiations with the Archbishop with a view to acquiring it, but Archbishop Walter, though an old friend and an experienced servant of the crown, was first and foremost concerned to protect the rights and privileges of the church which had been entrusted to his care. At some stage Richard lost patience. He seized the manor and began to build. The Archbishop protested. Richard took no notice. Eventually on 7 November 1196 the Archbishop set out for Rome in order to lay his grievances before the Pope.

Meanwhile, Richard fortified the Isle of Andeli and built a palace there which became his favourite residence during the last two years of his life. Opposite on the right bank he laid out a new town (now Petit-Andelys), and then on the three-hundred-foot limestone crag overlooking Petit-Andelys and the Seine and linked to them both by a series of outworks, there rose what he himself called either his 'fair castle of the Rock' (*bellum castrum de Rupe*) or his 'saucy castle' (Château-Gaillard). The whole complex of defences was completed by a stockade built across the river on the south side of the rock. Richard himself supervised the entire operation and allowed nothing to stop it. Among his other protests the Archbishop of Rouen had imposed an interdict on the duchy. This meant that most church services were banned and, in consequence, said Roger of Howden, 'the streets and squares of the towns of Normandy were littered with the unburied bodies of the dead'. But at Andeli the hodmen, the water-carriers, the limeworkers, carpenters, quarrymen, stone-cutters, woodmen, miners, watchmen, warders and smiths worked on. In October 1197 Pope Celestine lifted the interdict and a settlement between King and Archbishop was arranged. At Andeli work went on as before. In May 1198, says William of Newburgh, a shower of blood fell from the sky, spattering the unfinished walls. Some of Richard's advisers were alarmed, taking it to be an evil omen, but the King was unmoved. Not for a moment would he allow the masons and engineers to slacken the pace of their work. 'He took such pleasure in the building that, if I am not mistaken, if an angel had descended from heaven and told him to abandon it, that angel would have been met with a volley of curses and the work would have gone on regardless.' Richard's close personal involvement with Château-Gaillard makes it possible to use its design as evidence – if evidence were needed – of his deep practical knowledge of the craft of siege warfare. The increasing, and increasingly effective, use of siege-machines in the twelfth century had made military architects more sharply aware than ever of the threat posed by 'dead angles', spots which could not be reached by the defenders' missiles. Château-Gaillard's most distinctive feature, still clearly visible today, is the elliptical inner citadel with its remarkable curvilinear enclosing wall. Here there is no dead angle to be found; the fire of the garrison could cover all approaches. The choice of the site, the overall structure of the fortifications, stockade, island town, castle, each element a harmonious part of the whole – and the details of the design of walls and towers – all indicate the hand of a masterbuilder. Untroubled by modesty, Richard claimed that it was so perfectly designed that he could hold it even if its walls were made of butter.

Impressive though they are at first sight the ruins of Château-Gaillard give no real indication of the castle's importance. There are other castles whose ruins seem to be equally formidable. But this is misleading because, taken as a whole, the fortifications at Andeli are quite extraordinary. In the first place the modern appearance of most castles, whether they are reasonably intact or in a ruined state, reflects the labour of generations: castles, like cathedrals, were generally a long time a-growing. The ruins of Château-Gaillard, however, are the ruins of a fortress built in just two hectic years – and built only five miles distant from Philip's castle at Gaillon. We can get some idea of the importance which Richard attached to this work from the settlement he reached with Archbishop Walter. In exchange for the one manor of Andeli he gave the church of Rouen not just two manors but also the flourishing seaport of Dieppe. An even better picture of its importance comes from the fortunate survival of the account recording expenditure at Andeli in the two years ending September 1198. In this period recorded expenditure was approximately £11,500. In order to obtain some inkling of what this means it is necessary to compare it with expenditure on other castles. On rebuilding the walls of the town of Eu – the next largest piece of construction work recorded in the 1198 account roll – Richard spent nearly £1300. Turning to English castles, for which the surviving financial evidence is much more complete, we find that Richard spent just over £7000 on *all* English castles during the *whole* of his reign. The most that was spent on any one English castle in this period was the £8250 spent on Dover – and that was spread over the fifty years from 1164 to 1214. Measured in these terms Château-Gaillard completely dwarfs every other castle in Europe. The vast sums which he was prepared to spend show beyond all doubt that the building of Château-Gaillard was of overwhelming importance to Richard. The question has to be asked: why? Why so much money on one site?

The conventional answer to this question is that the fortification of Andeli was intended to plug the gap in the Norman defences which had been caused by the fall of Gisors. Seen in this light the role of Château-Gaillard was a defensive one; its function was to block the direct route to Rouen. Obviously there is something to this – but it is by no means the whole story. This was the role which, as it turned out, the fortress was called upon to play in John's reign when there was a general collapse of the Angevin position in Normandy. In the demoralized atmosphere of distrust and uncertainty created by that king, the six months' defence put up by the isolated garrison of Château-Gaillard was one of the few creditable episodes. But it does not follow from this that Richard *intended* Château-Gaillard to perform a primarily defensive function. In the years 1196–9 he was thinking not about defending Normandy but about conquering the Vexin. A place has to be found for Château-Gaillard within the framework of a strategy of aggression. Men and supplies could be sent here from the main Norman arsenal at Rouen, either by river or – since the Seine's meanders and the direction of its current were alike unfavourable – by the well-defended Seine valley road, via Pont de l'Arche, Vaudreuil and then over the bridge at Portjoie to Andeli. Richard's interest in this route was shown when he built himself a residence at Portjoie and rebuilt the Seine bridge after Philip had fled across it in July 1195, breaking it down behind him. Château-Gaillard protected the forward base from which Richard was to deliver hammer blows against Philip's castles.

In that same summer of 1196 when Richard laid his plans for the fortification of Andeli, he also entered into negotiations with Count Raymond VI of Toulouse, negotiations which were to end in a diplomatic revolution. Ever since 1159 the Angevin Dukes of Aquitaine had been in a state of almost permanent war with the

Counts of Toulouse. The Dukes argued that Toulouse was theirs by hereditary right and although they were unable to make good this claim, they had generally been successful in holding on to the Quercy. But no self-respecting Count of Toulouse could resign himself to the loss of this valuable region around Cahors and so whenever the Duke of Aquitaine was in difficulty or had his hands full elsewhere, the Count of Toulouse stepped in and did his best to take advantage of the situation. This was an essential element in the standard political pattern of the 1180s and 1190s and obviously it was one which suited Philip Augustus down to the ground. In 1195 Richard was given the chance to reshape the pattern because at the beginning of that year Raymond VI succeeded his father, Raymond V, as Count of Toulouse. But the terms of the Peace of Louviers make it clear that 1195 had been yet another year of war between Aquitaine and Toulouse – though it was a war which lay outside the scope of the Angevin chroniclers. It may have taken the setbacks which he suffered in Normandy in 1196 to persuade Richard that if he was to reconquer the Vexin he would have to be able to concentrate his resources in Normandy; and to be free to do this he would have to pay the price required by the Count of Toulouse, particularly since King Sancho of Navarre had now immersed himself in a war with Castile and, in consequence, was no longer a reliable ally in the south. Moreover, the death of Alfonso II of Aragon in 1196 may also have suggested that the time had come to reshape the alliances of south-western Europe. By October 1196 the negotiations were completed. Raymond VI came to Rouen and there married Richard's sister Joan. Richard renounced his claim to Toulouse, restored the Quercy and gave them the county of Agen as Joan's dowry. Agen was to be held as a fief of the duchy of Aquitaine in return for the service of 500 knights for a month should there be war in Gascony. These were generous terms, calculated not simply to neutralize a former enemy but to turn him into a friend and ally. From a financial point of view it made sense for the lord of Bordeaux to be at peace with the lord of Toulouse, so that the river-borne trade of the Garonne could flourish and be a source of profit to them both. At least one English historian, William of Newburgh, recognized the significance of this marriage alliance. It marked, he said, the end of forty years of exhausting war, the end of the old hatred – and it meant that Richard could turn with greater vigour to the struggle with King Philip.

At about the same time as his negotiations with Toulouse, Richard imposed an embargo on trade with Flanders. Some English merchants who were detected exporting corn were heavily fined. Flanders was the most densely populated and highly industrialized region in north-western Europe. Bruges, Ypres, Ghent and Lille were great manufacturing centres, with more mouths than the fields of Flanders could feed. For their very existence they depended upon imported foodstuffs, and also, since their chief industry was cloth manufacture, upon the import of wool. Close as were the economic ties between Bordeaux and Toulouse, the ties between Flanders and Eastern England were even closer and more vital. England supplied both grain and huge quantities of high quality wool. All this meant that the Count of Flanders was a prince of great wealth – but also one who was peculiarly vulnerable to economic pressure. Baldwin of Flanders and Hainault had been with Philip at Issoudun in 1195 and at Aumâle in 1196; he was now beginning to feel the effects of Richard's displeasure.

In April 1197 Richard renewed the war with a raid on the Count of Ponthieu's port of St Valéry. He burned the town and carried off much booty, including the relics of the saint. In the harbour he found some English ships, loaded with grain and other food-stuffs. The sailors were hanged, the ships burned and their cargoes seized. The King intended to see that his economic sanctions were properly enforced. But Richard did not want men to measure only what it cost to be against him; he also wanted them to know how much they could gain from being with him. He understood how to be generous – as he had shown in his 1196 negotiations with Tou-louse, and as he showed again in negotiations with Flanders in 1197. In 1194 he had offered Baldwin a pension, but the young Count had remained true to his father's French alliance, and the pension had not been paid. Now, if Flanders came over to the Angevin side, the crippling trade embargo would be lifted and Baldwin would receive full payment of the arrears of his pension, as well as substan-tial gifts, 5000 marks and a large quantity of wine. By midsummer discussions were far enough advanced for an embassy headed by William Marshal and Peter des Préaux to be dispatched to Flanders armed with 1730 marks to spend on the King's behalf. It is clear that Count Baldwin's advisers and kinsmen were also to be given a taste of the benefits to be gained from an alliance with the rich King of England. By July a formal treaty had been drawn up. Richard and Baldwin agreed that neither would make a truce or peace with the King of France without the other's consent. The alliance was a triumph for Richard's wine and cash diplomacy. The shift in the balance of power which it implied is made clear by the presence of three Norman marcher lords – Count Robert of Meulan, William of Caïeux and Hugh of Gournay – among those who stood surety for Richard's observance of the treaty. In 1197 they were just as sensitive to the way the wind was blowing as they had been when they joined Philip in 1193. In the estimation of Rigord of St Denis the alliance was the cause of a thousand ills to France.

Even before the Flanders alliance was formally sealed the fact that it was known to be on the way meant that Richard held the initiative in eastern Normandy. In May 1197 he was at Gournay and from there led a raid into the Beauvaisis, capturing the castle of Milli. According to the *History of William Marshal* the hero of the assault on Milli was none other than William himself, and when it was all over he was reproved by Richard. 'Sir Marshal, a man of your station ought not to risk his life in adventures of that kind. Leave them to the young knights who still have a reputation to win.' But according to the same source Richard had had to be forcibly restrained from plunging into the thick of the fray himself. While Richard and William Marshal were at the storming of Milli, another Angevin contingent, led by Mercadier and Count John, brought off a still greater coup: they captured Philip's cousin, the Bishop of Beauvais. On crusade Philip of Beauvais had been closely associated with Conrad of Montferrat and Richard had disliked him ever since then. He put the Bishop in prison and refused to release him. Protests on the grounds that this was no way to treat a churchman were countered by the argument that Philip had been captured not as a bishop but as a knight riding to war, for he had been fully armed and helmeted. The Bishop of Beauvais was indeed a notoriously militant bishop. He was later to take an active part in the Battle of Bouvines – though William the Breton excused him by saying that he was on the battlefield only by chance and happened, equally fortuitously, to have a mace in his hand. After this highly successful raid Richard returned to Normandy, where he took Dangu, a Vexin castle only four miles away from Gisors.

These were useful gains but more was to come once the Flanders alliance had been finalized. The western part of Flanders – the district known as Artois, including towns as rich as Arras, St Omer and Douai – had been in French hands since the death of Count Philip at Acre. If Baldwin invaded Artois, there was a good chance that Philip Augustus would rush to its defence, leaving Richard free to choose the time and place of his own attack. In July Baldwin attacked in the north-east while Richard made his move in the south, in Berry. Philip, however, began by coolly ignoring both threats. Only after he had recaptured Dangu did he turn north. By this time Douai had fallen already and Arras was under siege. When Philip advanced to the relief of Arras, Baldwin retreated and the King of France chased after him, determined to punish a disloyal vassal. But in his indignation Philip went too far. In a series of skilfully executed manœuvres Baldwin broke down the bridges behind and in front of Philip's army and cut off his supply routes. Eventually Philip realized that he had been drawn into a trap from which there was no escape and he sued for peace, promising to give Baldwin what he wanted if he would break with Richard. The Count of Flanders would not do this, however, and instead it was agreed that there should be a conference of all parties in September between Andeli and Gaillon. Baldwin and Richard met at Rouen and then went to the conference together. Richard certainly was not yet ready for a final peace but he was willing to agree to a truce on the basis of keeping what he held. While Baldwin and Philip had been busy in Flanders he had captured several castles – as many as ten, according to Roger of Howden – in Berry, including Vierzon. In the Vexin, moreover, despite the failure to retain Dangu, there seems to have been some advance. The records of the Norman exchequer show that Richard was spending money on the castles of

Gamaches and Longchamps; the frontier between him and Philip was gradually being pushed back.

In theory the truce made in September 1197 was meant to last untill January 1199. Inevitably it did not and, equally inevitably, the months of peace were filled with preparations for war. Richard pressed on with his two main tasks: castle-building and coalition-building. His search for further allies in the struggle with Philip became entangled with the central question of European diplomacy – the election of a new German King to succeed Henry VI, who died of a fever at Messina on 28 September 1197, aged only 32. Since Henry's son, the future Emperor Frederick II, was less than three years old it was a golden opportunity for the enemies of the Hohenstaufen to reassert themselves. At their head were Richard's Welf kinsmen and his allies, the princes of the Lower Rhineland. They invited Richard to take part in the business of choosing a new king and it was at his suggestion that they eventually plumped for his nephew, Henry the Lion's younger son, Otto of Brunswick. Otto had spent most of his youth at the Angevin court and had recently, in the summer of 1196, been made Count of Poitou. In the absence of his elder brother on crusade he was, however, effectively the head of the Welf family and a natural choice for king-makers looking for someone to oppose the Hohenstaufen candidate, Henry VI's younger brother, Philip of Swabia. So, in the course of the spring and summer of 1198, two kings were elected in Germany: one supported, financially and diplomatically, by the King of England, the other therefore by the King of France. On the whole it was Richard rather than Philip who gained from the disputed election since it strengthened his ties with a number of princes from the Low Countries – with Dietrich, Count of Holland, Henry, Duke of Limburg, Henry, Duke of Brabant and Adolf, Archbishop of Cologne as well as with Baldwin of Flanders and Hainault – while Philip's friends in Germany lived too far away to worry Richard. But the weight of this hostile political bloc on his north-eastern border gave Philip cause for concern, particularly when more of his own vassals judged it wise to join the Angevin bandwagon, notably Renaud, Count of Boulogne and Hugh, Count of St Pol. And not only in the north-east did some of Philip's frontier vassals go over to Richard's side; so also did Geoffrey of Perche and Louis of Blois. Naturally Philip did not remain idle. He struck back in traditional fashion by entering into an alliance with two of Richard's Aquitainian vassals: Aimar of Limoges and Ademar of Angoulême. But there can be no doubt that in this diplomatic warfare it was Richard who held the upper hand. Finally there was the fact that Richard's support for Otto meant that his envoys could count on a friendly reception at Rome. The newly elected Pope, Innocent III, though at this stage doing his best to preserve a façade of neutrality, in fact preferred a Welf to a Hohenstaufen Emperor. Since Innocent was also at odds with Philip of France over the repudiation of Ingeborg, he was unquestionably well disposed towards the King of England, even though the latter's matrimonial affairs were not entirely straightforward. In a letter written in May 1198 the Pope promised Richard that he would try to persuade Sancho of Navarre to return the castles of St-Jean-Pied-de-Port and Roquebrune, which Sancho's father had given to Richard as Berengaria's dowry. This isolated fragment of evidence, hinting at tension between Richard and Sancho of Navarre, suggests that the settlement with Toulouse may well have been part of a major realignment of alliances among the countries bordering the Pyrenees. If this is so then it is possible that by 1198 a question mark was hanging over Richard's childless marriage with Berengaria. Inevitably we are in the realm of speculation but it may be that she was barren. If this was the case then her future must have been in doubt since there were few positions more precarious than that of a queen who bore no heir and who represented an alliance which was no longer wanted.

While Richard's diplomats were busy in Germany and at Rome, his administrators were fully occupied with the tasks imposed by the King's insatiable demands for money and soldiers. In December 1197 Hubert Walter summoned a council meeting at Oxford and passed on Richard's requirement that the barons of England should supply him with a force of 300 knights prepared for a year's service at their own expense, while the towns should provide 500 men-at-arms. Measures of this kind were a rationalization of the feudal system which, in theory, required the service of more knights – ten times as many – but for a period which was so short as to be useless except for purely local purposes. Demands such as these naturally provoked opposition – and the political and legal arguments are often well covered by contemporary writers. But while chroniclers record the debates, exchequer records show that the King and Hubert Walter got their way. Moreover, the chroniclers make it clear that although they disliked the level of taxation, they none the less sympathized with the policies which made the taxation necessary. To them it seemed right and proper that a king should strain every nerve to recover the lands of which he had been treacherously deprived.

The war began again in Setember 1198. Once more Baldwin of Flanders invaded Artois, capturing Aire without a fight and then laying siege to St Omer. The citizens of St Omer sent a message to Philip, saying that they would have to surrender unless he came to their aid. Philip wrote back, promising to come by 30 September; if he did not, they were at liberty to make the best terms they could. In fact, as before, the allies had opened a war on two fronts and Philip was detained in the Vexin throughout September. On 4 October Baldwin marched into St Omer. Meanwhile, in Normandy, the King of France had been defeated twice. On the first occasion he had led his army on a raid into the Norman Vexin but was outmanœuvred by Richard and Mercadier and had to flee to Vernon, leaving some twenty knights and more than sixty men-at-arms to fall into Angevin hands. Richard immediately followed up this success by fording the River Epte at Dangu on 27 September and invading the French Vexin. He captured Courcelles and Boury on that day and then returned to Dangu, while another force took Sérifontaine. The capture of Dangu and these three other fortresses meant that a net was closing around Gisors. Philip had received news of the attack on Courcelles and, on 28 September, he set out to its relief, not knowing that it had already fallen. As it moved north from Mantes the French army was detected by patrols which Richard had sent to reconnoitre the land east of the Epte while the bulk of his forces rested at Dangu. Richard, as so often, was out with the patrols himself and as soon as it became clear that Philip was not planning to attack the Angevin army at Dangu but intended to continue on his northward path, apparently unaware of what was happening around him, Richard decided to use the advantage won by good reconnaissance and attack the French army while it was still in marching order. He sent orders for the troops at Dangu to join him as quickly as possible. As Philip carried on marching, however, Richard could see his advantage slipping away. The French King was bound to realize what was going on when he reached Courcelles – if not before – and so Richard gave the order to charge while some of his reinforcements were still on the way. According to the *jongleur* who wrote the *History of William Marshal* he led the attack like a starving lion which catches sight of its prey. For the second time within a week or two Philip took to his heels, galloping northwards to the one place of refuge left to him, the castle of Gisors. So hot was the pursuit that the bridge at the gate of Gisors collapsed under the weight of French knights struggling to reach safety. Twenty knights were drowned, wrote Richard in a letter reporting his victory, and Philip himself was believed to be among those who had to be dragged out of the river. 'We ourselves un-horsed three knights with a single lance and have them prisoner.' Another hundred or so of Philip's knights were captured, as well as warhorses and men-at-arms. According to Angevin sources Richard had attacked a numerically superior army – though one which had been taken unawares before it could get into battle forma-tion. On the other hand, William the Breton says that Philip fought so courageously against great odds that the honour of the day belonged to the few against the many. Despite this special pleading it is clear that Philip was outmanœuvred in his own land – within the French Vexin – and suffered a humiliating reverse. In Rigord's view God was punishing Philip for allowing the Jews into his domains. Richard did not have the equipment to lay siege to Gisors so he returned with his prisoners to Dangu; only the fact that Philip had escaped – helped, it was said, by the clouds of dust kicked up on the summer roads – diminished his triumph.

The war continued. Philip took his revenge by mustering another army and raiding Normandy south of the Seine. Richard retaliated by sending Mercadier to plunder the town of Abbeville, where many French merchants had gathered for the fair. Still in October William le Queu, the castellan of Lyons-la-Fôret, captured a French force which Philip had sent to garrison Neufmarché – in itself not a major confrontation but typical of the dozens of unrecorded incidents which must have marked Richard's advance into the Vexin. That Richard was still gaining ground is suggested by two other events which Roger of Howden happens to mention – an attempt by the Earl of Leicester to recover his castle of Pacy which had been lost since 1193, and Philip's decision to fortify Le Goulet, a decision which suggests that he was being driven back along the banks of the Seine. Philip's own assessment of the situation can be deduced from the peace terms which he offered in the autumn of 1198. He simply did not have the resources to stand the strain of a war on two fronts and if he was to recover the territory he had lost in Artois then he would have to make peace with Richard, even if this meant renouncing his conquests. So he offered to hand back everything which he had taken except Gisors. But Richard refused to make a separate peace in breach of the terms of his alliance with Flanders. Philip had to make do with a truce to last until 13 January 1199, at which date the two Kings agreed to meet in the hope of working out an acceptable peace treaty.

Late in December a papal legate, Peter of Capua, arrived on the scene. Innocent III had proclaimed a new crusade and was anxious to see an end to the Angevin-Capetian quarrel. Richard, however, refused to make peace while Philip still held Norman territory and when the legate tried to talk him into a compromise, arguing that all the time their war continued the Kingdom of Jerusalem remained in danger, Richard angrily reminded him of the circumstances in which Philip had invaded his lands. 'If it had not been for his malice I would have been able to recover the whole of Outremer – and when I came back from crusade, what protection did the church give to me then?' According to the *History of William Marshal*, Peter of Capua then made things even worse by asking Richard to free the Bishop of Beauvais. At this point the King exploded with so violent a wrath that the legate fled, afraid that if he stayed a moment longer he would be castrated. Eventually, however, Richard was prevailed upon to agree to a truce for five years. Philip could keep the Norman castles which he still held, but Richard ordered his captains to prevent the Capetian garrisons from coming out to collect provisions and revenues from the surrounding countryside. If this were done efficiently the castles, far from being an asset to Philip, would become a drain on his already over-stretched resources. The *History of William Marshal* says that William le Queu carried out this policy so effectively that it was he, not Philip's castellan, who collected the rents from Gisors, while the garrison of Baudemont was afraid even to draw water from the spring just outside their castle. This may be poetic exaggeration, but it would none the less be true that on terms such as this Philip would find peace as expensive as war.

Although, as a gesture of help for the projected crusade, they had agreed on a five years' truce, it was extremely unlikely that it would last for as long as five months. Richard sent Mercadier south to help his seneschal cope with the Limoges-Angoulême revolt, but *en route* his company was ambushed by some French counts. As a result Richard accused Philip of breaking the truce – possibly unjustly in view of the general loathing for bands of mercenaries. But when Richard himself moved off southwards Philip took the opportunity to begin building a new castle on the Seine between Gaillon and Andeli. He agreed to demolish it when warned that unless he did so the truce would be at an end, but obviously in this atmosphere of mutual suspicion and recrimination hostilities were likely to start again at any moment. One more attempt was made to find a peace settlement which left Gisors in Philip's hands and yet which Richard could accept. The King of France's rights over the church of Tours had been a constant source of irritation to the Angevins; perhaps if he were to give these up then Richard might reconcile himself to the loss of Gisors. So, with the legate's help, a treaty on these lines was drafted. Philip's son, Louis, would marry one of Richard's nieces, a daughter of the King of Castile, and Richard would grant them Gisors as a marriage gift. As well as giving up his rights in Tours, Philip would also agree to abandon his ally Philip of Swabia and instead help Richard's nephew, Otto of Brunswick, in his fight to win undisputed possession of the German crown. Whether or not Richard would have ratified these terms we shall never know. He had left these preliminary discussions to his officials while he himself went to join Mercadier in Aquitaine.

Philip's allies, the Count of Angoulême and the Viscount of Limoges, had not been included in the truce – a truce which left Richard free to suppress their rebellion. In March 1199 Richard brought up his troops to lay siege to the Viscount's castle at Chalus-Chabrol.

On the evening of 26 March 1199, although daylight was beginning to fade, Richard, relentless as ever, ordered his soldiers to press on with the attack. His archers and crossbowmen maintained a steady rate of fire, forcing the defenders to keep their heads down, while the sappers concentrated on undermining the castle walls. Only one member of the garrison, a crossbowman using a frying-pan as a shield, was brave enough to show himself on the ramparts. It was a splendidly makeshift gesture of defiance but to the professional soldiers under Richard's command his occasional shots could be nothing more than a minor irritant. By now the siege was in its third day. Every now and then a piece of stonework came crashing down over the heads of the besiegers, but the sappers, protected by specially constructed covers, worked steadily on. Threatened by the imminent collapse of the castle walls, the forty men and women within were clearly on the verge of surrender.

After supper Richard left his tent in order to observe the progress of the siege and to exercise (as he often did) his own skill with a crossbow. Because he was not riding into battle he wore no armour except an iron headpiece, relying for protection on the rectangular shield which was carried before him. The lone figure of the crossbowman with the frying-pan was still visible on the parapets of the doomed castle and Richard could not help applauding as the man sent a well-aimed bolt in his direction. As a result he was fractionally late in ducking behind the shield and was struck on the left shoulder. Not wishing either to alarm his own men or to give heart to the defenders, he made no sound. Calmly he returned to his tent as though nothing had happened. Once inside he tried to pull out the bolt but succeeded only in breaking off the wooden shaft, leaving the iron barb, the length of a man's hand, deeply embedded in the flesh. Then a surgeon arrived. Working by the flickering light of torches he managed to remove the bolt; but the shoulder was badly hacked about. The wounds from the bolt and the surgeon's knife were then treated and bandaged up. Richard stayed in his tent, allowing only a few of his most trusted associates to enter, and indulging in his usual pleasures. This was flouting the advice of his doctors but it did at least provide an explanation for the fact that he took no further part in the siege. Soon afterwards Chalus-Chabrol fell. But it was no longer a victory. The king's wound turned gangrenous and daily the infection spread. Richard had seen too many men die not to know what was happening to him. He wrote to his mother, Eleanor of Aquitaine, and she came in haste. He forgave the man who had shot him, then confessed his sins and received Extreme Unction. At Chalus on 6 April, as evening came, he died.

13

CONCLUSION

WITHIN five years of Richard's death, John had lost Normandy and Anjou to Philip Augustus, and come within a hair's breadth of losing Poitou as well. This rapid collapse has led many historians to believe that the seeds of decline must have been planted before 1199 – a belief reinforced by the twentieth-century fashion for seeing John as an efficient and business-like king. No king as competent as John, the argument runs, could have been so quickly defeated if the empire he was defending was not already in poor shape. This has led to an interpretation of Richard's reign as a period of stress during which irreparable damage was done to the fabric of the Angevin Empire. The fault, it is said, was Richard's. He preferred the romantic illusion of the crusades to the hard, but fruitful, work of domestic administration. In his absence his lands were buffeted by a series of blows. On his return he initiated a policy of financial oppression which so exhausted his subjects' resources that they were incapable of resisting King Philip's renewed onslaught. Richard's irresponsibility meant that John never had a chance.

On every count this is a mistaken interpretation. John is the most overrated king in English history. He appears to be efficient only because the beginning of his reign coincides with the beginning of a much more bureaucratic system of record-keeping than had existed hitherto and the survival of these records permits historians to look, for the first time, at the daily routine of the King's government at work. Compared with his predecessors John's days *appear* to be crowded with business but this, of course, does not mean that he actually worked harder or more effectively than they had. Yet although they know this perfectly well, historians have allowed themselves to give the impression that John was unusually competent. In fact he was a very poor king, incompetent where it really mattered, in the field of man-management.

That damage was done during Richard's absence is obviously true. But this was not because he chose to go on crusade and neglect his dominions; if he had returned from crusade, as he expected, in January 1193, he would have found his empire intact. The damage was done because he fell into the hands of his Christian enemies, among them his own treacherous brother John. He remained in prison for more than a year and – for all anyone knew in 1193 – might have stayed there much longer. The essential point, however, is that the territorial losses of 1193–4 were not permanent. By the end of 1198 Philip had been driven out of most of his Norman conquests and was prepared to give up the rest, with the one exception of Gisors – and to keep Gisors he was willing to pay a heavy political and diplomatic price. Elsewhere too Philip was steadily losing ground – to Baldwin in Artois, and to Richard in Berry. Richard's acquisitions in Berry are particularly important because they mark not merely an improvement on the position in 1194 but an improvement on the position in 1189. Strategically they were valuable because they blocked Philip's approach to Loches and the Loire valley castles which lay at the heart of the Angevin Empire. The period between spring 1194 and Richard's death was a period of recovery and even, in some areas, expansion. If he had survived, there is every reason to believe that the momentum of the last four years would have been maintained.

Most historians, however, would not agree with this. They believe that the recovery was bought at too high a cost. Crushed by the intolerable burden of paying first for the crusade, then for the ransom and finally for the unrelenting war in France, Richard's dominions inevitably fell an easy prey to a ruthless enemy. By 1199 the crippled empire was incapable of paying for its own defence, and not even Richard's warlike spirit could have sustained it for much longer. This, again, is a mistaken argument. From England, the only part of the Angevin dominions for which we can compile a series of figures for the King's minimum annual revenue, the evidence shows that John was able to collect large sums – notably the £57,000 derived from one tax alone, the thirteenth of 1207. Indeed it is partly on the basis of his financial administration that historians have argued that John was a competent and business-like king. What such figures do clearly show is that the English taxpayer was not exhausted in 1199. For the rest of the Angevin Empire there is simply no evidence to enable us to judge one way or the other. It is true that after 1199 treasure was sent from England to Normandy, Anjou and Aquitaine but this may also have been the case much earlier as well. Since England was generally at peace, it is hardly surprising to find money raised there being dispatched to provinces in the war zone. It would have been nonsensical to insist on each province paying for its own defence while reserves of English silver were available.

What many historians seem to forget is the fact that it was not only the Angevin taxpayers who were hard pressed. Philip too had to pay for his wars. At least one contemporary believed that the burdens which Philip imposed on the churches in his lands were more severe than the burdens which Richard imposed. According to John of Belmeis, in comparison with the French King Richard was as demanding as a hermit. John had been treasurer of York, Bishop of Poitiers and Archbishop of Lyons; he was a cosmopolitan and much-respected churchman whose views were worth listening to carefully. It is true that we know John's opinion only because it was quoted by an English historian, William of Newburgh, and it might fairly be argued that an English chronicle is not the best place to look for an objective estimate of the French King. It is none the less striking that even Philip's own biographer, Rigord of St Denis, had to go out of his way in order to defend his master against charges of greed, which he admits were widespread. Of course any king who was not accused of greed would be a peculiar and possibly unique ruler, but the point here is that there is nothing to show that Richard was a more oppressive king than Philip, or that his dominions were any more exhausted. What evidence there is suggests that, if anything, it was Philip's territories which were feeling the strain more severly in 1198-9.

This problem is closely linked with another one: the question

of the relative wealth of the Capetian and Angevin lands. Which
of the two Kings possessed the greater resources? A glance at the
map would seem to indicate that Henry II and his sons were far
richer than Philip, yet this apparently obvious conclusion has been
denied by some modern scholars – most recently, and most em-
phatically, by Professor J. C. Holt, the leading historian of Angevin
England. He has argued that from the 1170s onwards the balance
between Angevin and Capetian was steadily shifting in favour of
the latter and that one vital reason for this was the improving
financial position of the French monarchy. He has compared the
French royal accounts for 1202–3 – the earliest ones to survive –
with the accounts of the English and Norman exchequers and come
to the conclusion that Philip was richer than either Richard or John.
The analysis, however, contains several errors and there can be no
doubt that Richard was a much wealthier king than Philip. This
is evident from the history of their crusade as well as the history
of their subsequent war. When hiring mercenaries, building castles
or courting allies Richard always had more to spend. When we
are assessing his success in the military and diplomatic campaigns
of 1194 to 1198 this is clearly a fact of prime importance.

But this brings us back to the original problem. If the Angevins
were richer than Philip Augustus why did their empire fall apart
so soon after Richard's death? In part it was because John's character was such that he and his barons lived in an atmosphere of mutual
distrust. 'The Normans in the old days were grain,' said the author
of the *History of William Marshal*, 'but now they are chaff; for since
the death of King Richard they have had no leadership.' Thus in
the years 1202–4 the Normans were blown about by every puff of
wind from France. But there were other underlying reasons. In
trying to rule the whole Angevin Empire John was trying to hold
together lands which did not automatically belong together. Henry
II's empire was a recent creation. It was not yet a traditional part
of the European political scene and it was not expected to survive.
Accidents of marriage and birth had brought it together; these same
accidents could equally well pull it apart again. For example, when
Henry II gave his daughter Eleanor in marriage to Alfonso VIII of
Castile in 1170 he seems to have granted her Gascony as her

marriage portion. It was a gift which was to become operative after
Eleanor of Aquitaine's death – or so King Alfonso claimed when
he moved into Gascony in 1204. Similarly Richard renounced the
Quercy and gave the Agenais to his sister Joan when she married
Raymond VI of Toulouse in 1196. When Richard and Philip drew
up the Treaty of Messina in March 1191 Richard envisaged having
more than one son and dividing his dominions between them. What
such arrangements show is that princes were more concerned about
the interests of their family than about the unity of their lands. If
they could provide for the members of their family in this way then
they would do so. They could not carve up England, or Normandy,
or Anjou, or Poitou, because these were established political and
social communities where the leading landowners had a sense of
solidarity – of being English, or Norman, or Angevin, or Poitevin
– but in this sense the whole empire was *not* a single political community and it could be broken up into its constituent parts as the
interests of the ruling dynasty required. This essential divisibility
of the Angevin Empire was glossed over by the circumstances in
which Richard succeeded his father in 1189, but there was no reason
why it should not come to the fore again when he died. This indeed
was what happened. His mother Eleanor remained Duchess of Aquitaine; Anjou, Maine and Touraine declared for Arthur; England
and Normandy accepted John. John's problems began with a succession dispute.

The responsibility for this is commonly laid at Richard's door.
He is said to have created trouble by negligently failing to leave a
clear-cut successor. If there were any truth in this it would be a
grave charge, since there can be no doubt that succession disputes
were the most frequent cause of serious political unrest in twelfth-
century Europe, as in seventh-century Europe or in seventeenth-
century Europe. Contemporaries knew this and worried about it.
When, after a period of doubt, an heir to the throne was born there
was general rejoicing. The birth of an heir held out the promise
of stability. The legend of the birth of James of Aragon in 1208,
as told by the later Aragonese chronicler Ramon Muntaner, makes
the point vividly. James's father, Peter II of Aragon, avoided his
wife, Marie of Montpellier, because he was in love with another

young lady. This so alarmed the people of Montpellier – 'for if the king should die and there should be no heir it would be a great hurt for all his country' – that they approached one of the King's household knights and persuaded him to tell the King that the lady he loved was waiting for him in a darkened bed chamber. In reality it was, of course, the Queen who was placed there. Not content with this, about fifty of the notables of Montpellier knelt all night long outside the lady's bedchamber, praying that the King was doing his duty inside. In addition all the city churches remained open so that the whole population could join in this night of fervent prayer. Needless to say not until dawn came and fifty witnesses barged into the bedchamber did King Peter recognize his Queen. She bore a son nine months later, of course, and no one could deny that he was the legitimate heir to the throne of Aragon.

Roger of Howden's story of the hermit's warning to Richard suggests that some of his subjects watched the progress of his marriage to Berengaria with similar concern – if with less ingenuity. Although Richard had an illegitimate son, in eight years of marriage there were no children – and they did not live apart all the time. Was this childlessness the result of Richard's political irresponsibility? That it was seems to be the implication of those who say that Richard was homosexual: he enjoyed the pleasures of the present with no thought for the future of his dominions. But there is no evidence that he was homosexual and some that he was not. If he was, then it is truly remarkable that Gerald of Wales failed to mention the fact. In the latter part of his life Gerald was a disappointed man who systematically dragged up every scandal he could in order to blacken the reputations of the Angevin kings. But homosexual or not, what could Richard have done if his wife was barren? Have the marriage annulled? This would certainly have been normal political practice, but it would also have been unwise for as long as the Navarre alliance kept its value – in the years 1193–4 it had been extremely useful. Only after the alliance with Toulouse in 1196 did a break with Navarre become conceivable and it is possible that by 1198 Richard was considering an annulment. In the meantime, since he did not expect to die, there was no reason to make anything other than provisional arrangements for the succession – though this was no easy task in view of the youth of his nephew Arthur and the unreliable behaviour of his brother John in the years 1189–94. It is, however, clear that by the autumn of 1197 Richard had recognized John as heir presumptive, and he confirmed this arrangement on his deathbed. On the whole, it seems fair to conclude that what could be done to clarify the question of the succession had been done, but given the complex political and legal structure of the Angevin dominions it could not be taken for granted that one heir would scoop the lot. This was still something which would have to be fought for – as Richard had fought for it between 1183 and 1189.

If, on the other hand, it was a king's chief duty to stay alive until he had a son to succeed him then there can be no doubt that Richard had his faults. He was not as careful of his health as he might have been; by King Philip's standards he was positively reckless. There were times when he was prepared to take risks. In this context the fact that he was not wearing armour at the siege of Chalus-Chabrol is irrelevant. Knights, even in the midst of war, wore their coats of mail only when they had to and the shield carried before him should have given adequate protection. None the less his active and whole-hearted participation in every aspect of warfare meant that he was sometimes in danger of being wounded or, more seriously, of being captured. This comes across very clearly from his record as a crusader. Ambroise recorded a conversation supposed to have taken place in the autumn of 1192 when Hubert Walter went on pilgrimage to Jerusalem and met Saladin. The two men discussed Richard. Hubert Walter praised him, emphasizing his prowess, chivalry and generosity:

>   'Sire, I say with pride
> That my lord is the finest knight
> On earth ...'
> The sultan heard the bishop through
> And answered: 'Well I know 'tis true
> That brave and noble is the king,
> But with what rashness doth he fling
> Himself! Howe'er great prince I be

I should prefer to have in me
Reason and moderation and largesse
Than courage carried to excess.'

Richard's bravery was not, however, nothing more than the use-less self-indulgence of a warrior who shared Bertrand de Born's appreciation of the excitements of hand-to-hand combat. Doubtless this was part of it but it was also linked with a sense of honour, an unwillingness to ask his soldiers to run risks which he himself would not. Such courage was, moreover, useful. His men fought better knowing that their lord was with them, that he would not run away. As a result the morale of Richard's troops was high and, other things being equal, they had a good chance of winning their skirmishes and their battles. The author of the *History of William Marshal* acknowledges that French knights were normally recog-nized to be the best in Europe but says that when Richard was their leader thirty of his knights would confidently take on forty Frenchmen, and beat them too.

As we can see from the words attributed to Saladin, there were contemporaries who criticized Richard's apparent indifference to his own safety, but most men judged him with their hearts rather than with their minds, and it is clear that it was precisely because he was prepared to plunge into the thick of danger that he became a hero in the eyes of his own followers. If he had asked them, said one contemporary chronicler, his soldiers would have waded through blood as far as the Pillars of Hercules for his sake. Above all else this was the quality which made him a legend in his own lifetime and which kept his memory alive in subsequent centuries. But we should not be blinded by the brilliance of the legend and be made incapable of seeing anything else. Judged as a politician, administrator and war-lord – in short, as a king – he was one of the outstanding rulers of European history.

To assess Richard fairly we have to see him in the company of his contemporaries. If the least a king could do was to avoid the disgrace of losing his patrimony – the land he inherited from his father – then it is clear that he was a much more successful ruler than either his brother or his father. Both John and Henry II died in the midst of political chaos which they themselves had created. If this comparison seems unjust to his father – a great king but one who lost his touch towards the end of a long reign (a fate which might also have befallen Richard) – then we might recall that Richard was king for less than a decade. Henry II enjoys a great reputation as the king who shaped the common law of England and did much to strengthen the position of the crown. But most of the reforms on which his reputation rests came in the second and third decades of his reign. If he had died in 1164, after a reign as short as Richard's, he would have done very little to make himself famous. Most kings needed time to establish themselves – but not Richard. Within two or three years of coming to the throne, his crusade had already made him world-famous. In 1189 he was, of course, an experienced soldier and politician. He had learned a great deal in the hard school of Aquitaine. In judging him we should never see him only as the crusader king; most of his life he was Duke of Aquitaine and – as is clear from the circumstances of his death – the politics of his mother's duchy was always one of his chief concerns.

As it happened, he died in a rebellion behind which we can see the hand of Philip Augustus. For most of his political life this was the man against whom Richard was measured. In some ways it is not easy to compare them for one died early, while the other reaped the rewards given to those who outlive their enemies. On the other hand, in the years 1194–9 their struggle was the main strand in the politics of north-western Europe and it is possible to study their performances in this arena. Both Kings were experts in the art of siege warfare. As the man in possession of the castles in dispute Philip held an advantage. Moreover, he had the interior lines of communication. None the less these two advantages were insufficient to give him the initiative. In the first place Richard was the better all-round soldier, as much at home on the battlefield or on a reconnaissance patrol as he was in the trenches of a siege. This meant that Philip was afraid to meet Richard in open country or to risk battle against him – and he was right to be afraid. In the second place Richard's financial resources enabled him to bring massive pressure to bear against Philip's castles. He had enough siege-artillery, crossbowmen, archers and assault troops to put the fear of Richard into the constable of any castle.

Richard won his wars not simply by deeds of prowess on the battle-field, but also by being able to transform the economic resources of the Angevin Empire into military supplies and ensure that these supplies were in the right place at the right time – in other words by sheer administrative competence. The image of Richard as a knight in armour, good at fighting but at nothing else, is an image based upon a romantic and unrealistic view of war. Campaigns were not won by displays of mindless courage. Twelfth-century warfare, revolving around the control of stone castles and fortified towns, was as precise a discipline as warfare in the age of Vauban. To master this discipline a man required many skills: a grasp of military tactics and strategy, the ability to pick good subordinates and the ability to inspire their confidence and loyalty. Obviously Richard made mistakes – the appointment of Gilbert de Vascœuil as constable of Gisors, for example – but taken as a whole his record was a re-markable one. In tactics his march from Acre to Jaffa was a model of its kind, as was the manner in which he exploited efficient recon-naissance in order to drive Philip in utter confusion into Gisors in 1198. In strategy he showed himself capable of organizing a crusade, planning an attack upon Egypt, and conducting the overall defence of the Angevin Empire. In politics and diplomacy he was able to outmanœuvre Philip by making the crucial alliances with Flanders and Toulouse. In administration he was ultimately responsible for picking such men as Hubert Walter and Geoffrey FitzPeter in Eng-land, Robert of Thornham in Anjou, Geoffrey de la Celle in Aqui-taine, while the case of William FitzRalph as seneschal of Normandy makes it clear that he did not recklessly dismiss all his father's senior officials out of hand. These justiciars and seneschals did not only collect money on Richard's behalf; they also spent it, chiefly – as the King himself did – on war. Efficient administration is not simply a matter of collecting large quantities of money without arousing too much opposition, it is also a matter of spending money effec-tively so that the desired end is achieved. In this sense Richard him-self was a fine administrator who knew the political, diplomatic and military value of open-handedness.

It would be very odd if we shared twelfth-century values; none the less it is in the light of values which are not our own that we must try to understand Richard and his contemporaries. We might think, for example, that the crusades were a terrible waste of human life and that the time spent on barbarous and intolerant wars could have been much better employed. But in the twelfth and thirteenth centuries even the best educated and most humane Christians thought otherwise. In going on crusade to recover the Holy Land, the patrimony of Christ, Richard was living up to the standards of his own day. So, too, contemporaries accepted that it was right and proper – if unpleasant – that they should be required to pour out their treasures to pay his ransom and to pay for the wars to recover his patrimony from the aggressions of Philip Augustus. Thus William of Newburgh observed that although Richard taxed his subjects more heavily than his father had done, they did not complain so much about it. They trusted him to spend money in ways that made sense to them – just as later generations trusted those other successful warrior-kings, Edward III and Henry V. But Richard tackled and solved far greater logistical problems than ever confronted either them or, to take the example of another famous soldier, William the Conqueror. He took a fleet and an army not just to the other side of the Channel but to the other end of the Mediterranean and there he fought on equal terms with no less an opponent than Saladin. Since Saladin had access to much greater reserves of men, money and supplies near at hand in the Middle East, this was an astonishing achievement. Because Richard failed to recapture Jerusalem his crusade, in the purely emotional terms of a crusade, is seen as a failure, but as an example of administrative efficiency it is superb. For this reason it is appropriate to leave the last word not to an English or a French chronicler but to a Muslim one. In Ibn al-Athir's judgement 'Richard's courage, shrewdness, energy and patience made him the most remarkable ruler of his times.'

SELECT BIBLIOGRAPHY

Among earlier biographies of Richard, one is still well worth reading: K. Norgate, *Richard the Lionheart* (London 1924). J. Gillingham, *The Life and Times of Richard I* (London 1973) is worth looking at for the sake of its illustrations. Unfortunately the most recent French life – by R. Pernoud, *Richard Coeur de Lion* (Paris 1988) – takes virtually no account of work done in the last ten years.

Much the best brief assessment of Richard as ruler is J. O. Prestwich, 'Richard Coeur de Lion: *rex bellicosus*' in *Riccardo Cuor di Leone nella storia e nella leggenda*, Accademia Nazionale dei Lincei, Problemi attuali di scienza e di cultura 253 (Rome 1981). See also J. Gillingham, 'The Art of Kingship: Richard I' *History Today* 35 (April 1985).

W. L. Warren, *Henry II* (London 1973) is both massive and readable. It is useful for Richard's relations with his father and his career as Duke of Aquitaine.

L. Landon, Itinerary of King Richard I (London: Pipe Roll Society N.S. vol. 13, 1935) provides the indispensable chronological framework.

J. T. Appleby, *England without Richard* (London 1965) chronicles events in Richard's absence.

J. W. Baldwin, *The Government of Philip Augustus* (Berkeley, California 1986) is an important study of Richard's great opponent.

Like its predecessors this biography is based chiefly on well-known contemporary narrative sources. Of these the most important are:

Roger of Howden, *Gesta Henrici II et Ricardi I*, ed W. Stubbs, 2 vols (R[olls] S[eries] 1867)

Roger of Howden, *Chronica*, ed. W. Stubbs, 4 vols (R.S. 1868–71)

Ralph of Diss, *Radulfi de Diceto Decani Londiniensis Opera Historica*, ed. W. Stubbs, 2 vols (R.S. 1876)

Ralph of Coggeshall, *Chronicon Anglicanum*, ed J. Stevenson (R.S. 1875)

Richard of Devizes, *Chronicon*, ed. and trans. J. T. Appleby (London 1963)

William of Newburgh, *Historia Rerum Anglicarum*, ed. R. Howlett in *Chronicles of the Reigns of Stephen, Henry II and Richard I*, vols 1 and 2 (R.S. 1884)

Histoire de Guillaume le Maréchal, ed. P. Meyer, 3 vols (Société de l'histoire de France, Paris 1891–1907)

Œuvres de Rigord et de Guillaume le Breton, ed H. F. Delaborde, 2 vols (Société de l'histoire de France, Paris 1882–5)

Geoffrey de Vigeois, *Chronica*, ed. P. Labbe, *Novæ Bibliothecæ Manuscriptorum* II (Paris 1657)

Ambroise, *L'Estoire de la Guerre Sainte*, ed. G. Paris (Paris 1897). Translated by M. J. Hubert and J. La Monte as *The Crusade of Richard Lionheart* (New York 1941)

Itinerarium Peregrinorum et Gesta Regis Ricardi, ed. W. Stubbs (R.S. 1864)

To all those chronicles which were written in England and Normandy during this period A. Gransden, *Historical Writing in England c.550–c.1307* (London 1974) provides an exceptionally useful guide.

CHAPTER NOTES

CHAPTER ONE. THE LIONHEART OF LEGEND

'Medieval history was always slowly turning into Romance' and a stage
in this process can be seen in the *Crusade and Death of Richard I*, ed.
R. C. Johnston (Anglo-Norman Texts, vol. 17, 1961). The thirteenth-
century Romance of Richard's life survives only in a fourteenth-century
Middle English version, ed. K. Brunner, *Der mittelenglische Versroman
über Richard Löwenherz* (Vienna 1913). The legendary Capetian view
of Richard is encapsulated in Guillaume Guiart's fourteenth-century
verse history, *Branches des royaux lignages*, ed. J. A. Buchon (Paris
1820). Some of the earliest legends were told by Roger of Wendover,
Flores Historiarum, ed. H. G. Hewlett, vol. 3, pp 21–27 (R. S. 1886–9).
B. B. Broughton, *The Legends of King Richard I* (The Hague 1966), is
a thoroughly prosaic survey of the king's place in medieval poetry and
legend. On the Blondel legend, L. Weise, *Die Lieder des Blondel de Nesle*
(Dresden 1904), pp xix–xxxviii. On the continuing influence of these
stories see J. Gillingham, 'Some legends of Richard the Lionheart: their
development and their influence' in *Riccardo Cuor di Leone nella storia e
nella leggenda* (already cited). For a child's view of Richard see such
statements as 'Richard was not a good king. He cared only for his
soldiers,' L. Du Garde Peach, *Richard the Lionheart* (Ladybird History
Book, London 1965).

CHAPTER TWO. AT THE CASTLE OF CHALUS-CHABROL

The full text of Bernard Itier's vital testimony together with the charter
evidence for the Paris-Limoges-Angoulême alliance was printed more
than a hundred years ago by F. Arbellot, *La vérité sur la mort de Richard
Coeur-de-Lion* (Paris 1878). Unfortunately the work of this Limousin

historian never received the attention it deserved and in consequence
knowledge of his conclusions for long remained restricted to other local
historians, e.g., P. Patier, *Le siège de Chalus-Chabrol par le Roy Richard
Coeur de Lion, L'an 1199. Étude des deux châteaux de Chalus* (Limoges
1973). The argument of this chapter was elaborated and detailed references given in J. Gillingham, 'The Unromantic Death of Richard I'
Speculum 54 (1979).

On the kind of medical treatment Richard might have received see
L. Paterson, 'Military Surgery: Knights, Sergeants, and Raimon of Avig-
non's Version of the *Chirurgia* of Roger of Salerno (1180–1209)' in ed.
C. Harper-Bill and R. Harvey, *The Ideals and Practice of Medieval
Knighthood II* (Woodbridge 1988).

There is still no good study of the twelfth-century viscounts of
Limoges, though there is some information, presented in a confusing
fashion, in G. Tenant de la Tour, *L'Homme et la Terre de Charlemagne
à Saint Louis* (Paris 1942). On the counts of Angoulême see R. C. Watson,
*The counts of Angloulême from the ninth century to the mid-thirteenth
century* (Ph.D. thesis, Univ. of East Anglia, 1979).

CHAPTER THREE. THE HOUSES OF ANJOU AND AQUITAINE

Two helpful general guides to the political scene in medieval France are
E. M. Hallam, *Capetian France 987–1328* (London 1980) and J. Dunba-
bin, *France in the Making 843–1180* (Oxford 1985). The latter is particularly good on the principalities, on which see also K. F. Werner,
'Kingdom and principalities in 12th-century France' in T. Reuter, ed.
and trans., *The Medieval Nobility* (Amsterdam 1979). On the Angevin
Empire see J. Boussard, *Le gouvernement d'Henri II Plantagenêt* (Paris
1965); J. Le Patourel, 'The Plantagenet Dominions' *History* 50 (1965);
J. Gillingham, *The Angevin Empire* (London 1984); and R. Benjamin,
'The Angevin Empire' *History Today* 36 (February 1986). On Anjou
itself J. Boussard, *Le Comté d'Anjou sous Henri Plantagenêt et ses fils
1151–1204* (Paris 1938) remains useful but there is still no equivalent
study of the Angevins as dukes of Aquitaine in the second half of the
12th century. In the meantime we have to rely upon the relevant sections
of the old study by A. Richard, *Histoire des Comtes de Poitou 778–1204*
(Paris 1903), though there are some pointers in R. Hajdu, 'Castles,
castellans and the structure of politics in Poitou 1152–1271' *Journal of
Medieval History* 4 (1978). A forthcoming work by J. Martindale on the
earlier dukes of Aquitaine will contain much of value; in the meantime
local insights are offered by C. Higounet, *Bordeaux pendant le haut moyen*

age (Bordeaux 1963); G. T. Beech, *A Rural Society in Medieval France: the Gâtine of Poitou in the Eleventh and Twelfth Centuries* (Baltimore 1964); and, in particular, by G. Devailly, *Le Berry du Xe siècle jusqu'au milieu du XIIe siècle* (Paris 1973) and A. Debord, *La Société laïque dans les Pays de la Charente X–XII siècles* (Paris 1984).

On relations between the Angevins and Toulouse see R. Benjamin, 'A Forty Years War: Toulouse and the Plantagenets, 1156–96' *Historical Research* 61 (1988); also E. Mason, ' "Rocamadour in Quercy above all other churches": the healing of Henry II' in ed. W. Sheils, *Studies in Church History* xix (Oxford 1982).

On the wine trade the fundamental work remains R. Dion, *Histoire de la vigne et du vin en France des origines au XIXe siècle* (Paris 1959). See also some of the essays in Y. Renouard, *Études d'histoire médiévale* (Paris 1968). On the rise of La Rochelle, R. Favreau, 'Les débuts de la ville de la Rochelle', *Cahiers de Civilisation Médiévale* 30 (1987).

The 'guidebook' for pilgrims to Compostella was edited by J. Vielliard, *Le Guide du pèlerin de St Jacques de Compostelle* (Macon 1969), but it needs to be read in the light of the cautionary tale told by C. Hohler, 'A Note on Jacobus', *Journal of the Warburg and Courtauld Institute* 35 (1972). On the Angevins and Santiago see K. Leyser, 'Frederick Barbarossa, Henry II and the hand of St. James', *English Historical Review* 90 (1975).

For the kind of education Richard would have received, I used Gottfried von Strassburg's *Tristan* in the English translation by A. T. Hatto (Harmondsworth 1960). More generally see now N. Orme, *From Childhood to Chivalry. The education of the English kings and aristocracy 1066–1530* (London 1984). On Richard as a song-writer see P. Dronke, *The Medieval Lyric* (2nd edn., London 1978). On tournaments see J. R. V. Barker, *The Tournament in England 1100–1400* (Woodbridge 1986) and G. Duby, *William Marshal. The Flower of Chivalry* (London 1986). On the whole subject of chivalry and the chivalrous outlook there is now the fine study of M. Keen, *Chivalry* (London 1984).

Richard's inner life is, of course, beyond our reach but, to all appearances, he was pious in the conventional manner of kings. See Coggeshall, *Chronicon*, p. 97; Howden, *Chronica*, iv, 299–90, *Gesta Regis Ricardi*, 146–7; Adam of Eynsham, Magna Vita, pp 101–5; Robert of Auxerre, *Monumenta Germaniae Historica* SS XXVI, 259; *Chronicon Turonense Magnum* (Recueil des Chroniques de Touraine ed. A. Salmon, Tours 1854), p. 144. On his deathbed Richard forgave the man who shot him, Coggeshall, p. 96, and the letter of Radulfus Presbiter printed by C. Kohler, 'Notices et extraits de manuscrits', *Revue de l'Orient latin* 5 (1897). During both his stays in England as king he went out of his way to visit Bury St Edmunds. See also *The Chronicle of Jocelin of Brake-*

lond, ed. H. E. Butler (London 1949), p. 49, and Ambroise, *The Crusade*, p. 91. On Richard's relations with Hugh of Lincoln see K. J. Leyser, 'The Angevin Kings and the Holy Man' in ed. H. Mayr-Harting, *St Hugh of Lincoln* (Oxford 1987).

There are comments on the relationship between the crown and other bishops in D. Walker, 'Crown and Episcopacy under the Normans and Angevins' *Anglo-Norman Studies V* ed. R. A. Brown, (Woodbridge 1982) and D. Spear, 'The Norman Empire and the Secular Clergy, 1066–1204' *Journal of British Studies* 21 (1982).

On Richard as a patron of the monastic orders see E. M. Hallam, 'Henry II, Richard I and the Order of Grandmont', *Journal of Medieval History* 1 (1975) and her *Aspects of the Monastic Patronage of the English and French Royal Houses c.1130–1270* (unpub. London Ph.D. thesis 1976) where Richard appears as rather more generous than both Henry II and Philip Augustus. On the building of Richard's churches at Bonport and Petit Andeli see L. M. Grant, *Gothic Architecture in Normandy, c.1150–c.1250* (unpub. London Ph.D. thesis 1986). On his association with the Order of St Thomas at Acre see A. J. Forey, 'The Military Order of St Thomas at Acre', *EHR* 92 (1977). One indication of the close relation between Richard and the Cistercians can be seen in A. D. A. Monna, 'Diagnose van een omstreden 13e eeuwse kalender uit de Servaasabdij te Utrecht' *Archief voor de Geschiednis van de Katholieke Kerk in Nederland*, 25 (1983).

There is a good, brief introduction to the problem of courtly love in C. Morris, *The Discovery of the Individual 1050–1200* (London 1972). See also L. T. Topsfield, *Troubadours and Love* (Cambridge 1975) and P. Dronke, *Medieval Latin and the Rise of the European Love Lyric* (2nd edn., London 1986). There is a useful selection of translated troubadour songs in A. R. Press, *Anthology of Troubadour Lyric Poetry* (Edinburgh 1971). On Eleanor's grandfather both as poet and as politician see J. Martindale, ' "Cavalaria et Orgueill" Duke William IX of Aquitaine and the Historian' in Harper-Bill and Harvey, *Ideals and Practice* (already cited).

CHAPTER FOUR. FAMILY CRISIS 1167–74

Richard's mother has always attracted biographers, but the more recent ones add little to the well-known accounts in A. Kelly, *Eleanor of Aquitaine and the Four Kings* (London 1952) and R. Pernoud, *Eleanor of Aquitaine* (London 1967). Both take an over-romantic view of her, as does also – despite its elaborate scholarly apparatus – E. R. Labande, 'Pour une image véridique d'Alienor d'Aquitaine', *Bulletin de la Société des Antiquaires de l'Ouest* 4th ser. 2 (1952). On Eleanor's position as Duchess of Aquitaine see J. C. Holt, 'Eleanore d'Aquitaine, Jean-sans-Terre et la succession de onze cent quatre-vingt dix neuf' in *Cahiers de Civilisation Médiévale* (forthcoming). Useful, though at times excessively sceptical of the chronicle evidence, is H. G. Richardson, 'The letters and charters of Eleanor of Aquitaine', *EHR* 74 (1959). See also B. Lees, 'The letters of Queen Eleanor of Aquitaine to Pope Celestine III', *EHR* (1906). There is a brief, sensible and down-to-earth appreciation of Eleanor's character by E. A. R. Brown in *Eleanor of Aquitaine: Patron and Politician*, ed. W. W. Kibler (Austin 1976). See also F. M. Chambers, 'Some legends concerning Eleanor of Aquitaine', *Speculum* 16 (1941). Andrew the Chaplain's much misunderstood treatise, *De Amore*, was translated into English under the title *The Art of Courtly Love* by J. J. Parry (New York 1941). But the idea that Eleanor established 'a court of love on a grand scale' was effectively criticized by J. F. Benton, 'The Court of Champagne as a Literary Center', *Speculum* 36 (1961) – despite the attempt by J. H. M. McCash, 'Marie de Champagne and Eleanor of Aquitaine: a relationship re-examined', *Speculum* 54 (1979) to salvage what can be salvaged. Literary historians seem to find it difficult not to exaggerate Eleanor's influence, e.g. R. Lejeune, 'Le rôle littéraire d'Alienor d'Aquitaine', *Cultura Neolatina* 14 (1954) and 'Le rôle littéraire de la famille d'Alienor d'Aquitaine', *Cahiers de civilisation medievale* 1 (1958). See also the essays by R. Baltzer, M. Lazar and E. S. Greenhill in the collection edited by W. W. Kibler. However the importance of the Angevin court is clear enough. See, for example, R. R. Bezzola, *Les Origines et la formation de la littérature courtoise en occident*, Part 3, *La société courtoise*, 2 vols, where volume one devotes 310 pages to the Angevin court while volume two deals with the courts of France, Sicily and Outremer in just 220 pages.

On Eleanor's first husband see M. Pacaut, *Louis VII et son Royaume* (Paris 1964).

On the Lusignan family there are two genealogical studies by S. Painter, 'The houses of Lusignan and Châtellerault, 1150–1250', *Speculum* 30 (1955) and 'The lords of Lusignan in the eleventh and twelfth centuries', *Speculum* 32 (1957), both reprinted in *Feudalism and Liberty: Articles and Addresses of Sidney Painter*, ed. F. A. Cazel (Baltimore 1961).

Richard's installation as duke of Aquitaine has been variously dated to 1170, 1172 and 1179. The chronology of Geoffrey of Vigeois makes it clear that 1172 is correct. On the political context of such ceremonies see H. Hoffman, 'Französische Fürstenweihen des Hochmittelalters', *Deutsches Archiv* 18 (1962).

The account of the revolt of 1173–4 is based largely upon Roger of

Howden, Ralph of Diss and Robert of Torigny, *Chronica* ed. R. Howlett, *Chronicles of the reigns of Stephen etc.*, vol. iv (R. S. 1889). La Rochelle's role can be inferred from the agitated words of Richard the Poitevin, *Recueil des historiens des Gaules et de la France*, vol. 12, pp 418–21.

CHAPTER FIVE. DUKE OF AQUITAINE 1174–83

The best book on the conduct of war in the middle ages remains R. C. Smail, *Crusading Warfare 1097–1196* (Cambridge 1956). Most of his insights apply as much to war in Western Europe as to war in the Middle East. See also J. Gillingham, 'Richard I and the Science of War in the Middle Ages' in ed. J. Gillingham and J. C. Holt, *War and Government in the Middle Ages. Essays in honour of J. O. Prestwich* (Woodbridge 1984). For an extremely useful general survey see P. Contamine, *War in the Middle Ages* (Oxford 1984). G. Duby, *Le Dimanche de Bouvines* (Paris 1973) is provocatively written and sometimes illuminating. On the role of castles in warfare see N. Hooper, 'Strongholds and Strategy' in ed. R. A. Brown, *Castles. A History and Guide* (Poole 1980) and C. Coulson, 'Fortress Policy in Capetian Tradition and Angevin Practice. Aspects of the Conquest of Normandy by Philip II' in ed. R. A. Brown, *Anglo-Norman Studies VI* (Woodbridge 1983). On the relationship between war and chivalry see J. Gillingham, 'War and Chivalry in the History of William the Marshal', in eds. P. R. Coss and S. D. Lloyd, *Thirteenth Century England: II* (Woodbridge 1988).

On the 1175 siege of Castillon-sur-Agen and not, as is commonly stated, Castillon-sur-Dordogne, see Howden, *Gesta*, vol. 1, p. 101, and J. Andrieu, *Histoire de l'Agenais* (Agen 1893), vol. 1, pp 38–42.

On the Cornish connections of the Viscounts of Limoges: Geoffrey of Vigeois, ed. Labbe, pp 309–10; T. D. Hardy, *Rotuli Litterarum Clausarum* (Record Commission 1833), pp. 429, 437. On tin mining see G. R. Lewis, *The Stannaries* (Harvard 1906), especially Appendices J and L.

It is debatable whether Richard should be credited with the defeat of Vulgrin's Brabançons in 1176. According to Ralph of Diss the Brabançons entered Poitou in their usual obnoxious fashion but then received the fate they deserved in a battle at Barbezieux at the hands of forces raised in Richard's absence by Bishop John of Poitiers and Theobald Chabot, *princeps militiæ Ricardi ducis* (Diceto 1, p. 407). This is the most detailed account and historians have generally accepted it, but it contains one rather odd feature. Barbezieux lies south of Angoulême – hardly on the route of an invasion of the diocese of Poitiers. Roger of Howden's version (*Gesta* 1, pp 120–21), clearly based upon a contemporary official account,

mentions neither Bishop John nor Theobald Chabot, but simply says
that Richard overcame the Brabançons in a battle between St Maigrin and
Bouteville – which is not a bad way of describing the site of Barbezieux. It
is, of course, possible that there were two separate clashes in the same
area, but perhaps more likely that the same event was recorded from two
very different points of view. Ralph of Diss, writing some years later than
Howden, saw the episode through the eyes of Bishop John; we know that
he sought and obtained information from him (Diceto 1, pp 5–6).

We know very little about the subjugation of the Limousin by Henry
II and Richard in 1177. Since both father and son were there, Roger of
Howden lacked his usual source of information – the reports sent by
Richard to his father in England. There is, however, one piece of evidence
which has hitherto been overlooked by historians of the Angevin Empire
and which can probably be dated to this year. This is a letter written by
Abbot Archamband of Solignac, a Benedictine house just south of
Limoges, and printed in *Recueil des Chartes de l'abbaye de Stavelot-
Malmédy*, ed. J. Halkin and C. G. Roland (Brussels 1909), vol. 1, pp 506–
7. The editors' dating of this letter to 1170–76 can be disregarded since
it is based on the hopelessly unreliable list of abbots of Solignac in *Gallia
Christiana* II, 570.

On Henry II's acquisition of La Marche see G. Thomas, *Les Comtes
de la Marche de la maison de Charroux*, pp 49–51.

The history of the southern border of Aquitaine is almost totally veiled
in obscurity. Spanish historians have understandably been absorbed by
the story of the Reconquista and have, in consequence, neglected their
northern borders. I have used: F. W. Schirrmacher, *Geschichte Spaniens*,
vols 3 and 4; P. Tucoo-Chala, *La Vicomté de Béarn et le problème de sa
souveraineté* (Bordeaux 1961); C. Higounet, 'La Rivalité des maisons de
Toulouse et de Barcelone pour la préponderance méridionale', *Mélanges
d'histoire du Moyen Age dédiés à la mémoire de Louis Haphen* (Paris 1951).

On the Young King see O. H. Moore, *The Young King Henry Plantagenet 1155–1183* in *History, Literature and Tradition* (Columbus 1925).

The standard edition of Bertrand de Born's poems is now G. Gouiran,
L'Amour et la Guerre. L'Oeuvre de Bertrand de Born (Aix-en-Provence
1985).

The tentative explanation offered here for the curious Clairvaux
episode is chiefly based on parallels with the Saint-Rémy-sur-Creuse
inquest, *Archives historiques du Poitou*, vol. 8, pp 39–53, and on the
little that we know about the earlier history of Clairvaux: C. Chevalier,
'Cartulaire de l'abbaye de Noyers,' *Mémoires de la Société archéologique
de Touraine* 22 (1872), pp 402, 476, 486, 505–6, 528–9, 626; 'Documents
concernant le prieuré de St Denis en Vaux', *Archives historique du Poitou*,
vol. 7, p. 347. For Geoffrey of Vigeois's account of the 1182–3 revolt it

is best to refer to *Recueil des historiens des Gaules et de la France*, vol. 18, pp 212–20.

CHAPTER SIX. THE UNCERTAIN INHERITANCE 1183–9

Study of Richard's quarrel with Raymond v of Toulouse in the 1180s was put on a new basis by R. Benjamin's discovery (and re-dating) of a treaty between Richard and King Alfonso of Aragon, R. Benjamin, 'A Forty Years War' (already cited).

On Henry II's attitude to the crusading movement see H. E. Mayer, 'Henry II of England and the Holy Land', *EHR* 97 (1982). For some contemporary views of Richard's attitude see E. Siberry, *Criticism of Crusading 1095–1274* (Oxford 1985), pp 52–63.

Historians have been inclined to give Gerald of Wales's account of Henry's last days (*Giraldi Cambrensis Opera*, ed. J. S. Brewer and G. F. Warner, R.S. 1861–91, vol. i, 8off.; iv, 369–72; viii, 286–305) more credence than it deserves largely in the belief that, however, biased, he was at least an eye-witness. It is, however, clear that he left Henry's court after the burning of Le Mans and headed north to Normandy while the king turned south. For an analysis of the dramatic shape which Gerald gave to his account of Henry's last days see R. Bartlett, *Gerald of Wales 1146–1223* (Oxford 1982), pp 84–91.

CHAPTER SEVEN. PREPARING THE CRUSADE 1189–90

On William Marshal see S. Painter, (Baltimore 1933); G. Duby, *William Marshal. The Flower of Chivalry* (London 1986) – on which see my comments in 'War and Chivalry' (cited above); and D. Crouch, 'Strategies of Lordship in Angevin England and the Career of William Marshal' in Harper-Bill and Harvey (cited above).

On Baldwin of Béthune see the *Histoire des ducs de Normandie et des rois d'Angleterre*, ed. F. Michel (Paris 1840), pp 99–100.

On Richard's brothers see W. L. Warren, *King John* (London 1961) and D. L. Douie, *Archbishop Geoffrey Plantagenet* (York 1960). A good study of William Longchamp is long overdue. In the opinion of F. J. West, *The Justiciarship in England 1066–1232* (Cambridge 1966), he was 'plainly an efficient superintendent of royal business'.

The evidence for the complicated story of Richard's betrothals (both to Alice and Berengaria), and for his supposed homosexuality is set out in J. Gillingham, 'Richard I and Berengaria of Navarre', *BIHR* 53 (1980). So far as I am aware the first writer to state that Richard was homosexual was J. H. Harvey, *The Plantagenets* (London 1948). Since then it has generally been accepted as fact, indeed enshrined in the *Encyclopaedia Britannica*, (15th edn. 1980). For one of his more recent biographers, J. Brundage, Richard's supposed homosexuality was an indication of his 'emotional immaturity', *Richard Lionheart* (New York 1973), pp 88–9, 202 and 257–8. So it is hardly surprising that Richard now figures in histories of homosexuality, e.g. N. I. Garde (in drag?), *Jonathon to Gide* (New York 1974); A. L. Rowse, *Homosexuals in History* (London 1977); and J. Boswell, *Christianity, Social Tolerance and Homosexuality* (Chicago 1980). It is in this guise that he appears in films – e.g. *The Lion in Winter* – and in popular historical novels, though for a recent exception in this genre see M. Rofheart, *Lionheart!* (New York 1981). I have discussed the implications of this view of Richard in 'Some legends' (cited above). The subject of marriage in the twelfth century has been dealt with, fascinatingly but also somewhat erratically, in two books by G. Duby, *Medieval Marriage. Two Models from Twelfth-Century France* (Baltimore 1978) and *The Knight, the Lady and the Priest* (Harmondsworth 1985).

On Richard's illegitimate son Philip see *Archives historiques de Poitou* vol. 4, pp 21–2 and Howden, *Chronica* iv, 97 – though in view of the silence of the Limousin sources, Bernard Itier and Giraut de Bornelh, there is room for scepticism about Howden's statement that Philip avenged his father's death by killing the viscount of Limoges.

CHAPTER EIGHT. SICILY AND CYPRUS 1190–91

On Roger of Howden, the single most important chronicler of the reigns of Henry II and Richard I, see J. Gillingham, 'Roger of Howden on Crusade' in ed. D. O. Morgan, *Medieval Historical Writing in the Christian and Islamic Worlds* (London 1982); D. Corner, 'The earliest surviving manuscripts of Roger of Howden's "Chronica"', *EHR* 98 (1983); and D. Corner, 'The *Gesta Regis Henrici Secundi* and Chronica of Roger, Parson of Howden', *BIHR* 56 (1983).

Much of what F. Braudel has to say about weather, sea and ships in his classic book, *The Mediterranean and the Mediterranean World in the Age of Philip II* (London 1972), esp. pp 246–65 is relevant to 12th century conditions. In this area particularly important work is now being done by J. H. Pryor. See his articles on 'The Transportation of Horses by Sea during the Era of the Crusades' and 'The Naval Architecture of Crusader Transport Ships' in *The Mariner's Mirror* 68 (1982) and 70 (1984), both reprinted in J. H. Pryor, *Commerce, Shipping and Naval Warfare in the Medieval Mediterranean* (London 1987) as well as his *Geography*, *technology and war. Studies in the maritime history of the Mediterranean 649–1571* (Cambridge 1988).

On Sicily in this period see J. J. Norwich, *The Kingdom in the Sun* (London 1970); E. M. Jamison, *Admiral Eugenius of Sicily* (London 1957); and D. Abulafia, *The Two Italies* (Cambridge 1977). D. Clementi, 'The circumstances of Count Tancred's accession to the Kingdom of Sicily', *Mélanges Antonio Maronqiù* (Palermo 1967) and 'Some unnoticed aspects of the Emperor Henry VI's conquest of the Norman Kingdom of Sicily', *Bulletin of the John Rylands Library* 36 (1954) throw light on the problems facing Tancred of Lecce.

On Richard's conquest of Cyprus see G. Hill, *A History of Cyprus*, vol. 1 (Cambridge 1940). For the suggestion that the conquest must have been in Richard's mind from the outset see J. O. Prestwich, 'Richard Coeur de Lion: *rex bellicosus*' (already cited).

CHAPTER NINE. ACRE AND ARSUF 1191

The most useful short history of the crusades is H. E. Mayer, *The Crusades* (2nd edn., Oxford 1988). On the Third Crusade in particular see S. Runciman, *A History of the Crusades*, vol. 3 (Cambridge 1954). On the politics of the kingdom of Jerusalem see J. Riley-Smith, *The Feudal Nobility and the Kingdom of Jerusalem 1174–1277* (London 1973); J. Prawer, *Histoire du royaume latin de Jerusalem*, 2 vols (Paris 1969–70); J. Richard, *The Latin Kingdom of Jerusalem* (London 1979); R. C. Smail, 'The predicaments of Guy of Lusignan, 1183–1187' and B. Z. Kedar, 'The Patriarch Eraclius', both in *Outremer – Studies in the History of the Crusading Kingdom of Jerusalem presented to J. Prawer* (Jerusalem 1982). On the siege of Acre see R. Rogers, *Latin Siege Warfare in the Twelfth Century* (unpub. D.Phil. thesis, Oxford 1984).

R. C. Smail, 'The international status of the Latin kingdom of Jerusalem' in *The Eastern Mediterranean Lands in the Period of the Crusades*, ed. P. M. Holt (Warminster 1978) has investigated the circumstances in which Richard and Philip exercised governmental powers in Outremer. On this see also J. Gillingham, 'Roger of Howden on Crusade' (already cited).

On Saladin see M. C. Lyons and D. E. P. Jackson, *Saladin. The Politics of the Holy War* (Cambridge 1982) and H. Möhring, *Saladin und der Dritte Kreuzzug* (Wiesbaden 1980). An English translation of Baha ad-Din's *Life of Saladin* was published by the Palestine Pilgrims' Text Society (London 1897). There is a useful selection of translated extracts from Baha ad-Din, Imad ad-Din and Ibn al-Athir in F. Gabrieli, *Arab Historians of the Crusades* (London 1969).

An attempt to clarify the extraordinary complexities of the interrelated Old French chronicles of Outremer generally known as the *Estoire d'Eraclès* and the *Chronique d'Ernoul* was made by M. R. Morgan, *The Chronicle of Ernoul and the Continuations of William of Tyre* (Oxford 1973).

On Richard's quarrel with Leopold of Austria see H. Fichtenau, 'Akkon, Zypern und das Lösegeld für Richard Löwenherz', *Archiv für österreichische Geschichte* 125 (1966).

When Richard learned that Philip was returning home, he sent a group of his own servants back to Europe. They took with them a letter giving authority to a Pisan banker to raise large sums of money on their behalf. Since Richard's most trusted captain of mercenaries, Mercadier, was among them, there would appear to be little doubt that they were, very sensibly, being sent back to meet the attack which Philip was almost certain to launch. This, at least, is the implication of a letter, dated 3 August 1191, and listed by Landon, *Itinerary*, n. 359. Unfortunately, the letter seems to have been written, not by Richard in Acre, but by a forger in Paris in the 1840s. In 1840 Louis-Philippe opened a gallery in the Palace of Versailles in order to celebrate the part played by the French people in the history of the crusades; coats of arms of aristocratic families with crusader ancestors were put on display. But next year the gallery had to be closed owing to the storm of protest raised by those nobles who had been left out. Louis agreed to make four more rooms available and, starting in 1842, a flood of documents – possibly as many as 2000 – came on to the market in Paris, enabling the families who bought them to 'prove' their right to have their coat of arms displayed in the gallery of Versailles. One such coat of arms was that of the Walsh family – and among the men named as Mercadier's companions was Philip Walsh. See Comte de Belley de Blancmesnil, *Notice sur quelques anciens titres suivie de considérations sur les salles des croisades au musée de Versailles* (Paris 1866). Three hundred and fifty of these technically brilliant forgeries are now in the *Archives Nationales* in Paris: R. H. Bautier, 'La collection de chartes de croisade dite "Collection Courtois"', *Comptes rendus des séances de l'Académie des Inscriptions et Belles-Lettres* (Paris 1956). The forging of this letter may have had an academic as well as a commercial purpose. In 1841 a French historian published a paper on Mercadier commenting that he did not appear to have gone on crusade with Richard: H. Géraud, 'Mercadier: Les routiers au treizième siècle', *Bibliothèque de l'Ecole des Chartes* 3 (1841). Then this letter 'appeared' and Géraud printed it in the *Bibliothèque de l'Ecole des Chartes* 5 (1843), p. 36. Since this is the only piece of evidence for Mercadier's presence in the Holy Land (on which see Powicke, *The Loss of Normandy*, p. 232, Brundage, *op. cit.*, p. 218) it would clearly be wiser to return to Géraud's view of 1841.

CHAPTER TEN. JERUSALEM AND JAFFA 1191–2

On Richard's plan to invade Egypt see the writs issued at Jaffa on 11 October 1191 (Landon, *Itinerary*, nos. 363, 364) printed in C. Imperiale di Sant 'Angelo, *Codice diplomatico della reppublica di Genova*, vol. 3 (Rome 1942), 19, no. 7; Ambroise, *The Crusade*, pp 379–81; and the *Itinerarium*, pp 381–2. The two writs have been discussed by H. E. Mayer and M. L. Favreau, 'Das Diplom Balduins I. für Genua und Genuas Goldene Inschrift in der Grabeskirche', *Quellen und Forschungen aus italienischen Archiven und Bibliotheken* 55/56 (1976), pp 89–92. See also H. E. Mayer, 'Die Kanzlei Richards I. von England auf dem Dritten Kreuzzug', *Mitteilungen des Instituts für österreichische Geschichtsforschung* 85 (1977) and J. Sayers, 'English charters from the third crusade' in *Tradition and Change. Essays in honour of Marjorie Chibnall* (Cambridge 1985).

On the re-building of Ascalon, D. Pringle, 'King Richard I and the Walls of Ascalon', *Palestine Exploration Quarterly* 116 (1984).

On the Assassins see B. Lewis, *The Assassins* (London 1967) and C. E. Nowell, 'The Old Man of the Mountain', *Speculum* 22 (1947). On Conrad of Montferrat, J. Riley-Smith in the *Dizionario biografico degli Italiani* 29 (1983).

For an example of Richard's close association with local military experts see J. Riley-Smith, *The Knights of St John in Jerusalem and Cyprus c. 1050–1310* (London 1967), pp 107–15.

CHAPTER ELEVEN. PRISONER IN GERMANY 1193–4

The most vivid and detailed account of Richard's journey from Acre to Vienna is Coggeshall, *Chronicon*, pp 52–6. This account is, however, problematical. A marginal note seems to give it the authority of an eyewitness report – but so far as I am aware the eyewitness named, Anselm the Chaplain, is not known from any other source. (The view that Anselm was the author, or at least part author, of a now lost life of Richard – see *Itinerarium*, p. xxxiii and Gransden, *Historical Writing in England c. 550–c. 1307* (London 1974), pp 228, 239, 330 – is a mistake.) It is not clear whether Coggeshall claimed that he had obtained the whole story from Anselm, or just the two anecdotes on pages 54–5, originally written on an erasure. Alternative sources for the rest of Coggeshall's account could be Hugh Neville, whom he had earlier cited as his authority for his long and vivid description of the struggle for Jaffa (pp 41–51), or William de l'Etang, who had also distinguished himself at Jaffa and was one of Richard's companions on the journey home. These and other problems suggest that it is probably safer to rely on Roger of Howden, *Chronica* iii, 183–6 and Henry VI's letter to Philip Augustus (*ibid.*, p. 195). On this letter, correcting Landon, *Itinerary*, p. 71, n. 1, see G. Baaken, *Die Regesten des Kaiserreiches unter Heinrich VI.* (Cologne 1972), n. 271. It is possible that when Richard reached Corfu he was already in Norman territory: Abulafia, *The Two Italies*, p. 81, n. 58. That he hoped to travel to Saxony through Bohemia, principalities at that time hostile to Henry VI, is suggested by Andrew of Marchiennes (MGH SS VI, 430) and by an Austrian source, the *Continuatio Admuntensis* (MGH SS 9, p. 587).

On Richard's involvement in German politics see: J. Ahlers, *Die Welfen und die Englischen Könige 1165–1235* (Hildesheim 1987); F. Trauz, *Die Könige von England und das Reich* (Heidelberg 1961); R. H. Schmandt, 'The Election and Assassination of Albert of Louvain, Bishop of Liège 1191–2', *Speculum* 42 (1967); A. L. Poole, 'Richard the First's Alliances with the German Princes in 1194', *Studies in Medieval History presented to F. M. Powicke*, ed. R. W. Hunt and others (Oxford 1948): W. Kienast, *Die deutschen Fürsten im Dienste der Westmächte* (Utrecht 1924); and H. J. Kirfel, *Weltherrschaftsidee und Bündnispolitik* (Bonn 1959).

On Hubert Walter see C. R. Cheney, *Hubert Walter* (London 1967).

For the song which Richard composed while in captivity I have used Kate Norgate's translation, with some amendments in the fifth stanza.

The text of John's treaty with Philip in January 1194 is in Rymer, *Foedera*, vol. i, p. 57.

CHAPTER TWELVE. RECOVERY 1194–9

The major work on the reign of Philip Augustus is now J. W. Baldwin, *The Government of Philip Augustus* (Berkeley, California 1986), though both here and in his article 'La Décennie décisive: Les Années 1190–1203 dans le règne de Philippe Auguste' *Revue Historique* 266 (1981) he probably exaggerates the extent of Philip's successes in the 1190s. See also the essay in ed. R. H. Bautier, *La France de Philippe Auguste – Le temps des mutations* (Paris 1982). On the problems connected with the wars between Richard and Philip Augustus, F. M. Powicke, *The Loss of Normandy*, 2nd edn. (Manchester 1961) is still indispensable reading. So also, on the French side, is E. Audouin, *Essai sur l'armée royale au temps de Philippe Auguste* (Paris 1913). On the Angevin side the most important documents are the Norman Exchequer rolls, ed. T. Stapleton, *Magni Rotuli Scaccarii Normanniae*, 2 vols (London 1840–4). On these see J. C. Holt, 'The Loss of Normandy and Royal Finance' in eds. J. Gillingham and J. C. Holt, *War and Government* (already cited). P. N. Lewis, *The Wars of Richard I in the West* (unpub. M.Phil. diss. London 1977) contains some figures for expenditure on war revealed in the English and Norman exchequer rolls.

Conceivably Philip's capture of Fontaine in June 1194 may have led the author of the *Histoire des ducs de Normandie* (p. 88) to believe that he besieged Rouen twice. Otherwise, despite Powicke (p. 97, n. 16), there seems to be no definite evidence for two attacks on the ducal capital. See the *Chronicon Rotomagense* in P. Labbe, *Novæ Bibliothecæ*, vol. 1, p. 369 and L. Halphen, *Recueil d'Annales angevines* (Paris 1903), p. 26.

On Richard's attitude to the Truce of Tillières (July 1194) see Landon, *Itinerary*, pp 176–7. Powicke's view that Arques and Drincourt remained in Philip's hands until January 1196 (*op. cit.*, p. 190, n. 77) seems to be untenable in the light of the terms of the truce of Tillières and the payments recorded in Stapleton, *Magni Rotuli* 1, p. 137 – payments for building works as well as soldier's wages. The number of payments for soldiers stationed at Bellencombre (*ibid.*, pp 137, 236–7) suggests that this castle may have been used as a base from which Arques and Drincourt were recaptured.

On the incident at Vaudreuil in July 1195 and the Issoudun campaign see: Howden, *Chronica* iii, 301; Newburgh, *Historia* ii, 445–7; *Histoire de Guillaume le Maréchal*, ll.10534–58; Rigord, *Gesta*, pp 130–3; Stapleton, *op. cit.* i, pp 136, 156; Landon, *Itinerary*, pp 100–3.

For an early hint of tension between Richard and Sancho of Navarre see J. A. Brutails, *Documents des archives de la Chambre des Comptes de Navarre 1196–1384* (Paris 1890), pp 1–3.

It will be apparent that I do not accept J. C. Holt's interpretation of the Angevin Empire as a ship sinking steadily from 1180 onwards, with Richard's return from captivity making 'little difference', 'The End of the Anglo-Norman Realm', *Proceedings of the British Academy* 61 (1975), pp 223–65, reprinted in J. C. Holt, *Magna Carta and Medieval Government* (London 1985).

The account of Richard's death is taken from Coggeshall, *Chronicon*, pp 94–6, on the assumption that Coggeshail's source was Abbot Milo of Le Pin.

CHAPTER THIRTEEN. CONCLUSION

The problems involved in weighing up the different types of evidence for John's reign are neatly set out by J. C. Holt, *King John* (Historical Association Pamphlet G 53). For an assessment of Richard based on the English and Norman administrative records see J. C. Holt, 'Ricardus rex

Anglorum et dux Normannorum' in *Riccardo Cuor di Leone* (cited above). Both of these are reprinted in Holt, *Magna Carta*.

That Richard's subjects believed themselves to be hard-pressed by his financial demands is not in dispute. See, for example, Coggeshall, *Chronicon*, p. 91: 'No age can remember or history tell of any king, even one who ruled for a long time, who demanded and took so much money from his kingdom as this king extorted and amassed within the five years after his return from captivity.' None the less Coggeshall believed that there was some justification for Richard's demands and presumably it is beliefs of this kind which explain William of Newburgh's observation that although the king exploited his subjects more thoroughly than his father had done, yet they complained less about it, *Historia*, p. 283.

A much more controversial question is whether or not the Angevin taxpayers were so exhausted by these policies that John found himself in the position of being a poorer king than Philip Augustus. The most recent contributions to the debate are J. C. Holt, 'The Loss of Normandy and Royal Finance', in Gillingham and Holt (already cited), J. Gillingham, *The Angevin Empire*, pp 71–6, and J. Gillingham, 'The Fall of the Angevin Empire' *History Today* 36 (April 1986). Few, if any, contemporary commentators believed that John's military problems were caused by inadequate financial resources. See, e.g., the clear statement on this point made by the author of the c. 1220 text known as *Flandria Generosa* (MGH SS IX, 330). This is also my opinion.

INDEX